The

Handball

Book

A publication of Leisure Press.
597 Fifth Ave., New York, N.Y. 10017
Copyright © 1983 Leisure Press
All rights reserved. Printed in the U.S.A.

Library of Congress Catalog Card Number 82-81813

IBSN 0-88011-065-1

Cover and book design: Brian Groppe
Typesetting: The Graphics Connection; Oakland, California

The
Handball
Book

Edited by
Pete Tyson
and
Jim Turman

Leisure Press
New York

CONTENTS

CHAPTER 1 *FUNDAMENTALS*

CHAPTER 5 *HANDBALL RULES ... REFEREEING, RULE INTERPRETATIONS AND COMMENTS*

APPENDIX

ACKNOWLEDGEMENTS

Organizing, writing, photographing and editing a project of this magnitude would not have been possible without the collective contributions of many individuals to whom we are truly indebted. Dr. James A. Peterson, the publisher, has provided us with the financial commitment, support and patience to make this book possible. In addition, he has allowed us extreme freedom to include a wide variety and comprehensive collection of photographs and diagrams to augment the text of this monograph.

Over six hundred pages of manuscript were typed by Ms. Margie Williams, Ms. Gwen Russell, Ms. Evelyn Turman and Ms. Barbara Turman. A special thanks to Ms. Williams who typed four of the six chapters during a four month period in her "spare" time on weekends and evenings. We are indebted to Mr. Calvin Turman for his contribution of $150 to help defray some clerical and duplicating costs.

Mr. Frank Walters, a retired newspaper journalist from the state of Washington and former Public Information Officer for the United States Military Academy at West Point, New York, who now resides in El Cerrito, California, deserves special thanks for his major contributions of time, energy and expertise in proofreading our entire manuscript. Mr. Walters unselfishly volunteered his professional and technical experience, as well as offered many helpful comments and cogent advice during his five months of involvement on this project. His encouragement and support helped us through many difficult times.

Many of the photographs were taken by Ms. Margaret Lucas and Glenda Huff, students in Pete Tyson's handball classes, and Ms. LeaAnn Fuson. Ms. Fuson also spent many hours assisting us in putting this book together.

We would like to extend our appreciation to the many great handball players whose pictures are in this book and to all the authors of the articles. Finally, we are indebted to the United States Handball Association for allowing us access to their photograph files where many pictures of the past champions were obtained and for their permission to reprint many articles from *Handball* magazine.

FOREWORD

During the past 35 years no other outside interest has captured such an important segment of my life as 4-wall handball. This singularly personal game has been a haven of comfort and confidence, and of fear and apprehensions, each a learning experience savored in its own way. Throughout the many years, it has provided me with a universal comradeship that time does not diminish; it has provided me with that special peace of mind and concentration within myself when I close the door and start playing the sport I have so dearly loved.

Handball players throughout the world have expressed to me the same sentiments, coupled with their desire to play a better game, or improve their technique and strategy. Each decade of players and champions have answers to these questions and bring to the game another element for the improvement of skills, conditioning and attitudes. And each decade should be "heard" by any handball player intent upon the betterment of his game. A serious player, whether tournament or recreational, would probably like to seek out the wide spread gems of advice on the subject, but time prohibits us from tracking down the names of books, the many articles, the photographs and films. The authors have performed a great service to the handball enthusiast by compiling in one volume their considered and expert opinions of the best past and current material available regarding 4-wall handball.

Pete Tyson and Jim Turman have not only given us a composite of the views and lessons of many of the great theorists and players, but have updated the art of 4-wall handball and added elements of their own expertise as exceptional players and instructors. They have published a book which will serve as a supplement to books on the market and probably for others to be published in the future.

I recall the intensity with which I bored the champions of my day in order to learn more about the game. I recall the many hours spent on a court trying to improve a single stroke or serve. I also recall with some joy and with some pain the hours of studying, observing and practicing a sport that seem unexplored during the early portion of my career. The authors are a little late for my time, but I congratulate them for giving us all who love the sport a significant work which will advance the teaching and play of 4-wall handball for generations to come.

James L. Jacobs

January, 1983

PREFACE

Handball is truly a dynamic sport that has piqued the intellectual interests and challenged the physical skills of people for over two thousand years. "Man" has continually had a fascination for developing sports and games with round, cylindrical objects of all different sizes and materials, but no ball sport has evolved that matches the physical simplicity and intellectual complexity of handball. Since handball does not require any physical extensions to the body, such as a racquet, to aid in the hitting of the ball, but does require ambilateral motor skills, learning to play the sport presents the player with complex and provocative learning problems unlike other ball sports. Therein lies the challenge of the "chess of the court sports," handball. This book is our effort to express that challenge.

For several nights in March of 1981, Pete Tyson and I sat up late in a hotel room near the University of Colorado in Boulder discussing the purpose of this book. We intentionally decided to limit the scope of the text to four-wall handball. In addition, we felt that there were several good books on teaching the fundamentals of handball and that it was impossible to coherently discuss every aspect of the game. As a result, we decided to gear our book towards the experienced player with the intent that it could be used as a valuable supplement to existing handball texts on fundamentals and teaching.

There is one aspect of editing this type of book that makes it particularly appealing and interesting; the end result is a consensus opinion about the sport from many authors, players and participants. Our bias is revealed through the process of editing, selection and presentation. Pete and I reviewed all the articles that have appeared in *Handball* and *Ace* magazines since they were first published. We discarded more articles than we included in the text, providing the reader with only those articles that had relevance and substance to the aspects of handball we felt were important. A few articles were included for their historical significance and thoughtful musings of some of handball's great players.

In an attempt to focus on the interests of the experienced handball player and set a logical pattern for all players to think about the total four-wall game, we separated the book into five broad subject areas: fundamentals, singles, doubles, mental, and rules. The other advantage to this format is that the reader can easily locate a particular aspect of the game he/she wishes to concentrate on. As a result, each chapter can be treated as a unique subject area complete with a bibliography for easy reference. For the advanced student of the game Pete Tyson has included at the end of the text a complete list of all the books, magazine articles, theses and dissertations he has collected over the last twenty years.

Finally, the keys to the importance of this book to handball players and to Pete and myself are the hundreds of pictures and diagrams that accompany virtually every article in the text. There are no other books that contain such an extensive collection of visual aids, many of which have never been published before. We believe that this text will be a must for every handball player from beginner to national champion. It is with great pleasure that Pete and I present to the reader, under one cover, the best of the best articles, pictures and diagrams, written, photographed and illustrated on the sport of handball for your enjoyment.

Jim Turman
University of California, Berkeley
January, 1983

CHAPTER 1
FUNDAMENTALS

HOW TO HIT
A HANDBALL
TERRY MUCK

Just as the universe is made up of atoms, your handball game is made up of strokes, hundreds of individual swings of the arm. The quality of those individual swings determines the overall quality of your game, just as the nature of individual atoms determines whether a substance is gold or feathers. Therefore, it is all important that you learn a sound, fundamental handball swing before you start to compete in matches.

One is reminded of Ted Williams when an adoring fan asked him what made him such a great hitter: "Two things," he said, "a willingness to work and attention to detail. Every little cock of the head, twist of the wrist, and tilt of the bat held great importance to me. I worked and worked until I found which cock, twist, and tilt worked best for me, and then I practiced them until they became ingrained features of my swing plane."

Jim Jacobs, perhaps the greatest four waller of them all, recounts how he used to spend hours in front of a full length mirror examining his stroke, trying to detect flaws that robbed him of power and accuracy. "No detail was too small. Even the fit of my gloves had significance. The successful handball swing must be built piece by piece with the building blocks provided to you: your body."

Good handball players all have good handball swings. But if you go to a tournament and watch good players, the first thing you will notice is they all have unique swings; they all seem to do it a little differently. You'll find yourself wondering how you can even learn the right way to hit the ball.

Don't despair. The fundamental handball stroke has certain features common to all the good players. Body types, styles, and extraneous idiosyncrasies all serve to make handball swings look different. But at several crucial points, sound strokes all adhere to the same basic principles. Those principles we will now examine. **(Photo 1-1A)**

Body Position
The stroke starts with body position. Your swing's effectiveness depends on how well you station yourself to allow a free swinging movement with the arm.

Photo 1-1A   **Photo 1-1B**   **Photo 1-1C**

Photo 1-1A: Face side wall and start with feet close together.

Photo 1-1B: Draw the hitting arm back with the elbow slightly bent. Note the left arm.

Photo 1-1C: Initiate the forward phase of the swing by striding into the ball.

Photo 1-1D   **Photo 1-1E**

Photo 1-1D: The ball should be at the centerline of the body after striding into the ball.

Photo 1-1E: Stroke the ball as if you were throwing a baseball sidearm. Contact the ball just below the base of the first two fingers and allow the ball to roll off the fingertips on the release.

Step number one for the sidearm stroke: face the side wall when hitting to the front wall. During a rally, the ferocity of the action tempts a player to flail away at the ball without taking the extra hop step necessary to face the side wall for the stroke. Make yourself do it!

The reason this step is crucial will become clear when we talk about stepping into the ball and transferring the weight; you can't do these two things when your body faces the front wall; therefore you lose control and power in your shots. Facing the side wall, on the other hand, makes stepping into the ball the natural thing to do, and as a bonus it makes it much easier to watch the ball rather than the front wall, another important element of a good swing.
(Photo 1-1B)

So you prepare for the upcoming shot by facing the side wall. Next you must align the body so that when it comes time to actually strike the ball, the ball and your hand meet at the center line of your body (the center line is where your nose, chin, and belly button are, in case you were wondering). This means you must judge where the center line will be after you take your step into the ball; generally one foot behind the ball is a good place to start your forward movement.
(Photo 1-1C,D)

Okay, now imagine yourself facing the side wall, a foot behind the ball as it drops into your striking zone (any height that is comfortable between the waist and the knees), and you're ready to swing. As you take your arm back, turn your shoulders back also, then open up your hips and rotate into the ball. Don't worry too much about this shoulder and hip action; it should come naturally. Hitting a handball should feel just like throwing a ball; the body movement is the same. Handball players almost always warm-up by taking a few throws against the front wall, because the similar movements prepare their bodies for the more difficult task of hitting the ball. In fact, a good way to practice your swing is to throw an imaginary ball into a full length mirror. Imitate that same throwing motion when you hit the ball.
(Photo 1-1E)

Leg Position

Handball players start to slip when their legs get old. This fact alone reliably indicates the importance footwork plays in the handball stroke. You must use your legs to get yourself in position for the shot.

First, the legs get you to the ball so you set up behind it preparatory to stepping into it. Secondly, the legs are the means by which you take that all important single step into the ball as you're hitting it. Through this step comes a very large share of whatever power you generate in the shot.

Photo 1-1F   **Photo 1-1G**   **Photo 1-1H**

Photo 1-1F: The wrist snaps through the ball and follows through. The weight has been transferred completely to the front foot although the back foot is still in contact with the floor.

Photo 1-1G: Only after the arm and shoulders have come through the ball should the head come up.

Photo 1-1H: Follow through so that the hand is pointed towards the opposite side wall. Note the shoulder rotation from Fig. 1-A through Fig. 1-G.

Proper footwork in hitting a handball is as beautiful as one of Bach's Brandenburg Concertos. The move is trumpeted with several short staccato steps to get in position, and then the smooth, violin-like step into the ball. Legwork makes all the elements of the shot blend together and the picture is one of effortlessness and grace.

Make sure your legs keep you an arm's length away from the ball so the swing remains free and uncramped.

In a sense, legwork initiates the handball stroke by getting your body to the right place on the court. Then comes the cocking of the arm, the backward rotation of the shoulders and hips; then the forward step that opens the hips and commences the forward position of the handball swing.

Many players find a little shuffle step helpful in relaxing and loosening the body for the shot. It serves the same purpose as the forward press in golf or the little hip wiggle some golf teachers suggest to initiate the golf swing. Or you might compare it to the shuffle a shortstop gives his feet after picking up a ground ball before throwing to first; he does it for balance and positioning.

In handball this movement usually consists of a little three-step hop into the ball. The extra steps get the legs moving and make the final step into the ball that much easier and much more fluid. It is a movement that helps especially on fly shots where getting set up properly needs to be done very quickly and so is particularly difficult. If you practice this little three-step movement, you'll find it feels very natural and helpful.

The final step into the ball transfers the weight from your back foot to your front foot at the same time the wrist snaps through the ball. If done properly, it all comes together for a firm, solid shot. This perfect feel when everything comes through at the same time is called good timing. *(Photo 1-1F)*

Head Position

During the entire stroke the head points directly towards the hand-ball. Don't neglect this point. If one element of the swing can be called crucial or ultra-essential, watching the ball is it. No swing succeeds without watching the ball. *(Photo 1-G,H)*

Solid head position helps the swing for two reasons. The first is obvious: if you don't see the ball, you can't hit it. The golfing advice that you should see the clubface strike the back of the ball holds true for handball as well: you should see your glove come into the back of the handball.

Secondly, a solid, steady head provides a fulcrum around which the rest of the body turns. Simple physics tells us that speed increases momentum. In order to generate the most power in your swing, it's necessary to get your arm and hand moving as fast as possible. Swinging the arm and trunk around a fixed axis increases the speed of the swing which leads directly to greater power.

Think of the body as a spinning top. The center of the top barely moves; the outside of the top must move very fast to keep up. Or think of your hand as the end of a golf club; it must swing very fast to keep up with the slower moving parts of the body nearer to the center axis such as the shoulder.

What happens if the head moves forward? The speed of the arm is decreased because it doesn't have to move quite so fast to whip around the head. Thus, if you lunge at the ball in an attempt to hit it harder, you're actually defeating your purpose; the arm will travel slower, and as a result the ball will travel slower.

A problem beginning ballplayers often have is trying to watch both the ball and the front wall, the place where they are aiming. You can't do both. The experienced ballplayer rarely looks at the front wall. He is either watching the ball for his own shot or watching his opponent hit the ball. One thing he does, however, is to imagine the front wall. In his mind he "sees" the area of the front wall he wants to hit and this visualization helps guide the shot to that area. This kind of mental practice has good documentation by psychologists who have performed numerous experiments showing that mental imaging of a desired result acts positively towards achieving that result. So keep the head still on the outside but active on the inside.

Hand Position

It all comes down to the hands; it should in a game called handball. Actually, it all comes down to a specific portion of the hands, the hitting area. *(Photo 1-2)*

The ideal hitting area is surprisingly small—an area roughly the size of the handball on the top part of the palm at the base of the two middle fingers. Good players hit the ball there almost all the time and have the callouses to prove it.

Five-time national champion Paul Haber has a callous on his right hand that has become legendary. Paul's big trick in bars, where he spends an inordinate amount of his time, was to extinguish his cigarettes on the palm of his hand, protected, of course, by his callous. This trick won Paul many drinks, another advertisement for the virtues of handball.

Hitting the ball in the sweet spot takes practice. It's a difficult task and will only come after long, hard practice. But it really pays off in terms of control.

The actual contact of hand and ball is not so much a collision as a caress. It is accomplished with a cupped hand, a position that lessens the impact of the ball and softens what can otherwise be a jarring joining. After the ball strikes the sweet spot it usually rolls up off the end of the fingers or off the side of the hand. Which way it rolls determines the kind of spin the ball will have.

During the stroke the hands and wrists should be loose and relaxed. This makes the snap of the wrist at impact much more pronounced. As the arm swings the hand down into the ball, the elbow leads the way; it reaches the centerline of the body before the hand. When the elbow reaches the plane of the ball, then the wrist and forearm snap the hand forward at tremendous speed. Remember, speed equals power. The rest of the swing is a natural follow through.

Another very popular method of hitting the ball is with the fist; the hand is fisted and the ball is struck on the cuticles of the two middle fingers. The first stroke is accomplished with a stiff wrist, and the power in the shot comes from the shoulder and the relatively hard surface off which the ball rebounds, the clenched hand.

Because the mechanics of the fist are much simpler than the free swinging, open-handed shot, it is very popular for use with the off-hand. Its major drawback is a marked loss of control.

Editor's note: Photographs for this article by Pete Tyson.

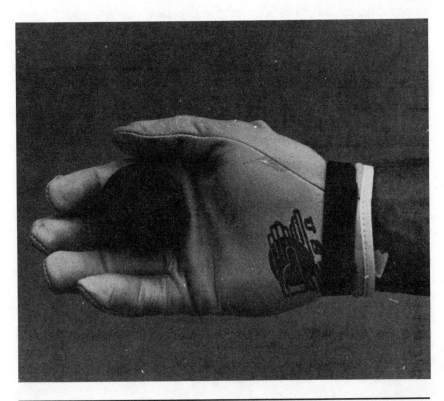

Photo 1-2: **Hand position and ball contact at base of first two fingers. Note hand is slightly cupped. Contact could also be made in the palm of the hand just below the base of fingers.**

HANDBALL
THE KIRBY WAY
PAT KIRBY

The proper dress for playing handball is a uniform consisting of shorts, singlet or tee shirt, good quality socks and good quality shoes—good quality socks and shoes will eliminate foot blisters, a common occurrence with most handball players. Gloves should fit comfortably; too tight a fit restricts the bending of fingers. It is better to have the gloves slightly large than too small.

Hand Position

When hitting the ball, hold your hand in a relaxed cup with your fingers together and the thumb lined up beside the index or first finger. Make certain not to tense your fingers so tight that your wrist will not flex. Your wrist should be loose and flexible for most shots.

Contact the ball at the base of the first three fingers—this is where you would grip the ball if you were going to throw it. Even though you can hit the ball further down in the palm area, you will have better control and leverage if you hit at the base of the fingers.

Strokes

On all strokes you should face the right side wall if you are hitting right handed, left side wall if left handed. Face the side wall, feet approximately 12 inches apart, flex your knees slightly and rest your weight on the balls of your feet, even though your entire foot is on the floor. Most of your weight is on the back foot at the start of your stroke and is shifted to your front foot as you stride towards the front wall to complete your shot. All your weight should be on your front foot at the end of your stroke.

Your arm should be completely relaxed. Your elbow should be bent, as much as 90 degrees, depending on what feels comfortable. The ideal point of contact is on line with the middle of your body. The ball should be far enough away from the body to allow the arm to pass comfortably between the body and the ball at the point of contact.

There are four basic strokes:
(1) the underhand;
(2) the low sidearm;
(3) the sidearm;
(4) the overhand.

Photo 1-3A: Sometimes you must use the underhand stroke to "dig up" your opponent's low hit shots as illustrated by Alvarado in this game against Vern Roberts.

Photo 1-3B: Fred Lewis using his underhand stroke to hit the ball low into the front left corner.

Photo 1-3C: **Dennis Hofflander hitting against Naty Alvarado. This is a superb example of the low sidearm stroke, the primary offensive stroke in the game.**

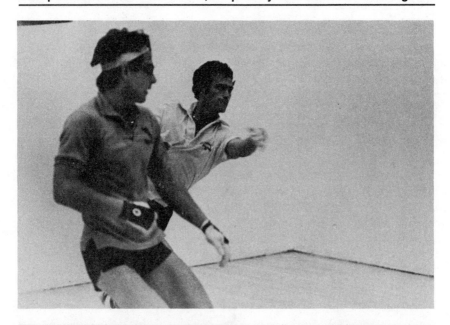

Photo 1-3D: **Professional handballer Gene Craft of Texas showing good form on the followthrough of his driving sidearm stroke.**

The Underhand

For the underhand stroke the ball is close to the body and the forearm and fingers point toward the floor before contact is made. The arm is raised to about head level on the back swing and then is brought forward and downward. *(Photos 1-3A,B)*

The Low Sidearm

With this stroke, contact with the ball is made from below the knees. A very effective stroke on the 20 ' x 40 ' courts, it is most often used in executing the kill. The knees and waist are bent to assume a low crouched position. The forearm is pointed towards the floor, with the fingers pointed towards the side wall. *(Photo 1-3C)*

The Sidearm

Again a very effective stroke on the 20 ' x 40 ' courts, this stroke is used to hit the ball between the waist and the shoulders. At the point of contact, the arm is almost fully extended. In preparation for the shot, the forearm and fingers point towards the side wall. You should crouch slightly when attempting this stroke. *(Photo 1-3D)*

The Overhand

This is used to hit and return high bouncing balls from a shoulder high, or higher, position and to hit ceiling shots on 20 ' x 40 ' courts. At the point of contact, the elbow should be pointing towards the front wall and downwards while the fingers are pointing towards the ceiling. The follow-through should be a downward pulling motion.

Footwork

Since the ball rarely comes to you in perfect position to be hit, you must move into your proper position. Footwork is one of the most important fundamentals of handball. Good footwork begins with an alert starting position. The body is slightly crouched, with the knees flexed and the weight on the balls of your feet.

The forearms are drawn up so that they are parallel with the floor. As soon as you see the direction of the ball, move quickly to the court position from which you will attempt your return. Remember, you should face the side wall when attempting your shot. So don't move directly behind the ball but to one side or the other of it, depending on which hand you will use for your return attempt. Always finish your move into position in such a manner that the weight of your body is travelling into the ball and towards the front wall. Prepare for your stroke as you are moving to the ball by drawing your arm back partially, and complete your back swing as you set your feet for the shot. Whether you are moving forward, backwards or sideways, keep your eyes on the ball at all times.

Stroking the Ball

Beginners often make the mistake of rushing shots and trying to hit the ball too soon. The best time to hit the ball is when it has reached the height of its bounce and is dropping towards the floor. It is difficult to hit the ball as it is bouncing upwards.

IMPROVE
YOUR TIMING
TERRY MUCK

A common losing complaint: "I'm sorry I couldn't give you a game today. I guess my timing's off." We know two things about this speaker: he is a sophisticated loser, because he knows the right things to say when he loses (loser rule number one: never give the winner credit). Also, he could be correct in diagnosing his troubles, because poor timing is a very common fault.

Good timing can be a matter of only a fraction of a second. Hitting a ball a little too early or too late can be the difference between hitting it firmly with accuracy and hitting it weakly and wildly. Timing means utilizing the snap of the wrist and the elbow to their maximum efficiency. During the swing, both the wrist and elbow cock backwards as the arm is drawn back; as they come forward, the elbow snaps forward and the wrist snaps around, just as the head of a tennis racquet is snapped forward in the forehand tennis stroke. A handball player making a good stroke hits the ball with his hand at the same moment the wrist snaps forward. This is called good timing. If he hits it before or after the wrist snap, bad timing results.

Besides the uncomfortable feeling of losing a game, there are several other things which indicate you have bad timing. Good timing produces the soft sound of leather striking rubber; poor timing produces a loud smack as the hand and ball meet. Good timing causes the ball to jump off your hand with very little effort; bad timing causes the ball to travel relatively slowly even though you swing with all your might. Good timing means good accuracy; bad timing means the ball will be flying all over the court and you have little idea of where it will go next.

An additional consequence of poor timing is the feared bone bruise. Some bone bruises come from lack of play; the time lag between matches allows the hands to soften and makes them more susceptible to broken blood vessels. But among those who play regularly, poor timing causes bone bruises because the hand and ball meet in a jarring collision. Heating the hands helps prevent bone bruises of the first sort, but only good timing will prevent those of the second class.

Several hints to improve your timing:

- **Practice hitting the ball against a wall by yourself.** At first this may seem a boring way to spend your court time, but all the great players did it when they started out and continued to do it throughout their playing years. One remembers Jim Jacobs' answer to a questioner asking him how he learned to hit a ceiling ball: "I went in the court at 9 in the morning and hit ceiling balls until noon," was Jim's reply. Jim wasn't being facetious. Developing timing means practice, practice, practice. By educating your muscles to the proper stroke during practice sessions, it will come naturally during games. During the heat of battle you forget to set up properly, watch the ball, and strike it in the center of your body. But if you have developed a good practice stroke, it will come back to you when you need it in a game.
- **Practice prolonged rallying.** An alternative to working in the court alone, this exercise removes some of the boredom of volleying alone by adding a partner. Decide between yourselves what shots you want to work on and hit them to one another. Without the pressure of winning and losing, you can devote all your mental and physical energies to hitting the ball properly, and your timing will improve. Try to keep volleys going with good crisp shots, concentrating on hitting the ball smoothly and with purpose. In these artificial volleys, never just hit the ball; always have a plan as to where you want to hit it and how hard you want to hit it.
- **Discuss your problems with a good player.** This is fun. Part of the fascination of handball is the comradeship which naturally develops between players of all levels. Timing is a problem shared by novice and pro alike. Although they have different levels of expertise, the principles of solving the problem are the same, and discussion can be mutually illuminating. Ask a better player how he deals with poor timing when it confronts him; his ideas will help you devise ways to cure your own woes. Other players will be happy to help. Almost every geographical area has at least one player who has gained some reputation as a teacher of handball, someone able to analyze the intricacies of the stroke. Get his help.
- **Watch other players.** One of the best ways to improve your timing is to watch players who hit the ball fluidly. Try to pick out reasons why this player hits the ball so well, and why that player hits the ball so poorly. You will discover that the size of the person and the size of his swing have very little to do with how well or how hard he hits the ball. Chicago's Wes Yee hits the ball as hard as anyone, yet he is one of the smallest players around. The secret is timing, timing which comes from smoothness and footwork. By watching the fluid hitters, you will pick up some of the reasons for their success. Have you ever noticed how players from the same

areas of the country seem to hit the ball the same way? Subconsciously they copy one another. The same thing will happen to you by watching good swinger's play. And it's an entertaining way to learn.

- **Relax.** Worry will make your timing trouble worse. Handball relieves tension: don't let it cause more. Swing easily, well within yourself. Try to make your swing as smooth and even as possible. Erase all other thoughts from your mind (the score, your opponent, the last point, the next point), and make this one swing the smoothest you can. Soon you will be stroking the ball as well as you can, and all the other phases of the game will fall into place. Imagine you are Fred Lewis hitting pass shots and Dennis Hofflander hitting kill shots. Imagine their relaxed strokes and their perfect timing. Yours will improve by osmosis.

Photo 1-4: **Perfect timing by Fred Lewis hitting a shot in the finals of the 1978 national championships. Note the wrist snap just after the ball is contacted.**

THE
BACK WALL
TERRY MUCK

Beginning handball players have trouble adjusting to the back wall shot in developing their initial skills. The shot requires a movement quite different from any other shot, a movement unique to the court sports.

Not only beginning players have trouble with the back wall. There is no other single shot in handball that is executed improperly as often as the back wall shot by both beginner and experienced player.

Photo 1-5: **Former national champion, Terry Muck, taking the ball "off the back wall." Muck is considered the fastest player of all time. He wrote several of the fine instructional articles in this book while he was editor of *Handball* magazine.**

Photo 1-6A
Photo 1-6B
Photo 1-6C

Photos 1-6A,B,C: Pete Tyson hitting a straight back wall shot. This shot should be attempted with the low sidearm stroke.

The difficulty lies in the timing. Usually the beginning player goes the wrong way when trying to hit the ball as it bounces out from the back wall. The secret to the shot is to add your momentum to the ball's momentum as it abruptly changes direction from reverse to forward.

Once you get the "feel" of the back wall shot, it will become one of your favorites. It presents many opportunities to the player for making both offensive and defensive shots. If shot correctly, it takes almost nothing out of your arm. It is a blessing to the meek player because you can hit the back wall shot hard, and for that fleeting instant you put everything you have into the shot, you'll think you're one of the big boys.

The back wall shot is essential to playing good handball. Needless to say, all the great players have had this shot; a few, such as Claude Benham and Steve Subak, have made it the focal point of their offensive game.

But even average players need a decent back wall shot. Players must use the shot frequently, for any shot that is overhit in the slightest goes to the back wall and rebounds out. Good players quickly learn that the back wall is a great friend in time of need, such as when the ball is hit by them and they have to turn around and chase that elusive ball. The back wall brings it back.

The back wall shot can be either offensive or defensive. Two things determine which it is: the angle the ball comes off the back wall and the distance it comes off the back wall. The really good back wall players are the ones who know when to go on offense and when to use a defensive return.

How can you go about developing this skill? The use of the back wall can be broken down into three areas: the proper way to use the body or push, the point of contact, and the placement.
(Photos 1-6A,B,C)

Push

The uniqueness of the back wall shot stems from the need to go back with the ball as it goes to the wall and then stop and come out with the ball as it rebounds towards the front wall. To make the shot effective, it is necessary to do this work, to get behind the ball so that your whole body weight is added to the shot. The result is a powerful push from the legs that makes the ball jump off your hand and crisply reach the front wall.

The most common error in executing the back wall shot is to reach back and try to strike the ball forward as your body is still going backward. *(Fig. 1-1)* This causes a weak shot, both in terms of power and direction. The reason this is a common error is because the proper movement takes work. The proper shot requires a certain amount of quickness (to get back with the ball), leg strength (to push out with the ball), and a few extra steps (to complete the movement).

You have to be willing to use your legs in this pushing motion in order to use the back wall effectively. To get the feel of this pushing movement, here are a couple of drills you can try when you have some time to practice by yourself: *(Figs. 1-2, 1-3)*

1) Throw the ball high and hard against the front wall, straight down the middle of the court, so that it rebounds off the back wall all the way to the short line *(Fig. 1-4)*. Throw the ball from about three-quarters court, and as the ball passes you on the way to the back, run along with it until you are about three feet from the back wall. Stop and reverse your direction so you are now running towards the front wall, and so that you are running along with the ball as it comes off the back wall. Don't try and hit the ball at first. Just run along with it and catch it as it nears the floor. The idea of the drill is to learn what it feels like to make the proper movement with your legs. Do this 25 times before you try and hit the ball. Get into the rhythm of moving in and out with the ball. In an actual game you might not move as far with the ball; you might wait for it out near the short line and then start moving with it. But this drill will teach you the importance of pushing out with the ball.

2) Stand about five feet from the back wall. Throw the ball into the floor a foot from the back so that it rebounds up into the back wall and towards you in the air. As you throw the ball to the floor, swing your weight to the foot nearest the back wall (this comes naturally as you throw), and as the ball comes back to you on the rebound, begin to transfer your weight to your foot nearest the front wall. Again, just catch the ball initially and get used to feeling this transfer of weight, which is really the purpose of moving out with the ball: to get the weight transfer. Do this 25 times until it comes naturally. Then try and hit the ball as it comes by you, still concentrating on the weight transfer and not worrying about where you hit the ball. You may have to shuffle

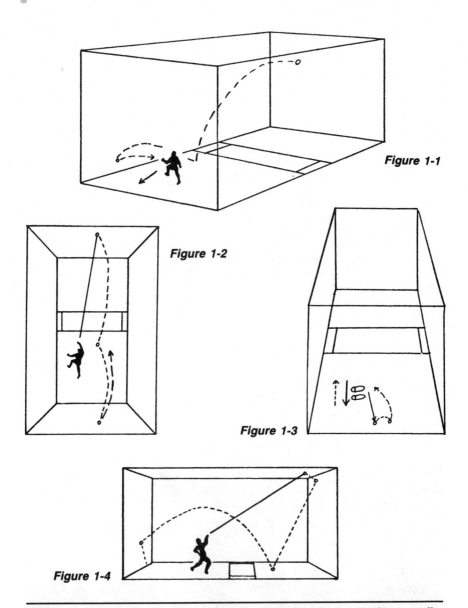

Figure 1-1

Figure 1-2

Figure 1-3

Figure 1-4

Figure 1-1: The most common back wall error is for the man trying to strike the ball to be moving backward while the ball is moving forward.

Figure 1-2: Practice this drill to get the feel of moving in and out with the ball off the back wall.

Figure 1-3: Practice transferring weight to back foot as ball is thrown back and to front foot as ball rebounds towards you.

Figure 1-4: A ceiling ball off the back wall bounces downward at a very sharp angle, and requires good position and fine timing to hit properly.

your feet slightly in order to get in comfortable position to hit the ball. This is all right, but still concentrate on the weight transfer from back to front. *(Photo 1-7)*

The footwork of this push may differ, depending upon the angle at which the ball is coming off the back wall. For the ball that comes straight out, such as the ones in the drills above, it is just a matter of moving straight towards the front wall with the ball, or slightly to one side or another if you wish to hit the ball down one of the side walls.

But the footwork becomes a bit more tricky when the ball goes into one of the corners and comes off the back wall at an angle towards one of the side walls. Two rules of thumb will help to guide you here. First, always face the ball; this means turn with the ball as it goes around the corner. Second, try to come out with the ball in the same direction as the ball is traveling, even if this means moving towards one of the side walls. If you follow these two rules, you will be assured of making good contact with the ball. It may limit the choice of shots you use but it will pay off in the end in terms of consistency and lack of errors. The skill of back wall corner play will come slowly at first until you learn the angles and the spin with which the ball is hit. Try to anticipate in advance where the ball will end up. This will give you more time to get back in position and push out with the ball. *(Fig. 1-3) (Photos 1-8A,B,C,D)*

Photo 1-7: **Naty Alvarado taking ball off the back wall with his offhand. Note the slightly bent arm backswing and how the hand is cupped.**

Photo 1-8A

Photo 1-8B

Photo 1-8C

Photo 1-8D

Photos 1-8A,B,C,D: Tyson hitting a shot as it ''comes out of the left rear corner.'' Note that the player pivots with the ball and attempts the shot with his dominant hand.

Another variety of back wall shot presents special problems. The ceiling ball that is hit a bit too hard comes off the back wall. But because of its sharp downward angle, it is a difficult shot to time properly. For this shot it is doubly important to get back to the back wall and move into and out with the ball. The movement here is a bit more subtle. Because the ball is traveling down at a sharp angle, the distance it comes out from the back wall is much less; thus you have less room to move out with it. *(Fig. 1-4)* The key here is to wait behind the ball and emphasize the weight shift rather than running out with the ball. Do not try to overhit this ball; just concentrate on making good contact as you move towards the front wall.

An additional problem with the back wall ceiling ball is loss of eye contact. The ball is coming down at a very sharp angle and this means it comes down much more quickly than the normal back wall shot. Also, the ball hits the back wall with a spin that makes it increase in downward speed. The result is that very often the eye loses contact with the ball; the head doesn't seem to turn fast enough to allow proper eye contact. It takes a special effort of concentration to keep this ball in eye range. A helpful hint here is to keep an arm's length away from the ball. Looking at the ball from the side is much easier than trying to watch it as it comes down from the lighted ceiling over your head down the back wall and into your hand. From the side this all flattens out, and you don't have to move your head so much to keep an eye on the ball. *(Photos 1-9A,B,C,D)*

Point of Contact

Now that you have your body in proper position to hit the ball, you need to become aware of where you should hit the ball in relation to your body.

A very common error in back wall play is a point of contact further back than it should be. Like the error of not getting back far enough so that you can push out with the ball, the error of reaching back comes from a laziness about getting into proper position for hitting the ball in the center of your body, the proper point of contact.

Another quite different cause of poor point of contact is over-anxiousness. Once behind the ball, a player may want to hit the ball too hard and may push out too far, getting ahead of the ball. When this happens, he has to reach back to hit the ball which is now behind him.

The cure for this malady is to concentrate on hitting the ball when it comes to the center of your body. In this respect, the back wall shot is just like any other shot. Your maximum effectiveness in hitting the ball comes when you hit it from a point in the center of your body. A good drill to instill this skill in your body's mind is to stand about ten feet from the back wall and throw the ball, in the air, to the back wall. The ball, after hitting the back wall, bounces once on the floor

Photo 1-9A

Photo 1-9B

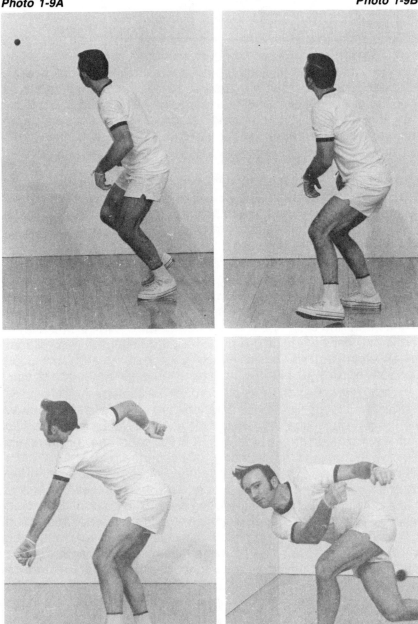

Photo 1-9C

Photo 1-9D

Photos 1-9A,B,C,D: **The great Paul Haber hitting his shot after ball rebounds from back right corner. Note the backswing in Photo #3 and how he stays low on followthrough.**

and comes towards you on the first bounce. Pushing out with it, let the ball come to a point in the center of your body and then strike it. Don't worry about where it goes, just make sure you are hitting it in the right place in relation to your body. Letting the ball bounce after it hits the back wall will give you more time to concentrate on a good point of contact. After you feel comfortable hitting the ball this way, then try and hit it in the same place while throwing the ball in the manner described in drill two. *(Figs. 1-5,6)*

Placement
Like any other shot, hitting the back wall shot in the right place spells the difference between effectiveness and ineptness. The decisions about which side of the court to hit the ball to and whether to make an offensive or defensive shot are of the utmost importance in utilizing the back wall game. Those decisions depend on two factors; the position of your opponent and the position of the ball.

If your opponent is in the front court it is normally foolish to go for the kill. While a flat roll out will win the point, anything short of that will be a set up, particularly since you are shooting from the rear of the court and are in poor position to cover a rekill. However, the further the ball comes off the back wall, the better the percentages for an attempted kill, because both your kill shot and your court position improve greatly with each step you take from the back wall.

Should you decide to kill off the back wall, the best kill is usually a straight kill to the side of the court you are on. *(Fig. 1-5)* That way the ball travels the least amount of distance, and should it be a little high it will slide down the side wall. A cross court kill is occasionally effective, but should be used only as a change-up from the straight kill down your side. It is too risky otherwise. If your position in the back court is poor, if the ball is very near the back wall or in one of the corners, or if the ball is a ceiling ball off the back wall, the best return is a pass shot. The most effective pass shot is the cross court V shot. *(Fig. 1-6)* This pass shot is particularly effective off the back wall because it needs to be hit with a fair amount of power, and the back wall momentum allows even light hitters to put some steam on the ball.

Occasionally, as a change-up, a pass shot that slides down the near wall can be used, but this is much harder to hit. If it catches the side wall it will pop out into the center of the court for an easy return.

In some ways the back wall is a risky shot. It provides so many wonderful offensive opportunities when the court factors are right. This can lead to players becoming too offensive with the back wall. You only have to miss a little off the back wall for your golden offensive opportunity to turn into a loss of the rally. When you shoot off the

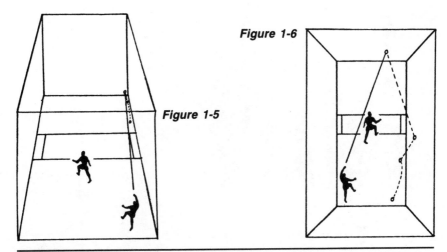

Figure 1-6

Figure 1-5

Figure 1-5: **The best percentage kill off the back wall is the straight kill down the side of the court from which you are shooting.**

Figure 1-6: **The V pass shot off the back wall.**

---

back wall the shot had better be good, because you are too far out of position to correct any mistakes.

That is the reason you see so many of the good players use the back wall as a chance to wear down their opponents with continued use of the hard V pass. While they may be passing up scoring chances on the kill, the V pass takes a lot out of their opponents; they have to run hard just to retrieve it, and the return is often weak.

In developing your back wall game, learn the physical moves first. After this becomes second nature, you can begin to map out strategy about how you are going to use the shot against certain players. You will also learn your weaknesses and strengths off the back wall. *(Photos 1-10A,B,C,D)*

Photo 1-10A

Photo 1-10B

Photo 1-10C

Photo 1-10D

Photos 1-10A,B,C,D: Several of top handball pros, Gordy Pfeifer, Stuffy Singer, Naty Alvarado and Vern Roberts preparing to execute their back wall shots. Note that all of the players are facing the ball as they let the ball drop below their waists.

THE OVERHAND

TERRY MUCK

Paul Haber didn't win any titles with it. Pete Tyson hasn't written an instructional on it. And, it hasn't ushered in a new era of handball. But all the same, the overhand shot has a definite role to play in four-wall handball.

Mention of the overhand shot usually brings to mind other sports, such as tennis, where the serve and smash are both executed with the overhand motion, or baseball, where the ultimate in pitching excellence often takes the form of the overhand fastballer, or badminton, where the overhand clear is a must for successful play.

Photo 1-11: **Lou Russo hitting overhand against Dennis Hofflander.**

In handball the overhand is not emphasized. It is used more often in three-wall than four-wall. Three-wall demands deep drives and overhand cut-offs. A good overhand makes or breaks the three-wall player. But the four-wall game also demands proper use of the overhand. In four-wall, however, the use is more subtle, so subtle in fact, its importance is often overlooked.

What is meant by the overhand shot? Any shot using the overhand motion. It can be used selectively as a lob, as a defensive pass or as an offensive drive. It can be hit hard or soft. As with other shots, the way you use it depends on your position and your opponent's position.

Although the ceiling ball is technically an overhand shot, we will not consider it in our discussion of the overhand, because the ceiling ball is so important and frequently used, it should be discussed separately. Analysis of the overhand can be broken down into three areas: the technique of hitting the shot, the touch that it requires and the theory of its use as it fits into the overall strategy of your game.

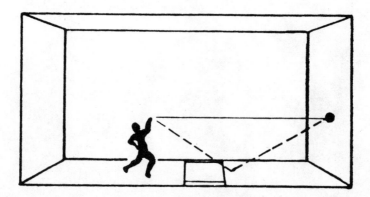

Figure 1-7: **The best way to get the feel of the overhand shot is to repeatedly hit the shot to the front wall. Engage yourself in a continuous rally of overhand shots from about mid-court. This should become second nature to you.**

Technique

The overhand shot requires the same fundamentals which apply to all other handball shots. You need to watch the ball descend into your hand, step into the ball, and follow through with a full arm motion and weight transfer. Failure in any one of these areas will result in a miss-hit shot.

As with the sidearm stroke, the overhand motion should feel just like you are throwing a baseball, except for the position of the head. Remember to keep your eye on the ball! This means your head is turned up to watch the ball strike your hand, instead of towards the front wall to watch where the ball hits.

Don't leave your feet when you hit the overhand. Players make this mistake on the overhand more often than on any other shot. Because the ball is above them they think they can get more power on the shot by jumping into it. The reverse is true; you lose power by leaving the ground.

Make sure you get in proper position to hit the overhand so you don't have to jump at it. The result will be a more powerful and more accurate shot.

Photo 1-12A

Photo 1-12B

Photos 1-12A,B: **Vern Roberts hitting overhand. Note in A how the elbow leads and in B how the wrist snaps after contacting the ball.**

The best exercise to get the feel of the overhand is repetitious hitting. *(Fig. 1-7)* Begin by throwing the ball overhand against the front wall 25 times with either hand. Next, hit the ball overhand 25 times with each hand. Stand at the short line and bounce the ball on the floor hard enough so that it rebounds over your head. Then step into the ball and stroke it to the front. Catch the ball and repeat the motion.

If you experience difficulty imitating the throwing motion, alternate throwing the ball overhand and stroking the ball overhand until the two begin to feel similar. The key to positive transfer of the motion is in the legs; you must concentrate on stepping into the ball with the left foot on right handed shots and with the right foot on left handed shots.

To complete this exercise, hit the ball to the front wall and instead of catching the rebound, hit it again with the same overhand motion. Continue this rally until you have hit the ball 50 times with each hand. Force yourself to move and get into position for each and every stroke.

Touch

Most players tend to overswing on the overhand. This is especially true when they attempt to drive the ball past their opponent down one of the side walls. Instead of gaining power and making an accurate shot, the overswinging usually causes a miss-hit or a loss of accuracy, with the ball hitting one of the side walls. When an overhand shot hits the side wall it is *always*, because of the spin on the ball, a set up. The spin makes it slow drastically and pop up to the center of the court.

Perhaps the temptation to overswing comes from expecting too much from the overhand. While at times power will pay off on the shot, usually placement is much more important. The shot must be hit crisply with a short overhand stroke. The ball will travel sufficiently fast to accomplish what you want it to with this short, firm swing.

Since the overhand is most effective hit down the ''short side'' of the court, that is, the side wall you are nearest to *(Fig. 1-8)*, quickness in the stroke is more important than raw power. Stroke the ball quickly so that it strikes the front wall about three to four feet from the floor and runs down the side wall.

Here are a few points to remember in deciding what role the overhand should play in your overall game plan:

- Don't hit the side wall with the overhand. We have already mentioned this point and the reason for it. When an overhand drive hits the side wall, it pops to the center of the court.

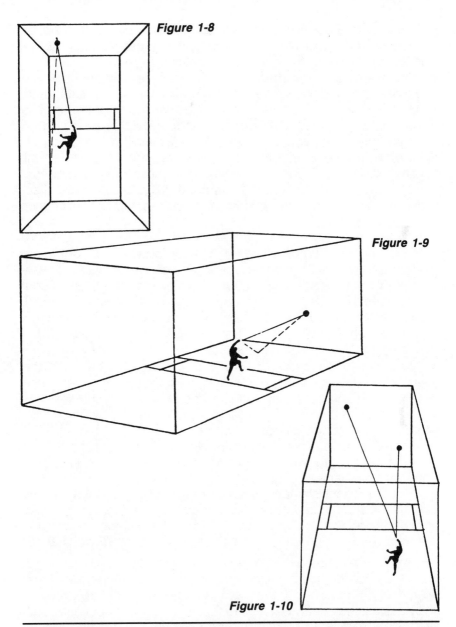

Figure 1-8

Figure 1-9

Figure 1-10

Figure 1-8: Most of your overhand shots should be hit down the short side of the court, that is, the side of the court with the least amount of distance between you and the side wall.

Figure 1-9: Hitting the ball on the half hop teaches you the timing so essential to hitting the overhand volley correctly.

Figure 1-10: Hit drives 3-4 feet high on the front wall and hit lob shots about 15 feet high.

- Don't try to kill with the overhand. This can be considered an absolute rule. For every kill you do get with this motion, you will miss twenty. This is not a good percentage.
- Don't overuse the overhand drive. Remember, you are using the overhand shot basically as a change of pace or as a shot to set up another better shot such as a kill or hard, sidearm pass. You are still looking for the rally ending shot and if you pass it up to hit the overhand, you are asking for trouble in the long run.
- When using the overhand shot as a drive shot, hit the front wall fairly low (3-4 feet high) and when using the overhand shot as a lob, hit the front wall high (15 feet high). *(Fig. 1-10)* To be effective, a lob shot has to bounce high and you can only get this bounce from a high angle.
- Aside from the serve, the lob shot should be hit sparingly. If your opponent is at all mobile, he will hit your lob shots out of the air, often killing them. If, however, your opponent does not take advantage of the time a lob shot affords him to cut off the ball, use it more because it is both easier and safer to hit than a ceiling ball.
- Remember, the overhand is basically a defensive shot. Rarely will it score you a point outright. So don't get too ambitious with the overhand. Use it, but use it selectively.

In order to discover just how and when you should use the overhand in your particular game, you must practice it under game conditions. This means that during some of your practice sessions you will want to try and use the shot more often than you normally should. Play a couple of games where you make it a rule to hit at least one overhand shot in every rally. Do not allow yourself a kill shot until you have hit an overhand of some kind. This drill will teach you when the overhand is effective.

The important element necessary for this stroke is timing. The ball must be contacted at precisely the right moment for the most efficient use of the arm movement. Hitting the ball too soon or too late means you won't get the most out of your shot. *(Figs. 1-9,10)*

A drill to teach you the proper timing is to hit the ball on the half hop, that is, as the ball is still traveling up after bouncing on the floor. *(Fig. 1-9)* Stand about 30 feet from the front wall and throw the ball softly against the front wall about 15 feet high so that it bounces about five feet in front of you. Try to hit the ball as it bounces up at you. This will require a quick, short swing, the same kind of swing you should use on all overhand shots whether they are hit on the half hop or not. Continue trying this shot until you find yourself making good contact with the ball.

Touch on the lob shot can be learned through the same kind of drill. Stand at the rear of the court and hit lob shots repeatedly to yourself until you gain the necessary feel to hit the shot high on the front wall and still be able to keep it off the back wall.

Theory

Where and when you use the overhand shot spells the difference between a good shot and a bad shot. Overuse of the overhand results in a useless rallying game that will only tire you out and will accomplish very little in trying to maneuver your opponent around the court. Hit to the wrong place, the overhand is simply a set-up.

For some players the problem with the overhand is one of overuse. You can decide if this is one of your shortcomings if you find yourself having trouble ending rallies, or you are constantly in the back court in long rallies. If overuse turns out to be your problem, make it a rule to hit an overhand only on alternate rallies, and even then limit yourself to one per rally.

Don't worry if these drills throw your game off for a little while. You will be better off because of the drill in the long run, and you will become even more conscious of your shot-making abilities and options.

Photo 1-13A

Photo 1-13B

Photo 1-13C

Photos 1-13A,B,C: Three action shots of Dennis Hofflander hitting the ball with his great "off-hand." Note his legs and how they are bent as he strides toward the front wall.

DEVELOPING
THE OFF-HAND

DAVE LYNCH

Our game of handball is a difficult one to master because it takes ability, agility, and *ambidexterity,* something that most sports do not require. Players give up the game and retreat to racquetball, or continue playing at the same plateau because they fail to develop the off-hand.

A good athlete coming from a basketball-baseball background can pick up the game of handball but it is only through practice, application, and dedication that one will develop the skills with both hands necessary to be successful. **(Photos 1-13A,B,C)**

In the last three years I have worked hard at developing the off-hand and I have some very concrete suggestions for the player of the perfect game, handball:

* **Observe in a full length mirror** the correct, detailed throwing pattern you use with the strong hand. Watch closely how the elbow leads in throwing, how the wrist cocks and how the hips and shoulders rotate to accommodate the throw. After doing this several times with the strong hand, repeat the throwing motion, with the off-hand, making a mental picture of what it should look like.

   Alternate in front of the mirror, using the strong hand for ten throws (without the ball, of course) and the off-hand for ten throws.

* **Practice on the handball court.** Take 15 minutes by yourself on the court and throw the ball with your off-hand. Start with the overhand throw and then go to the sidearm throw. Remember what you saw in the mirror and try to imitate the motion of your strong hand. If your club or court has a glass wall, throw it into that wall because it serves as a giant mirror to remind you of the proper form.

   If you don't practice and practice the correct technique you will never develop the off-hand. At our club we have many good players, but I have never seen any of them in the court practicing by themselves; everyone just wants to play games. You need 15 minutes by yourself per playing day to make any improvement.

- **Buy a dime store item called a "flyback."** For 25¢ you can purchase this great little trainer that I have used to help me tremendously. It is the small wooden paddle with a little red rubber ball attached with a 12 to 18 inch rubber band that kids use and mothers give out as birthday favors. Place that paddle in the off-hand and practice hitting that ball with the off-hand only.

   Begin with an underhand stroke with the paddle held about chest height and strike the ball straight up to the sky. Also practice hitting at waist level in a horizontal stroke similar to a ground stroke in tennis. Remember, all of this hitting is with the off-hand. See if you can make ten consecutive hits, then 20, and so forth. This is very essential in developing good hand-eye coordination.

   The brain must actually practice telling the off-hand to hit that little red ball. At first you start out like a klutz, just like you do in handball with that horrible-looking thing we call the off-hand. The carry-over to hitting the handball is truly amazing, and with constant practice it will improve your handball off-hand 25%.

- **Get a ping pong paddle and ball** using the same principle as the flyback for basically the same reasons. Place the paddle in the off-hand, hit the ball up, turn the paddle over to the other side and hit the ball as it comes down. Keep turning the paddle back and forth every time you hit the ball. Then hit the ball against a flat surfaced wall as you would in a ping pong game and alternate with a forehand hit and then a backhand hit. This sharpens the reflexes, develops the coordination between your eyes and the other hand and makes you a better ping pong player. (I teach PE and challenge kids at school in ping pong with either hand.)

- **Get three 4′ x 8′ plywood panels.** Nail these to a frame made from eight foot two-by-fours and erect this wall and fasten it to a fence or wall in your yard with bolts, nails, screws or whatever will hold. If you have a concrete slab or patio it is good to set the "court" in front of it. Keep a lefthanded glove with a ball in it by the backdoor and when you have five to ten spare minutes repeat step 2 right in your own backyard. This is an inexpensive wall (I built one for about $30) and can be used for many purposes also. You won't get any ceiling game practice, but you can wear out the bottom board.

- **Play only with your off-hand.** Select someone below your ability level and play against them using only your left hand. All shots must be hit with your off-hand, even the ones that would be natural set-ups for the strong hand. At times this causes frustration, but the continued hitting with the weak hand will do nothing but strengthen your game.

- **Use the off-hand in other sports.** Shoot baskets or dribble a basketball with the weak hand. Throw darts, serve a volleyball, pitch a softball or fling a frisbee with that off-hand. Get in the habit of using it and thinking of it as being as important athletically as the other hand, because in our game it certainly is. *(Photos 1-13 D,E)*

- **Treat the off-hand like one of the family.** If you had a kid brother who was locked in the closet for the first ten years of his life and you let him out one day to meet the neighbors he would be totally lost. It's the same with human anatomy—if you keep your off-hand in a closet when you play handball, your game will be lost and the off-hand will remain a liability to you all your handball playing days. When playing handball, use your off-hand frequently; at the very minimum when the ball comes to that side of your body. No matter how clumsy you feel, force yourself to hit that left hand shot and expect from it what you expect from the strong hand. If you expect less, you'll get less.

Photo 1-13D

Photo 1-13E

Photos 1-13D,E: Naty Alvarado demonstrating the low sidearm stroke with his off-hand. Note how the elbow is bent on his backswing and his good follow through after contacting the ball.

FOOTWORK
ALL IMPORTANT
GUS LEWIS

Footwork is the most important element in almost any sport you can name. Because handball is mainly a running game, the importance of good footwork, proper conditioning of the feet and legs, and of getting into the right court position are of evident importance and all are intertwined.

FACE THE BALL WHEN YOU HIT IT . . . If the ball is coming down the right wall, face the right wall. If it's coming down the left side, face left. If you're taking it off the back wall, face the back wall, pivoting as you swing.

Now, if it's coming straight at you from the front wall, shift your feet as you'll be facing right or left as you start your swing.

KEEP MOVING . . . Don't ever stop. In other words, don't ever come to a dead stop and plant yourself. And particularly, don't ever let your weight get on your heels—keep it on the balls of your feet. By this I do not mean on your toes, or you'll over-balance.

Special Exercise

Try this exercise . . . with your weight on the balls of your feet, move to your left with short steps, moving slowly. Then make a sudden take-off to your right. You will plant your left foot hard and drive off it to change direction. But because you had some motion the change of direction is easier.

You can change direction faster than you can start from a dead stop.

By getting into position you can stroke the ball rather than bat at it or stab at it.

ANTICIPATION . . . does not mean guessing.

If you hit a ceiling shot deep in the back court, you can be reasonably certain that your opponent (if he hasn't moved up to take it on the fly) will hit a high return. But you don't know for sure. And you don't know whether he'll hit it down the left or right, or whether he'll give you a twist shot out of the corner. He might even drive it low along either wall.

Photo 1-14: Two-time national singles champion "Lightning Gus" Lewis (right) shown here with Vic Hershkowitz receiving championship awards in the early 1950's. The presenter is Bill Clements, of Texas.

There's only one way you can anticipate where you should be for his return, and that is to watch the ball until he has hit it. Then you may have to turn your back on the ball to get into position—but never take your eyes off the ball or your opponent until he has swung.

Too many players make their break before the other player has hit, which brings me to another point: Never commit yourself in any direction at full speed.

Drift, Don't Run

If you've had to move close to the back wall for a shot, for example, you naturally want to get back to center, front court to be ready for anything. But drift back, for as soon as you break fast, your opponent will cross you up, catch you "on the wrong foot" as they say in tennis, and drive the ball behind you.

In this connection, here's a tip that may be of value. If you have to go to any wall at full-speed for a get, sometimes you save time by taking an extra step or two and then pushing yourself off the wall; it's frequently faster than trying to brake yourself, stop, and start back.

This may come under the heading of court strategy rather than footwork, but I'd like to point out that as the national championship matches near the final rounds, you see fewer and fewer players on the floor.

Dive Is Wasted

The best players have figured out that you can run to the ball faster than you can dive for it—if you keep your feet moving and keep your balance properly distributed. I can honestly say I've never fallen down in the court, unless my foot slipped on some perspiration; and I've never dived for a ball. You can get there faster with your feet than with you body.

In this connection, you will find—if you will believe it—that there's hardly a ball hit that can't be retrieved. You've played some baseball, no doubt, and you must have amazed yourself at least once by catching a fly on the dead run that you thought you couldn't reach. The same thing happens in handball. The ball "hangs" for that split second—or so it seems—and you'll get a large percentage of "impossible" returns if you persevere.

Proper Foot Action

The object of footwork is to get into position to stroke your shot. Now then, what should your foot action be when actually hitting the ball?

It's about the same action you use playing catch with a baseball. Your whole back foot is on the floor as you begin to swing, with your right hand, with the forward toe just touching the floor. As you swing, the weight is transferred, naturally and smoothly, from the back foot to the forward one, with the forward foot coming into full contact with the floor as power is applied. You hit "against" the leading foot just as you do with a baseball or golf swing. On almost every shot, the knees should be flexed slightly—more for low shots, of course.

Keep Weight Forward

The most important thing is that your weight be on the balls of your feet, even though the entire foot is in contact with the floor. This does not mean it should be on your toes, for if your weight is too far forward, you will be off-balance and will have a tendency to fall or lunge forward after the shot. You will also lose power.

Most handball shots, whether overhand, sidearm, or underhand, are more than an action of the hand and wrist. The whole arm, the shoulders, the back, the hips, the legs—and the feet—come into play.

No matter how much you love the game, you can't spend all your time in a handball court—and very few want to. But there are a lot of things you can do outside the court that will prove rewarding and beneficial to your game.

For Conditioning Legs

I had the tremendous advantage of being an acrobatic tap dancer in vaudeville for five years as a boy, and it's impossible to estimate how much the footwork I learned as a dancer helped my handball.

Not many take up acrobatic tap dancing, but I still do exercises I learned in those days, and I pass them along here as probably the most beneficial of all for both strengthening and limbering your legs for handball:

- Shallow knee bend or half squat.
- Rise up on the toes.
- Deep knee bends (full squat).

Repeat each exercise in various positions several times. This will develop ALL the leg muscles in a uniform way, making them strong enough to stand the stresses of handball, supple enough to respond to the many positions the game demands.

For further muscle development, coordination, and looseness, I list here a number of practice suggestions:

- Practicing alone with emphasis on facing the ball on every shot.
- Practicing alone, with emphasis on moving at all times with short steps, the weight on the balls of the feet.
- Practicing alone to retrieve "hangers." Stand near the left rear corner. Throw the ball into the right front corner six inches to a foot off the floor, then run for it—and don't give up. Vary this with shots from various points—but persevere on every shot.
- To build endurance and to strengthen your legs, running is good. But run a quarter mile or less at a time, ON YOUR TOES. Heel and toe running at long distances will not bring a tenth the benefit of sprints on the toes.
- Ballroom dancing, on the balls of your feet, will help you achieve a high standard of footwork. Imagine what handball players Fred Astaire and Gene Kelly would have made if they'd tried.

- Swimming is excellent, since it keeps your legs strong and supple, relaxes your muscles, and builds endurance. An older player who's relaxed will outlast a stronger, younger opponent who is tense. And remember, one tournament game takes as much out of you as half a dozen practice games because of the tension involved. Practice relaxing and pacing yourself, so you'll do it naturally in competition.
- Other sports. Basketball and soccer are both excellent because of the footwork and strategy involved. Soccer is especially beneficial in Ireland where you are allowed to kick the ball in handball. ALEX BOISSEREE, one of the best players in the Los Angeles area, was named soccer player of the year in China before the war (and was interned there throughout the war, incidentally).
- During calisthenics in the morning or evening, practice deep knee bends on your toes.
- Finally, take care of your feet. Wear one or two pairs of heavy wool sweat sox. Wear sneakers that have not worn smooth (some types actually serve as a squeegee if you hit a wet spot on the floor and prevent spills).

RUNNING
IN HANDBALL
TERRY MUCK

Next to kill shooting and serving, the most visable aspect of a handball match is the running. People can't help but notice the scurrying back and forth that takes place in a game, from corner to corner and front to back. Handball means running.

Fans can immediately identify the fast runners in a match. Identifying the naturally quick player requires no great skill. He stands out, and his particular talent gains recognition; someone blessed with a more subtle talent, such as anticipation, may not be as easily recognized.

Gus Lewis, one of the fastest of all our national champions, once characterized the runner as "a hardworking handball player. I should know, because I won my national title by running faster than anyone else. Quickness is perhaps the single greatest asset a handball player can have."

Whether you run fast or slow, you have to run to play the game. A thorough knowledge of the game can significantly reduce the amount of running you have to do, but total elimination is impossible. Older players who retain all their shotmaking and strategic skills must move to the Masters divisions when they lose their ability to keep up in the running department.

How do you keep up in the running department? Is running a natural talent that cannot be improved upon? The answer to this question is yes and no. Basically, speed is a natural talent. Certain training techniques can improve speed somewhat, and help you maintain it longer, but without the initial talent you will never be fast.

Even though slow stays slow, there are some principles of moving around the court which, if followed, can make a fast player appear faster and a person of average speed seem quick. Like any other skills, these principles take practice and discipline to learn. But they will help. **(Figs. 1-11,12)**

Wait before you run.

Oddly enough, the most important piece of advice you can get about running after the ball can be summed up in one apparently contradictory word: *"Wait."*

Wait and be sure you know where the ball is going before you start to run after it.

The average player has trouble doing this. He naturally wants to get about the business of chasing down his opponent's shots and he chomps at the bit to get started. So he starts running after the ball, thinking he knows where it's going when he really hasn't waited long enough to make his opponent commit himself to one shot.

This overeagerness comes from two sources: excitement and doubt. The excitement results from being pumped up for the match and it must be controlled. A couple of hard points and a little conscious effort will accomplish this. It's very much like overswinging at

Figure 1-11   *Figure 1-12*

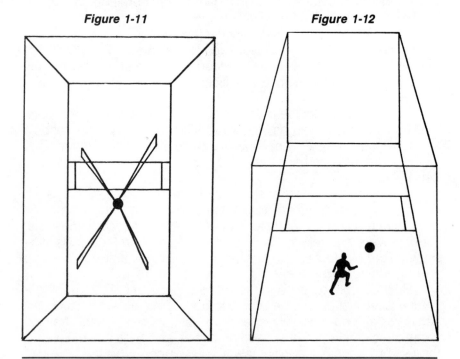

Figure 1-11: **Diagram of the movements of a successful handball player would show straight lines out to the ball from the center of the court, a step into the ball, and a straight line back again.**

Figure 1-12: **Try and set up behind the ball so you can stride into it on the stroke.**

the ball. You do it at the beginning of an important match because you want to play so well. It will go away.

Doubt is another matter. A person slow of foot or a person of average speed doubts whether he can get hard shots. So he mistakenly figures he can make up for his lack of speed by getting an earlier start. He ends up being fooled too often. Even a person with superior speed might find himself overreacting, trying to make the impossible retrieve upon which he has come to rely. This also is born of a lack of confidence, in this case a lack of confidence in the rest of his game. And it, too, has the effect of making a person slower than he really is.

He is slower because, although he looks like he is making some great running gets, he is really wasting effort, making a wrong start and then running wildly to get what should have been an easy shot in the first place.

The best example of the value of playing this waiting game is our current national champion, Fred Lewis. Fred does not have great natural speed, and yet he covers the court better than all but two or three of the top pros. He makes up for his natural lack of quickness by waiting until he is absolutely sure he knows where the ball is headed. Then he gets it. Although you will occasionally see a ball passed around Fred, you will very rarely see him fooled. So take a tip from the champ and wait.

Run in a straight line.

Once you know for sure the shot your opponent has hit, run straight to the ball.

This may sound like unnecessary advice, since running straight to the ball should be second nature, but you would be surprised how many players waste valuable steps by taking a looping, twisting path to the ball.

Part of the problem is unfamiliarity with the angles and bounces of a handball court. This is particularly true of a four-wall court where wrap-around and ceiling shots are the order of the day.

Figuring out where a particular shot is going to end up in a handball court can be learned. Just think about it. Analyze the different shots common to four-wall handball, and learn their ultimate destinations. By locking this information securely in your mind, you will soon find yourself economizing on the number of steps you take to reach the ball.

Another way to economize steps, and incidentally save time and energy, is to start your forays after balls from a good center court position.

As we have said many times before, winning handball comes from controlling the center portion of the court. Not coincidentally, center court is the best point from which to run after shots. You can get more shots from center court than any other place in the court.

If we were to diagram the movements of a successful handball player by lines on the floor of a court, the diagram would show hundreds of straight lines out to a point on the court and then back again to center court. *(Fig. 1-11)* All straight lines, mind you.

We need a word here on how to run. The best handball runners take short, quick steps, not long, graceful ones. The short steps allow for fast changes in direction (should a crack ball or hop ball call for it), and the good balance so essential for setting up to strike the ball.

One reason why little men as a group play better handball than big men as a group is the little guys naturally take short steps with their tiny legs and itty-bitty feet. They tiptoe through the tulips better, if you will.

Run behind the ball.

Now we need to refine our last principle a bit further: run in a straight line to a point behind the ball. We aren't just trying to reach the ball, we are trying to get in position to hit it properly. *(Fig. 1-12)*
To hit a handball with maximum power and accuracy, you must move into the ball with a last minute weight shift as the ball leaves the hand.

The more time you have to set, the further behind the ball you should go, so that on very simple shots you take a couple of steps into the stroke. Every handball player knows the feeling of power he gets when he can throw his whole body at a shot. It makes a shot much easier on the arm and shoulder.

Of course we're talking about an ideal situation. Many times you don't have all that time on a shot. But whenever you have any time at all, be conscious of running to the back side of the ball and stepping into it.

Stop running before you hit.

After writing several paragraphs telling you how to run and move into the ball, it may seem unusual to tell you now to stop running before stroking the ball. But that's the story. You make better shots when you are set before swinging. At the actual point of contact the body is stationary.

Some of you may remember Harvey Kuenn, the baseball player. Harvey was considered a great ballplayer not only because he hit for a fine average, but because he did it as a front foot hitter—he hit from his front foot while his body was still moving forward. Baseball men agree that you need to have both feet planted with the head still in order to hit at maximum efficiency.

The same principle applies to hitting a handball. A stationary head provides a fulcrum around which the rest of the body can rotate. More arm speed can be built up this way; none of it is dissipated with that fatal forward sway that golfers have come to dread.

After you make your strike into the ball, the arm swings around a stationary axis running vertically from the head down through the trunk of the body. The hips turn around that axis as do the shoulders. But the head remains steady.

A steady head does more than generate arm speed and thus increase power. It insures better contact because it keeps your eyes firmly rooted to the ball. It is a very logical sequence; if your head moves, your eyes move, and watching the ball becomes very difficult.

Another baseball analogy might help illustrate this point. Outfielders are taught to run on the toes of their feet when chasing fly balls. This allows them to carry their head on a more level plane, which in turn allows them to follow the ball more easily. Running flat footed or on the heels makes the head bounce up and down, so the eyes bounce up and down, and this makes the fly ball look like it's bouncing up and down.

Put simply, getting set before you swing makes a lot of good things happen. You maximize both your power and accuracy—which means you win more.

Naturally, you can't always set before you shoot. One reason your opponent tries to hit the ball where you aren't is to try and get you to hit on the run. Fight this strategy by working to get set before every shot. *(Photos 1-15A,B)*

Running as a strategy.

Paul Haber, after watching two young players dive, scramble, and run at breakneck speed during a match, once said, "If I had to run like that, I'd never win a match."

Paul wasn't saying he couldn't run like that. Paul was a very quick handball player; in his younger days he played a diving game. Paul's real point in this statement was this: running must be used properly and judiciously in order to win matches. More running doesn't mean better playing. The very opposite of this is often true.

The nature of a handball game is such that you work to eliminate as much running as possible. This means you control center court and are set when you shoot a large share of your shots. We have mentioned several ways of refining your running in this article. Here's one more: choice of shots.

Ceiling balls and deep court defensive shots slow down a game and reduce the amount of all-out running. The amount of running these shots reduce depends on how accurate you are with the shots.

But the point is this: in deciding on your strategy for a game, you may want to include more, or less, running. Offensive play increases running, defensive play should decrease it. In either case, running must be used properly and with as great an economy as possible. Remember, you win by being smarter, not faster.

Photo 1-15A

Photo 1-15B

Photos 1-15A,B: Vern Roberts preparing to dive for an attempted retrieve of a low kill shot and Naty Alvarado chasing down a pass shot. Both shots were hit by Fred Lewis who has a habit of making his opponents do most of the running.

BIBLIOGRAPHY

Kirby, Pat. "Handball the Kirby Way." Excerpts from *Handball,* 1980, Vol. 30, No. 2.

Lewis, Gus. "Footwork All Important." *United States Handball Association Guide and Directory,* 1961-62.

Lynch, Dave. "Developing the Off-Hand." *Handball,* 1977, Vol. 27, No. 5.

Muck, Terry. "How to Hit A Handball." *Handball,* 1979, Vol. 29., No. 4.

"Improve Your Timing." *Handball,* 1977, Vol. 27, No. 2.

"Running In Handball." *Handball,* 1979, Vol. 29, No. 1.

"The Back Wall." *Handball,* 1978, Vol. 28, No. 1.

"The Overhand." *Handball,* 1978, Vol. 28, No. 2.

CHAPTER 2
SINGLES

PART I
SERVES AND HOOKS

SERVING-THE PERCENTAGE WAY

PETE TYSON

In an article I wrote for *Handball* (Vol. 26, No. 5) entitled "The Five Situations of Handball," the word situation was defined as "anytime the ball is about to be hit." The five situations I listed were:
1. The Serve
2. Return of Service
3. Defense
4. Offense
5. Shot Anticipation (opponent is hitting the ball)
At the same time I discussed the five situations, I attempted to point out that there is a physical and mental aspect of each situation. "Physical" means hitting the ball where you are aiming, and "mental" means attempting the correct shot based on the best percentage play for the specific situation.

Articles on the five situations of handball will appear throughout this book wherever appropriate. The first situation to be discussed is the serve, or "Serving the Percentage Way." I have previously covered this topic to some extent in the article, "Pete Tyson Expounds on Importance of Serve" (*Handball Magazine,* Dec. 1973). Other articles have also been written on the serve and should prove valuable to you. These articles, written by three of the greatest players in the history of handball, Jim Jacobs, Vic Hershkowitz and Ken Schneider, can be found in Gordy Pfeifer's book, *A Lifetime Handball and Racquetball Reference Guidebook.*

It is difficult to say that any one particular shot is the most important shot in the game, because they are all necessary for success. However, the only way you can win a rally is (1) for your opponent to hit the ball into the floor or (2) for you to execute a well-placed kill or pass shot (not counting the flat crotch serve). It doesn't matter how well you can hit kill or pass shots, you cannot do so unless your opponent gives you a set-up. So, perhaps the most important shot in handball is the one that gains you the opportunity to end the rally with your offensive kill or pass shot. Thus, the serve can be your most important shot.

Good vs. Effective

Your opponent basically has five things he can do with the service return:

(1) Hit a kill shot.
(2) Hit a pass shot.
(3) Hit a defensive ceiling or 3-wall shot.
(4) Hit the ball into the floor.
(5) Give you a set-up.

Above all, when serving you want to place the ball in a position that eliminates his chances of #1 (kill) and #2 (pass). There are a number of serves that can accomplish this which were discussed in my earlier article on serving. These serves include the low power, changeup, lob and Z. If you execute these serves correctly, your opponent will have to attempt his return from very close to the side and/or back wall and this position allows him a very poor and risky chance of executing a kill or pass shot. When executed in such a fashion, these serves are GOOD serves, but that does not mean they will be EFFECTIVE. An EFFECTIVE serve, besides eliminating #1 and #2, also eliminates #3 (defense) and that leaves him with only #4 (hit into floor) and #5 (set-up), both of which are highly desirable for you, the server.

Photo 2-1: **A good low drive serve down the right wall can be very effective as illustrated by this photo of John Sabo's ''ace'' served to Dennis Hofflander in the quarterfinals of the 1981 National Championships.**

Which of your good serves will be effective? That definitely depends on whom you are playing. You want to serve your opponent a GOOD serve that he has difficulty defending, and that particular serve will depend on your opponent's defensive abilities. So, the more GOOD serves you can master, the better your chances of finding the EFFECTIVE one to use against that particular opponent.

The most popular serve is the LOW POWER SERVE. "Aces" (non-returned serves) are most likely to happen with this serve, because your opponent has less time to position himself to play it than any other good serve. If, however, you cannot keep it low enough so it will not rebound off the back wall, you will be much better off serving a well-placed lob or Z serve. The back wall is the enemy of the serve, especially power serves. The reason most power serves come off the back wall is the height at which they are contacted. If you closely watch Lewis, Singer, August, etc., execute this serve, you will see that contact is rarely made higher than 12 inches off the floor. This low contact allows the ball to hit lower on the front wall, and the lower the ball hits the front wall, the better your chances of keeping it from setting up off the back wall.

Control is most important, and yet I have observed most players take an average of 2-3 seconds in which to serve. The rules allow 10 seconds. Take advantage of them! By taking just a little more time, perhaps 6 or 7 seconds, you will have a better chance for greater accuracy and consistency with your serves. This is what you should be striving for—CONSISTENT CONTROL. Those two words are pretty good descriptions of Jacobs, Haber and Lewis (look in the record book if you fail to recognize those names).

Practice serving your low power serve down the right wall as well as down the left. More and more of the pros are using this serve to their opponents' strong hands, because many players do not defense as well with their strong hands as with their weak hands. However, you must learn to execute the low power serve without "giving it away." Learn to serve it from the same spot and with the same motion that you serve to the weak hand side. If you can control it so that it hugs the side wall and does not rebound off the back wall, you will often get some very pleasant results. But, perhaps you believe your opponent's strong hand is so terrific you would not dare serve that direction. I recently witnessed Lewis and Singer playing an exhibition in Philadelphia and watched these two great ballplayers ACE each other more than just a few times by serving low and hard to the right (they are both right-handed)! If it can work against the top pros, it can work against your opponent's "terrific strong hand."

Remember, just because the low drive serve is the most popular, that does not mean it will be the most effective. A good lob, Z or changeup will often achieve better results. Once again, it depends on whom you are playing.

I tried to point out in my "Five Situation" article that you lose rallies by making mistakes and that mistakes are either physical or mental. In serving, a physical mistake is hitting the serve in a manner that allows your opponent the opportunity to go on the offense. Physical mistakes are reduced by PRACTICE. Mental errors will often cause physical errors. Some examples of mental errors are:

- Not taking enough time to serve.
- Contacting your power serve too high off the floor.
- Not standing close enough to the side wall when attempting a lob serve down that wall.
- Not attempting some type of Z serve, if your first serve faulted.
- Attempting lob or Z serves to your opponent's strong hand.
- Always trying for the "ace."
- Serving with your off-hand.
- Not mixing up your serves as to speed and direction.
- Continuing a serve that your opponent has little difficulty defensing.
- Making your decision as to which serve to attempt as you are swinging.
- Believing that "your best serve" will achieve the same desired results against all opponents.
- Serving anything to Hofflander!

Sometimes you can get away with a mental error, but you have a better chance of reducing physical errors by eliminating mental ones. BETTER CHANCE—this is what we mean by PERCENTAGE HAND-BALL.

THE POWER SERVE

FRED LEWIS

It has been written that if there is any one time when an individual is in complete control of the situation during a handball match, it is when he is standing in the service box getting ready to serve. The server is going on offense, while the receiver may either play offense or defense. The special advantages a server has are:

* he is hitting the ball approximately 15 feet from the front wall;
* he has the option of serving from anywhere in the service box that he chooses;
* he has the option of hitting a wide variety of serves.

This article will focus on the power serve and its variations.

Photo 2-2: Classic backswing of Fred Lewis as he begins his low drive serve stroke. Lewis is one of the "greats" of the game having won six National Singles titles.

If you have ever marveled at the way some of the top players hit the ball so low and hard on the serve and wondered why you were having a difficult time, then this article might answer some of your questions. The prerequisite for hitting this serve effectively is having a sidearm stroke. Although there have been a few exceptions, the most gifted servers through the years have all possessed a good sidearm stroke—i.e., Hershkowitz, Collins, Jacobs, Decatur, August, Pfeifer. Each of these men had a different style and philosophy of serving, but the one element they all had in common was the basic, sidearm stroking motion.

The stroke itself can be broken down in this manner. Using the center of the body as the point of contact, the stroking arm is brought back approximately 2 to 3 feet from the center line (of the body). As the shoulder rotates the arm forward, the elbow and wrist are bent slightly backwards. As contact is made, the elbow and wrist snap forward. This is the common failing of most players. They don't get the snap from the elbow and wrist and therefore are unable to stroke the ball with needed force. After contact is made, the stroking arm follows through until the hand is pointing forward to the front wall. Too often players end their stroke with little or no follow through.

In the analysis of any stroke, the free hand cannot be ignored. It may or may not be used to toss the ball. Once the ball is tossed, the free hand's job does not end there. It is used as a guide to clear a free and unobstructed path for the stroking arm. A common error is to leave the free hand dangling at the player's side or to use it to grasp the knee as he is about to hit the ball. This restricts follow through and decreases the amount of momentum.

The last sentence leads to a discussion of a very important part of serving. Momentum is directly related to power. When momentum combines with force, power is produced. The force of the body combined with a little momentum can generate a lot of power. In handball, as in other sports, momentum comes from stepping into the ball. Usually, one or three steps are taken before stroking the ball. Taking one step keeps everything nice and simple; bounce-step-hit. The way to do this is to bounce the ball and let it come to its apex, pulling your arm backwards at the same time. As the ball begins to drop again, one step forward is taken with the front foot. Simultaneously, the arm begins its forward stroking motion. As contact is made with the ball, the rear leg pushes off the floor, driving the body toward the ball.

Three steps will give added momentum; however, complications may occur. It is important to toss the ball in front of the center of the body. Remember, you would like to hit the ball in the center of the body. After you've taken the third step, the ball should be right in the center for you to swing at. If you hit the ball off your back foot,

Photo 2-3B

Photo 2-3A

Photo 2-3D

Photo 2-3C

Photos 2-3A,B,C,D: Sequence of Fred Lewis executing the low power serve. Note his high backswing and how he allows the ball to drop very low before making contact.

the remainder of your body will be in front of the ball and much power will be lost.

Serving hard is only half the battle. Controlling the power is probably the most difficult part of the serve. Control means keeping the ball off the back wall and sending it close down the side wall. In order to keep the ball off the back wall, it must be hit very low on the front wall. Steve August has been accused of serving "kill shots." When he had his big serve working, he hit the ball so low and so hard against the front wall that it barely crossed the short line. In order to hit the ball that low, he let it drop just a few inches from the floor and then made contact. This required him to bend over very low at the waist and also at the knee. Keep in mind that Steve is 6 ft. 3 in. which means he had a long way to bend over in order to hit the ball. You don't have to serve "kill shots" in order to keep the ball from coming off the back wall. If the ball hits the front wall 3-4 ft. high, with sufficient power, it should cross the short line and never reach the back wall. Most effective serves land somewhere between the short line and the five foot mark. *(Photos 2-3A,B,C,D) (Fig. 2-1)*

Serving has often been compared with pitching a baseball. Good major league pitchers have great control and several different types of pitches in their repertoire. They move the ball around the plate, trying to keep the ball inside or outside. The strategy in serving is similar. The most effective serves are hit very close to the side wall without touching the side wall. Of course, the one exception is the crotch serve. The danger in going for the crotch is that if you miss and catch the side wall high, the ball will angle into center court and set your opponent up. Through the years, I have had a great deal of success with the crotch serve. Much credit is given to Marty Decatur, who perfected the crotch serve, and whom I tried to emulate. Marty probably ended more games with a crotch serve than anyone in the history of handball. It always seemed that when Marty was involved in a very close match, he was able to count on his ace serve in the clutch. After observing Marty for a number of years, I recognized that the key to his phenomenal accuracy was the fact that he stood not more than three feet from the left side wall. In other words, the ball had to travel a very short distance from the time it left his hand until it rolled off the side wall. We all recognize the fact that any target is easier to hit from a short distance away as opposed to a longer distance. Marty also would put a natural hook on the ball to insure that it would roll off the side wall. The natural spin forces the ball to stay down as it rebounds from the side wall.

Marty, being the intelligent player he is, knew that he could not rely on hitting twenty-one crotch serves in a row. He perfected a serve that ran straight down the left wall also. This serve was hit from the same position as the crotch serve but with a reverse spin. In other words, he turned his hand over the ball, rather than coming under it. This serve is very deceptive, because it starts out angling towards the side wall and then, all of a sudden, it straightens out after it hits the floor. As a result, the opponent is forced to return the serve with his opposite hand, while playing it very close to the side wall.

Occasionally, Marty would move to the center of the service box and serve a big natural hook to the left side of the court. The reason he moved into the center was because he wanted to give the ball more room to break without hitting the side wall. A hook serve is very difficult to return while it is in the middle of its break. If it hits the side wall, the spin is completely reversed and the ball jumps toward the center of the court for an easy return. By serving from center court, the chances of this serve hitting the side wall are diminished. Moving closer to the right wall may make this serve even more effective.

Much can be said for serving to the right side and your opponent's strong hand. Some of the most effective serves used by the pros are to the right side. The reason is most players do not defense well with their strong hand. They constantly go on offense with their strong hands and as a result get very little practice defensing the ball. A low, hard serve sliding down the right wall requires a good defensive return.

Gordy Pfeifer has one of the premier right side serves in handball. Gordy uses the same target theory as Marty. He stands 3 to 5 feet from the right side wall. When he goes for the crotch, he reverses the ball so when it hits the side wall, it rolls out. As you may recall, this is exactly opposite to what happens when attempting to hit a crotch serve to the left. Gordy also hits a natural hook serve to the right side. The ball straightens out and runs very close along the wall. This is also opposite to what takes place on the straight left side serve.

A discussion on power serving could not end without referring to Jim Jacobs. Jim possessed all of the aforementioned serves, along with a few others. He had some of the most vicious hook serves ever seen. Jim's serves were difficult to return because he could hook the ball either way, to any spot on the floor, from any spot in the service box. This provided him with so many different variations it was almost impossible for an opponent to anticipate what was coming. This is a plateau very few players can ever hope to reach. Most players should strive to develop two or three effective power serves. If your favorite serve is not working, you should be able to switch to one of the others until you find the serve that gets you the weak returns and aces.

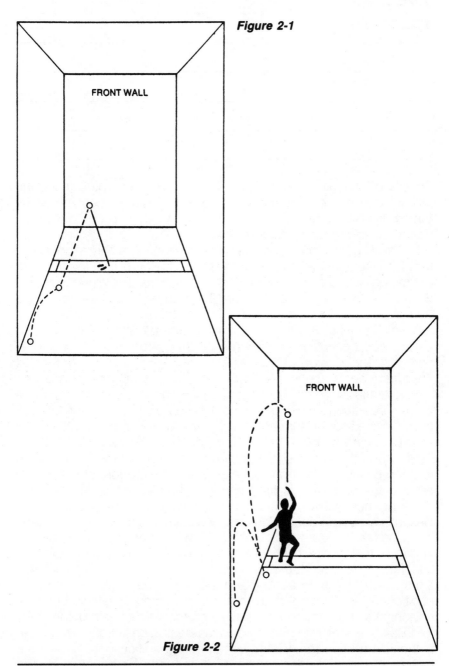

Figure 2-1

FRONT WALL

Figure 2-2

FRONT WALL

Figure 2-1: The low drive serve: Note that ball strikes floor close to the short line to keep from rebounding off the back wall.

Figure 2-2: The lob serve: Note that ball strikes floor just behind short line and remains close to side wall while angling to left rear corner.

THE LOB
TERRY MUCK

Several of the finest players in handball have successfully used the lob serve. Two come immediately to mind: Paul Haber and Stuffy Singer. Both hit it the same way, in a manner that can be described as the classic technique. *(Fig. 2-2)*

Standing very close to the left side wall (perhaps only a foot away) they face the front wall. Very few shots are hit with the shoulders square to the front wall, but the lob serve is one of them. The ball is dropped with a firm, downward toss so that it rebounds to a point above the right shoulder in front of the body. The exact height varies, from about a hand's height above the top of the head to just above the shoulder. Comfort and effectiveness will decide the proper height for you. A short, balancing step may or may not be taken with the left foot. I recommend taking one. The ball is struck at the height of its bounce with a gentle overhand flipping motion. It should strike the front wall about three-quarters of the way up and about a foot from the left side wall. On the rebound it should strike the floor just behind the short line, bouncing high to the left rear corner. *(Photos 2-4A,B,C,D)*

To be effective, the ball must hug the side wall without striking it. If the ball is too far from the side wall, your opponent can swing around and hit it with his strong hand. If the ball strikes the side wall, it will bounce out toward center court for a very fat set-up. Thus, because of its slow speed, precise location of the shot is all-important.

Once your opponent receives a few of your lob serves, he will anticipate them by quickly moving over to the left side wall in preparation for his return. You may find it necessary to counteract this anticipation by hitting a lob down the right side from your left side position. This is a dangerous shot. Not only are you hitting it to your opponent's strength, you are traversing the whole width of the court to do it. It's like throwing the cross-court pass in basketball. Therefore, it should be used rarely and with certain modifications; because it has such a long distance to travel, it needs to be hit lower on the front wall so its trajectory is flatter. This means it spends less time in the air, and there's less chance of it being returned out of the air.

At some levels of play, you see underhand lob serves. None of the top players use it. The only exception to this I can recall was Bill

Yambrick who occasionally hit an interesting underhanded lob serve. Standing about five feet from the right side wall, he hit the ball with an underhand scooping motion to a point very high on the front wall. The ball would kick up higher after hitting the front wall and come very close to the ceiling as it traveled to the back court. Bill would aim the ball so, instead of striking the floor first, it would hit the side wall low near the back wall; it would bounce out almost parallel to the back wall and be very difficult to return effectively with the left hand. An unorthodox shot, the classic style lob is more effective and easier to hit.

Photo 2-4A   **Photo 2-4B**

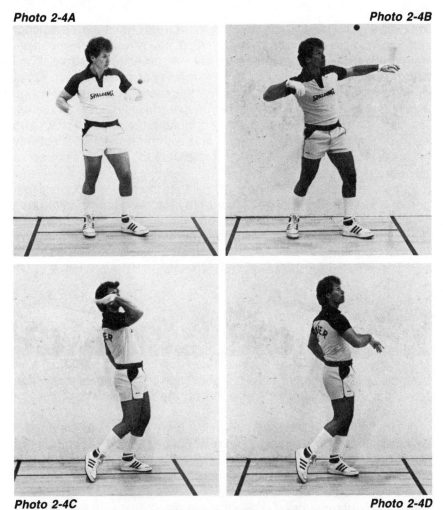

Photo 2-4C   **Photo 2-4D**

Photos 2-4A,B,C,D: Sequence of Stuffy Singer executing the lob serve. Note: (1) How close to the side wall his position is and (2) the angle of his arm and (3) how his shoulders are parallel with the front wall when he contacts the ball.

HANDBALL, THE KIRBY WAY

PAT KIRBY

Serves

The serve is the most important shot in handball because it puts your opponent on the defensive immediately. It may give you an immediate point or an ace. If it does not and yet it is an effective serve, it will bring a weak return, possibly setting up a kill or butt, a passing shot or some other non-returnable shot. For this reason it is vital to develop a good serve. By this I do not mean an extremely fast or vicious shot.

There are many effective ways of getting the ball into play, and each player must sort them out to find which one works effectively on his opponents. It is very important to vary the speed of the serve as well as the type.

I like to keep my opponent off balance by mixing up the direction and speed of my serves. Most of my decisive points have been slow serves that hugged the side walls. Or, after serving consistently down the left wall, I would serve a slow ball that would get lost in the right corner.

There are three basic serves:
- the low drive,
- the high lob,
- the scotch toss. *(Photo 2-5A)*

The Low Drive

Try to picture an imaginary line parallel to and about 12″ behind the short line. Your low drive should rebound from the front wall and bounce on the floor between the short line and the imaginary line. Make sure the ball will not rebound off the back wall or, if so, not higher than 30″.

This serve should not hit the side wall, but should be angled enough so as to hug the side wall as it enters the back corner. If this serve is directed to your opponent's weak hand, you will get a weak return from deep court.

This serve can be executed from several positions along the service zone, but most good players stand about half way between the side walls, so as to have the opportunity of serving the ball towards either near corner and at the same time commanding the all-important center court position.

The High Lob

This is a change-of-speed serve that hits the front wall higher than does the low drive, but is hit easier so it will rebound and bounce on the floor between the short line and the 12" imaginary line. Again, make sure it does not touch the back wall. This serve should be directed so as to force your opponent to attempt his return at chest height. *(Fig. 2-3)*

The Scotch Toss

The scotch toss can be executed by either overhand, side arm or underhand stroke. The server undertaking such a serve should stand about 6' from the left side wall if the serve is intended for the left rear corner. After contacting the front wall, the ball then strikes the right side wall and angles across the court to the rear left corner.

This serve should hit the front wall high enough for the ball to strike the floor halfway between the short line and back wall, and it should then hit the left side wall about 3' from the back wall.

Make sure to observe your opponent so as not to give him the chance to fly hit this serve. If he moves forward, anticipating the serve, give him the lob down the right. *(Photo 2-5B)*

Photo 2-5A

Photo 2-5B

Photos 2-5A,B: **Ken Schneider demonstrating the overhand "Z" serve and Fred Lewis preparing to a "Z" serve with his sidearm stroke.**

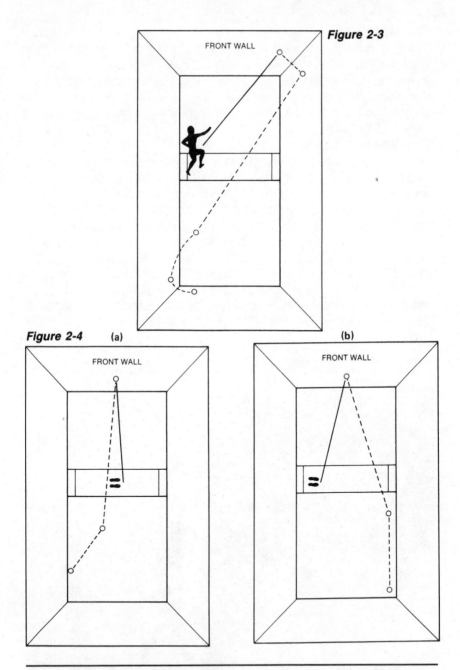

Figure 2-3

FRONT WALL

Figure 2-4 (a)

FRONT WALL

(b)

FRONT WALL

Figure 2-3: The Z-serve: Note that server is very near side wall, and ball strikes close to the corner of the front wall.

Figure 2-4: (a) The natural hook angled to left rear corner (hit with the right hand). (b) The natural hook angled to the right rear corner (hit with the right hand): Note that ball "straightens out" parallel to the side wall.

TOP DOUBLES PLAYER
COLLINS DISCUSSES
VARIETY OF SERVES
PHIL COLLINS

Photo 2-6: **Perfect form of 3-time National Doubles Champion, Phil Collins.**

Fortunately, I found that my baseball experience helped me quite a bit in learning the fundamentals of handball. Two common faults of most beginning players are failure to watch the ball in the air, and not keeping their eyes on the ball as it travels into the glove. In baseball, the good hitters follow the pitched ball all the way, and if they take their eye off the ball before swinging, they lessen their chances of connecting squarely. In handball, you can't hope to stroke the ball properly if you have your eye on a spot on the front wall where you may want the ball to go.

Remember, after serving the ball, you should turn your head and automatically guide your arm up, looking over your arm to protect you from being hit in the face. At the same time, you are able to know where the ball is and note the footwork of your opponent as he readies for the return.

The novice player should serve from the center of the court and after the serve, move about a foot back of the service line and about one or two feet to his weak side, blocking out that corner and forcing his opponent to return to the strong side or ceiling. If a ceiling return is made, the server should move back and return to the ceiling to keep his opponent in back court.

I wouldn't attempt to teach the novice any "hop" serves until he has mastered the fundamental serves. The most effective serve in the modern day game is the side arm smash serve, i.e, dropping the ball with the weak hand, and driving it with the strong hand *as the ball descends—not on the rise.* Follow through and you will obtain natural "English" on the ball. You will also keep your serve low and difficult to return.

I would definitely say that the success of a champion handball player is 50 per cent service, and 50 per cent in getting a weak return from the opponent. The side arm strong service will generally get weak returns. It can be varied with a lob overhand or underhand serve, deep and to the weak side of the opponent. You can also use a smash overhand serve in such a variety. There have been exceptions to the rule. We have seen tremendous retrievers, such as *Angelo Trulio* and *Gus Lewis,* who do not rely on powerhouse serves.

Change Serve

We should also mention the "Scotch Toss Serve," where the server stands to the left hand or right hand side of the serving lines and angles the ball so that it will hit front wall, side wall and come back high to the weak side of the opponent. The one glaring weakness of this serve is it leaves the server to one side if the opponent is able to return fast to the open side. Usually a server can hustle back to a good position before the return is made. This angle serve can be made side arm, overhand, underhand-fast or lob.

THE SERVE

MIKE DAU

Some players refer to the serve as the most important shot in handball. Others will counter that the most important shot is the one ending the volley. Regardless of the emphasis one wants to place on the serve, everyone must agree it is indeed unique. In many ways it can be likened to a penalty shot in soccer or hockey whereby a player has an uninterrupted opportunity to score a point against the goal tender. Certainly there is no easier way to score a point in handball than serving an ace against your opponent. Developing that skill is another matter.

Before discussing theory, it would probably best serve the purpose of this article to deal with fundamental mechanics. I will begin with those mechanics involved in the basic low hard serve executed with a side arm stroke.

- **Alignment in the Service Zone:** Body faces the side wall. Feet can be on the short line but not extended beyond. Weight primarily on the back foot.
- **Ball Drop:** There are two schools of thought: (1) dropping the ball with the stroking hand or (2) dropping the ball with the non-stroking hand. Without going into the merits of either, I will only discuss the non-stroking hand method. Place both feet on the short line, the left foot 3 or 4 inches in front of the right (for a right handed player). Take a short jab step forward with the right foot, then drop the ball with the non-stroking hand, minimizing spin, and forward of the center line far enough away from the body to accommodate the length of your stroke. The ball should not simply fall out of the hand but be purposely bounced so it will bounce higher than the level at which it is contacted.   The ball is not contacted at the apex of the bounce but on its downward flight.
- **Weight Distribution:** Most of the weight will stay on the back foot prior to contact. The forward movement of body mass must coordinate with stroke contact.
- **Arm Movement:** The elbow leads the arm and as both start forward, the hips should open. This can be accomplished by pointing the forward foot toward the front line. Opening the hips aids both control and power.

- **Hand Contact:** The ball should contact the hand at the base of the two fingers inside the thumb. This is not an absolute rule but rather a starting place. Many players contact the ball more toward the middle of the hand while others extend it further onto their fingers.
- **Eye Discipline:** If one fundamental can be considered more important than another, it has to be eye discipline. If asked, every player should be able to answer the following question after each serve. After dropping the ball, did you observe any spin on the ball as it rebounded from the floor? If a player cannot answer that question, how much better will his eye discipline improve once the ball is in volley?

Service Objectives

The primary concern in handball is service control. If a player consistently controls the serve, he increases his chances for any of the following: an ace, a weak return which provides an offensive opportunity, a defensive return executed by the receiver with his off-hand, or at the very least, prevents an offensive return by the receiver.

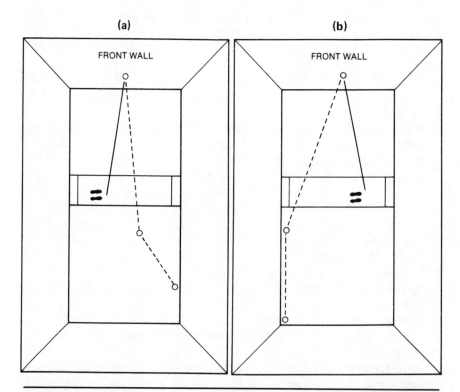

Figure 2-5: **(a) The reverse hook angled to right rear corner (hit with the right hand). (b) The reverse hook angled to left rear corner (hit with the right hand).**

Service Advantages

The server has several distinct advantages over the receiver: the server knows how he plans to execute the serve (speed, hop, etc.); the server has a front court position; and the server, as stipulated by the rules, is the only one able to score a point.

There are two distinct parts involved in the act of service. Part I, the serve itself (mechanics), and Part II, preparation for the return of serve. Both involve significant mental preparation prior to their execution. Before dropping the ball, a player should know exactly how he intends to serve (to include speed) and have a visual image of where the ball is directed. It is a gross error to drop the ball and then determine how and where the ball will be served. The rules permit the server 10 seconds in which to serve, and a segment of that time should be utilized for mental preparation. At the same time, the server should remind himself that after the serve has been executed he must "read and react" to the return of serve (Part II). A mental lapse at this point could mean the difference between gaining an easy point or a quick hand out.

Everyone has experienced serving "one that felt real good" as it left the hand, got a little smug, assuming it was an automatic point, only to have the serve returned and be caught flat-footed. The act of service must be viewed as an extremely critical time span, and the server must have his mental awareness operating at peak efficiency.

Initial movement after the serve (Part II) will be just behind the short line, equidistant from the side walls. However, this is not necessarily true when serving a lob or 3-wall serve unless they are poorly executed. The second phase of movement is to the pre-shoot position, the reaction to "reading" the receiver and the flight of the ball as it leaves his hand.

"Reading" the receiver simply means observing the manner in which he addresses the ball. Is he bending over to punch the ball to the ceiling; is he upright preparing to stroke the ball overhead; is he bending over to shoot, etc.? Does his body alignment tip off the direction in which the ball will travel?

"Reading" the ball as it leaves the receiver's hand must create a reflexive decision and movement. The flight of a handball is either propelled up or down. Movement to the back court is the reaction to a ball going up. Holding a position near the short line, preparing to attack the ball, is the reaction to a ball going down. There are some exceptions, most notably "Big V Returns" (see *Handball,* June 1977, "Specific Returns of Serve"), overstroked ceiling or wrap-around shots, or what I refer to as an "N.B." (no brain) return, one that goes up directly to the front wall and just as directly (after contacting the floor) to the back wall, the end result being a set up. Although the "N.B."

is propelled upward, it will not force the server into the back court. Experience will dictate other exceptions to the "up or down" reaction. Regardless of the reaction, the movement must be made with the utmost haste to a "pre-shoot" position.

Service Imagination

Players get into an unfortunate habit of serving one basic serve and usually at the same speed. The baseball pitcher who has only one pitch and nothing to complement it places limitations on his potential success. This holds true for the aspiring handball player. Changing speeds, developing hooks, controlling lobs, gaining some amount of consistency when hitting the crotch, effective 3-wall serves, hard low drives hugging the wall—all are essential tools in developing a more effective game. With a limited arsenal of serves, the server loses the element and advantage of surprise. Too many players view the serve as merely an opportunity to put the ball in play instead of acknowledging its scoring potential. The more points a player can score off his serve or off the second shot, the less he has to score via the rigors of volley.

- **The Safe Serve:** This is simply a 3-wall serve executed after committing a fault serve. The purpose of attempting a 3-wall serve at this time is it will prevent an offensive return by the receiver and has a low percentage of being short. Whenever this serve is attempted and the ball contacts the side wall first, thereby causing an out, players are encouraged the next time they serve to try the 3-wall serve again. The purpose is to regain confidence in this serve. As the game becomes critical and you have to rely on the safe serve, you do not want negative feedback from your last 3-wall attempt hindering your chance for success. This same principle could apply to other muffed serves.

- **Hop Serves:** The fundamentals involved in hopping a ball are very simple. The more spin the hand can impart on the ball, the bigger the hop. Creating spin on the ball relates to the amount of frictional hand surface making contact with the ball. Too often a player will rotate his wrist prematurely prior to contacting the ball, thus minimizing the hand surface contact. When executing a natural hop, the ball is contacted at the bottom of the palm and slides through the entire hand surface. When executing a reverse, the ball is contacted at the top of the hand with the fingers also contacting the ball on the outside. The hand rolls over the top and the outside of the ball. By definition, a natural hop by a right handed player makes the ball break to the left; a reverse hop makes the ball break to the right. **(Figs. 2-5)**

- **Bait Serve:** A player cannot make a steady diet of this type of serve, but it is useful occasionally. For this particular serve, the server attempts to hit the ball close to the right wall (approximately one foot), contacting the back wall about two feet high. The server is hoping to "bait" the receiver into attempting a kill return in the right corner. Unless it is a flat roll out, the server is in excellent position to rekill the kill attempt. A good time to attempt the bait serve is immediately after a long, hard volley. When the receiver is breathing hard, he is more prone to try to end the volley, given what appears to be an opportunity.

Service Drills

Practicing service control does not require much imagination. But as in any practice situation, I suggest you organize a definite plan, otherwise boredom sets in and little value is gained. For example, ten 3-wall, ten lobs, ten naturals to the left, etc. Practicing serves, like stroke mechanics, can be accomplished by yourself, but practicing "reading and reacting" to the service return requires another player. I refer to this exercise as the THREE SHOT DRILL. The server attempts any and every serve in his repertoire, and the receiver returns them any way he wants. The server "reads and reacts," taking his second shot. The server and receiver can exchange positions after a sequence of ten attempts.

The next opportunity you have to watch a match, regardless of the skill level of the players, observe closely the number of points won or lost on the serve or the second shot by the server. The margin of victory will more often than not reflect the winner's serve, Part I and Part II.

UNIVERSITY OF TEXAS COACH-TEACHER EXPOUNDS ON IMPORTANCE OF SERVE

PETE TYSON

Quite often when I am conducting a handball clinic someone will ask, "What is the best serve in handball?" To which I usually reply..."The one that works!" Now, I'm not trying to be a wise guy (or maybe I am). The point I'm trying to make is that no one particular serve can be called the best serve. Because serving in handball is so similar to pitching in baseball, I might counter the question with a question. "What is the best pitch in baseball?" And the reply is usually, "Well, it depends on who you are pitching against,"...which is usually correct not only for baseball but also handball. Who is your opponent and what are his own particular strengths and weaknesses? Maybe you know them before the game begins and you can plan your game accordingly. But maybe you don't know, in which case you should experiment with your various serves and attempt to determine his weaknesses by watching the effectiveness of his returns.

What does it take to be a good server? As in pitching, two things—control and variety. Naturally, it's nice to have good power, but power in itself is useless if it is not controlled. You need a variety of serves because, as in pitching, one serve may work very well against many players, but others may handle it easily. So you must be able to counter with another good serve if you hope to have success.

What kind of serves do we call "good serves?" The more advanced you become, the more advanced your competition is likely to be. Although the "Ace" (the serve that completely eludes the receiver) is ideal, you will find it very difficult to serve a ball an advanced player cannot at least return. So knowing he is probably going to return your serve, how do you know whether or not your shot has been effective? If his return allows you to remain close to the short line to make your next shot (either after the bounce off the floor or on the fly), your serve has accomplished what it should. Also, if his return gives you a back wall setup, your serve has been successful. What you manage to do with your next shot depends on your own skill, but at least you have gained the opportunity to win the volley, which means your serve was a good one. But if your opponent drives you into rear court with a well-angled pass or a ceiling shot, your serve advantage has been neutralized; even worse, he may have gained control of the volley since he will move up to the all-important front court while you retreat to the rear; remember, the player who controls the front court will usually win the volley.

Although there are different types of serves, most possess several common factors:

- Most of the time they should be directed towards your opponent's weak hand.
- They should remain close to the side wall on their path toward the rear corner (only the Z-serve varies a little on this one).
- They should be hit at such height, angle and speed that they do not allow your opponent the opportunity for a back wall return.

The first factor, hit serve to opponent's weak hand, sounds obvious, but perhaps it's not as obvious as it appears, because I believe your opponent has more than one weak hand...HE HAS THREE WEAK HANDS! (I think I just lost most of my readers here because they think I've been hit on the head by one handball too many—but give me a chance to explain what I mean by three weak hands.) Weak hand #1 is found when a player must attempt his shot from below the waist. Weak hand #2 is found when attempting a shot from between waist and shoulder height, and weak hand #3 is found when attempting a shoulder height or higher shot. A player can be very strong at one of these three positions and very weak at another. Even very good players will usually be weaker at one of the three positions. What you, the server, must do is discover which of your opponent's three hands is indeed the weakest, and then concentrate most of your serves to that "hand."

The serve that will force your opponent to use weak hand #1 (below the waist) is the *Low Drive Power Serve.* Remember to keep it low so it will bounce within about 5' of the short line or else it will rebound off the back wall.

The serve that forces your opponent's return from weak hand #2 (between the waist and shoulders) is what I call the *Changeup.* The angle of this serve is identical to the Low Drive except that it should be hit with a half-speed arm stroke so the ball will contact the front wall about 5' high. It must be stroked easy enough so it, too, will land close to the short line.

The serve that will force your opponent to use weak hand #3 (shoulder height or higher) is the *"Lob."* Anyone who has played against Paul Haber needs no introduction to this tantalizing serve. Most good players agree the receiver should charge this serve and hit it on the fly. However, if you can control the lob so the ball just clears the short line, it will be very difficult for your opponent to "cut it off" without stepping or reaching over the short line which is a violation (point for the server).

There is a fourth basic serve, the Z or *"Scotch Toss."* This serve can be executed both with the low sidearm and the overhand strokes. It should be hit hard and the ball should land on the floor about 8-10 feet behind the short line. Therefore, it is considered a safer serve, and most top players will use this serve if their first one was short. Unless your opponent has an exceptionally powerfull off-hand, this serve can be very effective. Remember the proper angle in order to keep it from rebounding off the back wall. One mistake some players make when hitting the Z serve is the position they take after the serve. Too often the server will move out to the exact middle of the court. Now this center court position is considered ideal most of the time. But the beauty of the Z serve is you can force your opponent to hit the ball with his weak hand into your strong hand area—if you will assume the proper position. This position is just behind the short line and on a straight line between where the receiver is going to contact the ball and left front corner, thus blocking that vulnerable alley down the left side wall. Of course, if the server is left handed, he would be between the ball and the right front corner.

Do you ever serve to a player's strong hand? If nothing else works, try anything! Some players have developed a very deceptive move when serving their low drive serve and have good success with an occasional surprise shot directed down the strong hand wall.

There is much more to the art of successful serving such as changing the speed of various serves. I suggest you read Jimmy Jacobs fine article entitled, "Jacobs Advises: 1—Change Speed of Serve...2—Don't Overswing...3—When to Concede Point." Other good articles on the serve are Vic Hershkowitz's, "Serve, Most Important Shot in Handball" and Ken Schneider's "Position Paramount—Control Down the Walls—Serve is Like Pitching in Baseball—Shoot Side Armed." All three of these articles appeared in earlier issues of *ACE* and they also can be found in the USHA's *Championship Handball plus Official Handball Rules.*

VARYING SERVE
TO FIND
VULNERABLE SPOT

HARRY PACKER

Underhand, overhand or sidearm, the server puts the ball into play from the server's box. Ideally, you serve the ball so your opponent cannot return it. Since you can score only while you are serving, if you can serve the ball 21 times in a row so your opponent cannot return it, you have got yourself the game. First, of course, you have to win the toss for serve. Unfortunately, I do not know any method that guarantees success in this.

Serving, then, is of prime importance to your game. It is, therefore, important to develop a good offensive serve that is hard to handle—one that puts your opponent on the defensive right from the start. If you can develop such a serve, your opponent's returns will be much easier to handle, and you may establish an edge that will give you an advantage throughout the game.

What is an effective serve? Any serve your opponent has trouble handling. You will reach to the point where you will be able to evaluate your opponent's weaknesses—then serve to those weaknesses. But until you are able to evaluate his game, serve to your opponent's weak hand consistently. When you have convinced him that you are going to continue "feeding" his off-hand, give him a serve to his strong hand, especially if he has begun overplaying the off-hand portion of the court.

This raises an important point. In serving from spot to spot, change the speed of your delivery and the direction in which you hit the ball. Look to one place on the court, serve to another. Keep your opponent off balance, expecting one kind of serve, receiving another.

Editor's Note: *Harry Packer is a veteran southpaw campaigner, astute student of the game and a handball enthusiast. He has authored the handball column for the Los Angeles Athletic Club Mercury magazine and was the 1974 club champ. He and Mike Dunne from San Francisco also won the 1974 Labor Day Open Doubles Tourney at San Jose.*

Practice all types of serves using all three basic strokes. The overhand enables you to lob the ball hard and high, making the ball hug a side wall on its rebound. (This is an excellent serving stroke, especially if your opponent has a very weak off-hand.) Try a sidearm serve that rebounds the ball low into one of the back court corners.

As you practice serves, concentrate on avoiding the serves that rebound to the back court, bounce to the back wall and come off in a perfect position for your opponent's sidearm return. Mix them up! Practice your aim. Pick out imaginary spots on the court and try to hit them with serves during your solo practice sessions.

Try hitting an overhand "Z" serve from the left hand side of the serving box. Hit the ball to the front wall far to the right. The ball will carom from the front to sidewall, bounce in center court and go back into the far left rear corner, where it will hit the left wall, then the rear wall and finally drop (with luck or skill on your part), completing a "Z" pattern, presenting your opponent with the difficult retrieve. However, this serve must be hit with speed and be placed accurately or it gives the receiver a set-up; so practice, practice and practice.

Use your imagination in practicing serves. Mix them up and when you find a certain serve works well for you, keep practicing it as you would a stroke, so that its execution becomes more or less second nature, enabling you to be more creative.

Players often inquire about "English": hooks, cuts, slices, reverse hops, etc. Applying "English" to the ball is a question that comes up more often from beginners than from seasoned players. I usually answer that you must control the other phases of the game before you attempt to put "stuff" on the ball. In learning the natural or reverse, it should be emphasized that such shots are useless if they cannot be controlled.

The natural hop is executed in the same manner that you would turn a door knob to open a door with a slight downward twist of the wrist. The ball is met low on its descent at the juncture of your forefinger, your thumb and first two fingers. In baseball, it would be similar to a throw from shortstop to second base, a sidearm throw.

The reverse hop is an unnatural motion—the hand, wrist, arm and shoulder rotating counterclockwise, like the screwball in baseball pitching. The ball is again met low on its descent with the wrist and hand movement rotating down and away from the body. This shot is hard on the arm for it takes a lot out of it. Many top players use it in conjunction with the natural hop, mixing up the serves to keep the opponent guessing. Defense for the hops? Do not commit yourself too soon. Let the ball break after it hits the floor and then make your move to the ball. Remember, if the ball is hit hard enough to come off the side or back wall before you hit it, the "English" will be taken off the ball as a result of hitting a wall after it bounces off the floor.

SERVE–
SWING–
VOLLEY–
JIM JACOBS

Concentrate continuously on changing the "speed" of your serve. We all change the place in the court where we serve the ball...down the left, down the right, three wall and so on. But of equal importance is the continuous change of the speed of the serve. If a ball is always fast, or slow, or simply at the same rate of speed all the time, your opponent must accustom himself only to the different places in the court you hit the ball.

In other words, he runs to the spot and swings away without one thought to timing his swing. However, if you hit two serves, hook or not, in the "IDENTICAL" spot on the court, but you have hit each at a different rate of speed, you require your opponent to adjust his timing to compensate for the speed you put on or take off the serve. The big difference, of course, is that you know in advance what you are going to do in the service box, while your opponent must make his adjustments in the timing of his swing "after" he sees the speed you have decided to use.

In conclusion, when you serve the ball to a different spot on the court, and you also change the speed of the serve, you are actually giving your opponent "twice" the problem he would have encountered had you simply changed the area to which you served, but kept the movement of the ball at the same rate of speed.

TAPE SESSION ON
THE HABER METHOD
COVERING OVERALL
COURT STRATEGIES
PAUL HABER

IMPORTANCE OF SERVE. PAUL, YOU DON'T NECESSARILY COUNT A LOT OF ACES OFF YOUR SERVE. WHAT DO YOU TRY TO DO, THOUGH?

–I try to force a weak return from my opponent's off-hand on the serve. Assuming most of the opponents are right-handed, I serve to the left with a reverse, and I try to keep from going to the back wall. In other words I want my opponent to hit the ball underhand with his left hand, hoping he'll get into a ceiling volley with me.

NOW, VERY FEW PLAYERS IN THE GAME USE "STUFF" ON THE BALL WITH THE SERVE OR DURING THE VOLLEY. DO YOU THINK IT'S POSSIBLE FOR THE CLUB A PLAYER TO LEARN HOW TO HOP THE SERVE?

–To learn how to hop the serve effectively is very helpful but I don't recommend that this player work on it. I think this should be the last step to learn after the rest of the game has been perfected. A hook takes a lot out of the arm and a great deal of control to be effective. Many "A" players hook the ball but it costs them points. You'll notice most of the players who hook the ball a lot lose speed from their arms in the second game of a tough match. One of the hardest hitters, Oscar Obert, hits a very hard ball but never uses a hook, and I think that's why he can always keep his arms so strong throughout a grueling tournament. I think if Oscar did employ a big hook, his arm would tire in late stages of key games.

With the amount of handball Oscar has played, one-wall, three-wall and four-wall, it is likely he would have suffered a lot of arm trouble with the use of hooks.

Editor's Note: *This article is an excerpt from the tape session referring only to Haber's comments on the serve.*

Photo 2-7: **Five-time National Singles Champion, Paul Haber, about to hit a back wall shot in the 1966 National Doubles Finals.**

COMBINATION LECTURES, IN-COURT DEMONSTRATION, FEATURES STORM MEADOWS A.C. FIRST SUMMER CAMP—INSTRUCTORS: JIM JACOBS AND STUFFY SINGER

MORT LEVE

Serves

We've heard it before, but it bears repeating. The importance of the serve cannot be over-emphasized. It is the ONLY time you have complete charge of the game. You're at the twenty foot line, while your opponent is back 37 to 38 feet from the front wall. Once in the service box, you have 10 seconds to concentrate on the speed and placement of your serve. You should experience little difficulty in propelling the serve to your opponent's weak hand. Often the serve in handball has been compared to pitching in baseball. You have available a full arsenal of shots; underhand, sidearm and overhand, which can be executed at various speeds with natural or reverse hooks.

ON THE REVERSE HOOK—a reverse hook by a right-hander results in a counterclockwise spin on the ball after it is struck by the right hand. The ball will then come off the front wall, hit the floor and jump to the right.

ON THE NATURAL HOOK—a natural hook struck with the right hand results in a clockwise spin on the ball. After rebounding off the front wall, the ball will hit the floor, sharply angling to the left. The amount of spin on the ball and, thus, the amount of the natural or reverse hook, is determined by the amount of friction transmitted from the hand to the ball, which results from the amount of glove-ball surface contact, speed of the swing and amount of wrist and elbow rotation.

There are many top tournament players who use little or no hook on their serves, but do have extreme accuracy with their power serves. An abbreviated list would include Steve August, Terry Muck, Lou Russo and Paul Haber.

THE LOB SERVE—the overhand lob serve is used more than the underhand. The ball is bounced high and preferably stroked as it descends to about eye level. The ball should hit high on the front wall and contact the floor directly behind the short line. This will result in the ball having a high arc prior to descending into either the right or left rear corner(s) of the court. Again, either the reverse or natural

96

can be put on the ball, making it rebound away or into the wall. The lob serve is very effective if it is controlled properly. The better players try to return it strongly as they do not want to give the server a set-up from his advantageous short line position. The so-called club player is content just to return the ball.

THE THREE-WALL, Z OR "SCOTCH TOSS" SERVE—a very "safe" serve. Usually, this type of serve is most effective when it is hit hard. A right-hander should serve from the left side of the service box so the ball will come off the left side wall parallel to the back wall deep in the back court. The speed makes it difficult for the receiver to react quickly and charge the ball before it hits the floor the first time. When using the Z serve from the right side of the service box against a left-hander, it is important for the server to move from his serving position; otherwise, the entire left side of the court is left open for the return of serve. Many players use the Z as a safe second serve. Again, the Z serve can be varied in speed to keep the receiver from anticipating fully. It can be executed overhand, preferably shoulder high to give a lower trajectory or sidearm.

In using the power serve, a player like Stuffy would rather short on the first serve than hit it too high so it comes off the back wall. The average player is inclined to hit that second serve too high as he concentrates on getting over the short line...the advice to him would be to work on the second best serve, a cross court or lob.

Editor's Note: *This article is excerpted by the editors from the many lectures and clinics given by Mort Leve.*

SERVE CAN BE
YOUR MOST IMPORTANT
WEAPON

VIC HERSHKOWITZ

The serve is the most important shot in handball, because the server is clearly on the offensive while the receiver is clearly on the defensive and the server is the only one who can score a point. In addition, serving may give you an immediate point as a result of executing an "ace." If it does not and the serve is a good one, it will probably bring a weak return possibly setting up a point on a kill, pass or some other non-returnable shot. For these reasons, it is vital to develop strong serves.

By this I do not mean an extremely fast or vicious shot. There are many effective methods of getting the ball into play and each player must "sort" them out, until he finds the method best adapted to his physique and style of game. Walter Plekan was the master of ball placement and the hook service. Angelo Trulio did his best work with an overhand high serve. Ken Schneider and Gus Lewis served underhand with plenty of "cut" on the ball. All of these men served differently, but effectively.

It is important, I believe, to vary the speed of service, as well as the general type of service. Plekan always kept his opponent off-balance, for example, by varying his service, similar to a baseball pitcher mixing his delivery. Some of Walter's most decisive points were slow serves that hugged the side walls or, after he had served consistently to the left side of the court, he would serve a slow ball down the right side wall deep in the right corner. If you can get a player all tensed up anticipating a hard serve down the left side wall, then give him a soft one down the right side wall, you have thrown him off-balance. Similarly, if you have fed him a steady diet of high scotch twist serves and then served him a sudden, fast, low ball, he cannot possibly be ready unless he is psychic.

I do not mean you must try to master all the various serves, but after deciding on the basic service best suited to your game, work to develop subtle variations within that general framework. My most effective serve is a hard one, usually quite low and short. To execute this serve with the right hand, I face the right wall with my feet parallel to the wall, shoulders in alignment with my feet. I stand about mid-

Photo 2-8: Vic Hershkowitz, the greatest all-around (1-wall, 3-wall and 4-wall) handball player in the history of the game.

way between the sidewalls, thus not disclosing which side I am going to serve to. At the same time, I am in position for the return of service.

Placement of the ball is controlled by the hips, shoulders and arms, not by the alignment of the feet. Aligning the feet differently for serves to the left or right side of the court will tip off your opponent where the serve is going. No unnecessary help should be given the opponent!

Whether the ball goes shallow or deep in the court does not depend on the height from which the ball is dropped, but depends on the follow-through. I usually drop the ball from a height of about 18 inches. This is quite low and many fine players drop it from greater heights. Trulio, for example, bounces the ball above his head for his overhand service and hits it when the ball is about level with the top of his head. A scotch twist serve is hit approximately shoulder high.

The backswing for the underhand serve is similar to the backswing in golf in that the contraction of the back muscles during the wind-up and the pivot of the hips in both sports is the same. Also, the arm is extended at about a 45 degree angle. As in golf, you should keep your head stationary and your eyes on the ball until after you have hit it.

Now, it is possible to keep your eye on a spot and still move your head. So, my advice is to point your chin at the spot where you are going to drop the ball and keep it pointed at that spot until you are well into your follow-through. Remember that important tip—point your chin!

RETIRED COLONEL DISCLOSES "SECRET" OF HOPPING BALL WITHOUT ARM SORENESS

COL. (RET.) MARTIN A. FOSTER

Sometime about 1959, Johnny Sloan was playing handball in the Pentagon Athletic Center in Washington, D.C. This fine young national champion was then in the Army, stationed in the Washington area, and played almost daily in the Pentagon Courts. He was agile, strong, swift, intelligent and deadly, and his serve, when he wanted it to be, was a gasp-provoker—hopping a yard. His gallery of analytical handballers learned a new lesson every day in the intricacies of this complex game. He was inspirational, creating new ambitions for handball perfection in all his watchers. But, innocently, Johnny probably ruined more of these players than he helped, driving some from the courts altogether, or into a lifetime of soft, well-placed but vulnerable serves, or into that handball players' limbo—racquetball. Everyone coveted that impressive "hop." *(Photo 2-9A)*

All through Johnny's tour of duty in the Washington area, I watched my fellow handballers working on new serves, emulating the young champion. They kept their wrists loose, their hands neatly cupped, and they attacked the ball. Each serve was marked by sharp hand action as they snapped their wrists, over or under, in or out, in an effort to spin the ball and make it hop. Few were successful. The proper timing at impact with the ball was too hard to achieve consistently with those flapping hands. They often got new speed on the ball but lost accuracy and the ball would bounce softly off the wall, or around the rear corners setting up easy returns.

Then disaster! The embryonic "hopartists" began to pay the price for those loose wrist, snapping serves. One after another they came up with sore elbows. Sore spots developed near the bony protrusion on the inner side of the joint and it became painful just to extend the arm. The loose serves were pure agony.

I was not a mere spectator at all this activity. I, too, was trying my damndest to copy the great Sloan—and my elbow was sore, sore, sore. The Flight Surgeon took one look, heard my story, hmmmmm'd a bit and said, "Tennis Elbow." He then gave me a quick lesson in "Bursitis—It's Causes and Cures."

Photo 2-9A

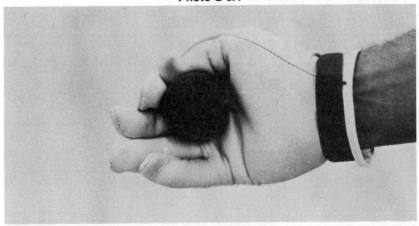

Photo 2-9A: Hand position for hitting a "natural" hook serve. Note that the ball will release off the thumb and forefinger.

Photo 2-9C

Photo 2-9B

Photo 2-9D

Photos 2-9B,C,D: Player showing the arm motion used in hitting a "natural" hook. Note the angle of the arm with the fingers pointing down and how the elbow comes in towards the player's mid-section as he imparts clockwise spin on the ball.

BURSITIS: Inflammation of the bursa, a small sac or cavity in the joint.

PROBABLE CAUSE: The wrist snapping action on the serves extended up to the elbow. The resultant jarring shocks in the joint distributed or damaged the bursa, producing painful inflammation.

CURES: Drugs, aspirin, and applied heat tend to reduce the pain, but the only sure cure—stop irritating the joint. The doctor suggested strongly I quit handball!

But, what sensible fanatic is going to quit handball? I kept playing but was reduced to the soft straight ball and a frustrating inability to score points. Some ailing players did quit. Others switched to games where they could still run and compete but without pain, contributing in the process to the growing popularity of racquetball.

Then I was hit with a paradoxically fortunate calamity. The orthopedic surgeon operated on my ailing left knee and took me out of handball competition for about five months. I was forced to rest my aching arm. This enforced rest cured my elbow. As soon as the cast was off my knee, however, I went limping back to the courts just to throw the ball to keep my arm muscles strong enough to preclude an injury or strain when I returned to playing. As my mobility increased, I began experimenting with my serve. The first wrist snap and the warning twinge in the elbow, however, convinced me I had to find another way to serve effectively. I had time. It would be eight to ten weeks before I'd be able to play a game. *(Photos 2-9B,C,D)*

In trying to analyze what makes a ball spin, I went back to my golfing experience. To hit the ball straight, the club face had to be straight, squared with the intended line of flight. If the face was open at contact, the heel of the club leading the toe into the ball, the ball took a clockwise spinning action and slice, or curved to the right. Conversely, when the club face was closed, the opposite spinning action resulted and the ball hooked or curved to the left. Reverse spin could be applied by hitting the ball below center, usually with a club face with more loft. The golfer need not snap at the ball. He merely hits through or across the ball to impart the spin. If the face is open, the ball slices; if it is closed, the ball hooks. I found, especially in the case of reverse spins, that a sharp, quick hit, not necessarily hard, produces a greater spinning action.

Applying this golf knowledge to my serving practice, I found that the same principles applied. Open the hand by turning the palm outward away from the body and strike the ball, hitting straight through along the intended line of flight, and the ball spins clockwise. When it hits the floor—it hops. Holding the palm inward toward the body as the hand hits the ball imparts a spin in the opposite direction and it hops the other way. There is no need to snap the wrist or to give any other hand action. The wrist is held straight, the hand does not snap forward, and there is no elbow shock—no pain.

During these weeks of convalescent serving practice, I experimented widely. I tried to find the effect of different hand angles and the reaction as the ball rebounded off the different spots on the hand. I found that each spot created a different action on the ball. Some were subtle—some sharp. Coupling the differing angles and spots, and adding other subtle differences like straight or bent fingers as I hit with them, created an infinite variety of serves.

I soon found the lush spot on the hand, though, and began to achieve my "Johnny Sloan hop." Well, it wasn't really that good, but the ball began to take a very gratifying hop, good enough when I was able to return to playing to get a few clear aces in almost every game.

The big muscular cushion at the base of the thumb, the lush spot, became my serving bonanza. With the hand slightly cupped and relaxed, the cushion is a soft hemisphere presenting a great variety of hitting angles. To capitalize on this cushion, I went back to my youth and the lessons learned on the pool table (at the YMCA) on how to make a cue ball spin. One diagram drawn for me showed nine distinct hitting areas on the cue ball.

Each spot, when hit by the cue stick, produces a different spin action, or "English," on the ball. For example, when the cue stick hits top center, the ball continues forward after making contact with the object ball. When the ball is hit on the low center spot, it tends to reverse itself after impact. Hit on the left, the ball spins clockwise; on the right, it spins counterclockwise. The expert, hitting a selected spot on the cue ball with exact desired velocity, can predict the path the ball will take after impact with the object ball or cushion to a predetermined spot on the table. He does not spin or twist the cue stick, but he hits, for the most part, through the desired hitting area. The hitting angle and the force of the hit created the spinning action on the ball. The most effective "English" results when the ball is hit with a quick, sharp motion such as would be used to strike a bell to get the greatest ringing resonance.

I began to visualize the same striking areas on the handball as are used in pool and billiards. When, by dint of concentration, I was able to hit the desired striking area with the hand cushion, I was delighted to see the ball doing new and different things. It would hop left or right, bounce high or low, depending on where I made contact with the ball on the serve. Best of all, I didn't have to hit hard or with any sharp wrist action to get the ball to hop. The only thing I had to insure was that I hit a specific aiming point with the big cushion and hit straight through the ball.

One particular spot on the ball gave the best hop, most nearly like the ones I'd seen Johnny Sloan apply. When I dropped the ball close to the body, then hit underhand with the elbow close to the body, contacting the lower left hitting area on the ball with the upper part of the hand cushion, hand turned outward, and hitting straight through the ball, it hopped sharply left after it hit the floor. The amount of hop or its quickness varied in direct proportion to the quality of the hand contact. If the ball was hit softly or smoothly, the bounce was soft—when hit sharply, with a quick bump, the leftward bounce of the ball was bigger and quicker.

When I began playing again after the long layoff, I found the new serving knowledge more than compensated for the loss in speed and mobility I suffered from the bad knee. I began gaining many points on the serve alone—a new experience for me. I also learned that, although the big hop was a very useful tool, it wasn't the only point getter. As long as the ball did something different on each serve, hopping softly or hard, bouncing high or low, moving in or out, all in varying degrees, the opponent's chances for a strong return were reduced and his mistakes increased. Frequently, he was unaware of the subtle differences applied to the ball and their effect on his timing and would blame my success on the "bad day" he was having.

In reality, my new-found serving skill (not great but far better than before) was only a spin-off from my attempt to learn to hit the ball effectively without jarring my elbow or straining my shoulder, thus incurring injury and pain. I was successful and now, 14 years later, I am playing as well as ever, with good company, and with no sore elbow. It seems that all players, young and old, should give careful attention to eliminating from their games any strokes which strain the shoulder or elbow. There are other effective ways to hit the ball. They'll play much longer and, very likely, a much better, controlled game of handball.

IMPORTANCE OF A STRONG SERVE

VIC HERSHKOWITZ

The top players watch the ball at all times, never taking anything for granted! If you follow the flight of the ball until your opponent has struck it, you will know if it is being angled and at what height it is being hit. Thus, you will get a jump on the ball, usually allowing you to get in a better position to return it.

To apply hop to the ball, one must either cut under the ball, twisting the wrist in a clockwise direction (for right-handed players) to apply natural spin to the ball so it will take off to the left, or roll your hand over the ball to apply reverse spin, making the ball bounce to the right. Left-handers obtain opposite results when putting "English" on the ball. *(Photo 2-10A)*

Many players have asked me where the ball meets my hand and just how twist or hop is applied to the ball. To put natural hop on a serve, the ball meets my hand on the heel or on the thumb and first finger, the hand being cupped to the same degree for all shots. To cut the ball to the right, I hit the ball in the meaty part of my hand between the first and second fingers while rolling my wrist over so that it covers the ball. For a left hop I hit the ball in the same spot while rolling my wrist under the ball in a clockwise direction. All of this, again, is for right-handed serves. Opposite hop results when you shift to stroke the ball with the left-hand. The hop and twist are applied solely through wrist action. The follow-through of the hips, shoulder and arm control the speed of the ball. *(Photos 2-10B,C,D)*

The question has come up whether the ball should always be made to hop toward the wall, depending on whether one is serving to the left or right side of the court. My answer is it should be made to hop both ways to either side of the court, because the main objective is to confuse your opponent for your advantage. Keep him guessing by varying the direction of the serve, the direction of the hop and the speed of the serve. Keep him off-balance at all times.

It is more desirable to try to hit a twist shot that will break into the receiver, "handcuffing" him. You have to study him closely to decide where he will be at a given time, because he may anticipate your shot or be agile enough to get into position for a fair return. In any case, when trying to handcuff your opponent, be sure the ball

Photo 2-10A

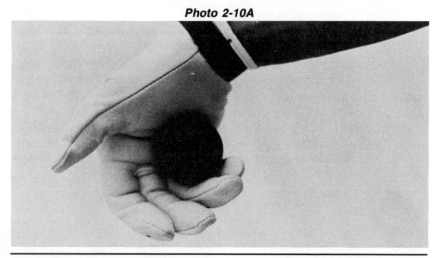

Photo 2-10A: Hand position for the "reverse" hook. Note that the ball will be released off the curled little finger.

Photo 2-10C

Photo 2-10B

Photo 2-10D

Photo 2-10B,C,D: Player's arm motion for hitting a "reverse" hook. Note how the elbow turns away from the body allowing the hand to "wrap" the outside of the ball.

is low enough so it does not come off the back wall as a set-up shot.

While mixing up your serves as to general placement and direction of hop, do not become so engrossed in the game or tense that you are trying to murder every serve. A major league pitcher who concentrates on sheer speed is soon in the showers unless he is a Walter Johnson or Bob Feller in his prime. Remember, there are times when there is much more spin on a let-up service than a fast one, and the hop will break very sharply, keeping the opponent off-balance.

BIBLIOGRAPHY

Collins, Phil. "Top Doubles Player Collins Discusses Variety of Serves." Excerpt from: *Official U.S. Handball Association Membership Directory and Guide,* 1961-62.

Dau, Mike. "The Serve." *Handball,* 1977, Vol. 27, No. 5.

Foster, Martin. "Retired Colonel Discloses 'Secret' of Hopping Ball without Arm Soreness." *Handball,* 1973, Vol. 23, No. 2.

Haber, Paul. "Tape Session on the Haber Method Covering Overall Court Strategies." Excerpt from: *Handball,* 1973, Vol. 23, No. 6.

Hershkowitz, Vic. "Importance of a Strong Serve." Excerpt from: *Official U.S. Handball Association Membership Directory and Guide,* 1961-62.

"Serve Can Be Your Most Important Weapon." *Handball,* 1973, Vol. 23, No. 6.

Jacobs, Jim. "Serve-Swing-Volley." Excerpt from: *Handball,* 1973, Vol. 23, No. 6.

Kirby, Pat. "Handball, the Kirby Way." Excerpt from: *Handball,* 1980, Vol. 30, No. 2.

Leve, Mort. "Combination Lectures, In-court Demonstration, Feature Storm Meadows A.C. First Summer Camp—Instructors: Jim Jacobs and Stuffy Singer." Excerpt from: *Handball,* 1974, Vol. 24, No. 4.

Lewis, Fred. "The Power Serve." *Handball,* 1977, Vol. 27, No. 6.

Muck, Terry. "The Lob." Excerpt from: *Handball,* 1979, Vol. 29, No. 2.

Packer, Harry. "Varying Serve to Find Vulnerable Spot." *Handball,* 1974, Vol. 24, No. 6.

Tyson, Pete. "Serving—The Percentage Way." *Handball,* 1977, Vol. 27, No. 1.

"University of Texas Coach-Teacher Expounds on Importance of Serve." *Handball,* 1973, Vol. 23, No. 6.

PART II
RETURN OF SERVE

RETURNING
THE SERVE
MIKE DAU

There must be a general understanding of offense and defense as it relates to handball shots before addressing the subject of service return. Handball shots fall into two basic categories: offensive shots, which are intended to end a volley and defensive shots, or those intended to continue a volley. Determination of an offensive or defensive shot when returning the serve will directly relate to the serve itself. If a serve is poorly executed and produces an opportunity to end the volley, an offensive shot is the proper choice. Conversely, if the serve does not provide an opportunity to end the volley, a defensive return is in order. The latter is certainly the most common situation, as part of the intent of service is to deny the receiver any chance to end the volley.

In developing an approach to the return of service, the receiver must be aware of the advantages in favor of the server.

- **The server knows how he is going to serve.** In most instances it will be an offensively-oriented serve, intended to prohibit any type of offensive return. Ideally, the server would like to score an ace, but, failing to do so, would then like to execute a serve producing a poor return with offensive possibilities on the next shot. The receiver's role is initially defensive in nature against a good serve. The receiver cannot manufacture an offensive shot; the offensive opportunity must be presented by the server.

- **The server has a floor position advantage.** *(Fig. 2-6)* The service zone is in the front half of the court, and after the serve the server will generally stand near the short line. Most points are won or lost in the front half of the court, and most serves are placed deep in the back half of the court. The receiver must acknowledge his poor floor position. *(Fig. 2-7)*

- **The server is the only player who can score points.** Loss of service is the server's penalty when unsuccessful. The receiver's penalty is much more severe; the server gains a point.

With an understanding of offensive and defensive shots and the advantages the server enjoys, how then should the receiver specifically approach the return of serve? The following sugges-

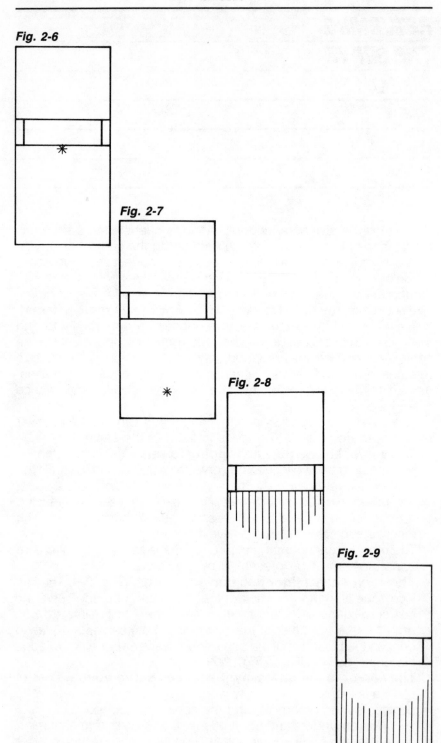

Fig. 2-6

Fig. 2-7

Fig. 2-8

Fig. 2-9

tions are recommended. The first consideration is the receiver's court-position. It should be five to seven feet from the back wall, equidistant from the side walls. Like all generalizations there are always exceptions, and they will be addressed later.

The next recommendation is one of movement. When the server makes contact with the ball, the receiver must start moving toward a preliminary "pre-shoot" position. There are several considerations taken into account when placing yourself in a "pre-shoot" position.

- Address the ball relative to the hand to be used, i.e. turn left for left hand, turn right for right hand.
- Get behind the eventual contact spot a step or two in order to drive into the ball.
- Get away from the line of the ball's flight in order to prevent restricting the intended stroke. In other words, avoid getting jammed.
- Place most of your weight on the back foot and bend the knees slightly.

The "pre-shoot" position must be determined as quickly as possible, and arrival at that spot must be almost reflexive. If the "pre-shoot" position is reasonably accurate and the bounce of the ball does not require any readjustment, there should be a temporary pause in body movement before driving into the ball. The ability to arrive at a good "pre-shoot" position, pause, then drive into the ball will greatly increase shot control.

What are the factors in determining whether to shoot the return of serve or attempt a defensive return? When reading the opponent's serve, the receiver must quickly analyze if the ball rebounding off the back wall will negate the advantage of the server's front court position. In other words, is the serve so poorly executed that the receiver will end up contacting the ball in the vicinity of the short line? An offensive shot is in order if such is the case. *(Fig. 2-8)* There are some obvious exceptions which must be taken into consideration and they are 1) ball hugging a wall (finger scrapers) and 2) ball very close to the wall and to the side of the receiver's off-hand. In both cases a wiser return would be a defensive choice.

When the serve forces a return from deep court, then a defensive return is necessary. *(Fig. 2-9)* Ideally the return would be directed to the server's off-hand. However, if the return fails to accomplish that, but still does not provide the server with an offensive opportunity, then for the most part the return of service would be termed a success. Everything possible must be done by the receiver to avoid giving the server two offensive shots in a row (considering the serve as the first).

Regardless of how the receiver mechanically returns the serve defensively, all defensive returns will generally have the characteristics of contacting at least three surfaces prior to contact with the back

Photo 2-12: **Naty Alvarado in position to receive service. Note that he is approximately 3 feet from the back wall.**

wall, two of which will be the front wall and the floor. Ideally the ball should contact either the ceiling or a side wall first. Contacting three or more surfaces does not automatically provide legitimate defensive return as every handball player has been victimized by a ceiling shot that caught a side wall and "hung" in the front court or by an overstroke wrap-around return, that after rebounding around the walls, arrived on or about the short line. The same can be said for an understroked wrap-around shot that provides a fly kill opportunity.

A service return contacting front wall, floor, back wall can be better phrased as a defenseless return, lacking intelligent planning.

In summary, the following sequence regarding return of serve is suggested:

1) Stand equidistant from side walls, 5 to 7 feet from back wall.

2) Determine the height the ball was contacted by the server and the initial left or right direction of the ball.

3) Turn left or right 90°, never taking eyes off the ball.

4) Get to a pre-shoot position.

5) Transfer weight to back foot, bend knees slightly.

6) Prepare to alter position if ball forces you to do so.

7) Return serve either offensively or defensively directly relating to the serve.

There are several basic defensive returns of service.

- Big "V" versus serves running close to a side wall and returned from the back 6 to 8 feet of the court.
- Overhand to ceiling versus lob serves.
- Punch to the ceiling versus 3-wall serves.
- Wrap-around return versus 3-wall serves and serves hooking into a side wall and carrying the back wall.

These will be covered in detail in the next article.

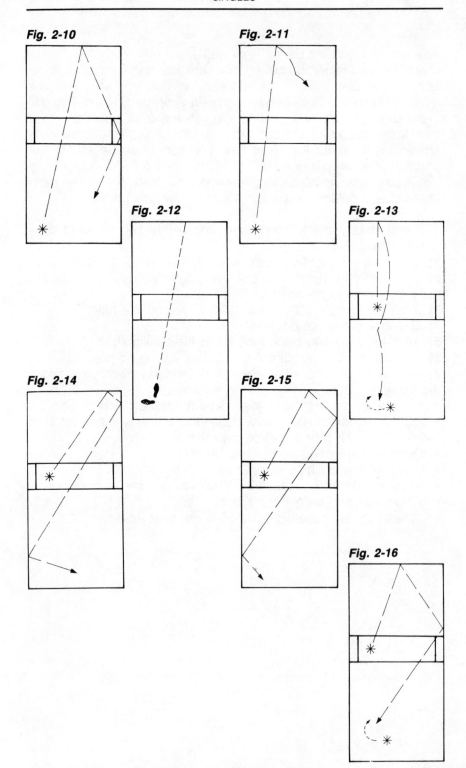

Fig. 2-10

Fig. 2-11

Fig. 2-12

Fig. 2-13

Fig. 2-14

Fig. 2-15

Fig. 2-16

SPECIFIC RETURNS
OF SERVE
MIKE DAU

In the article titled "Returning the Serve," I discussed the basic concepts and fundamentals of returning the service. This article will offer a variety of suggestions on the return of specific serves.

Photo 2-13: Vern Roberts attempting a back wall shot from the left rear corner. A good return would be the 2-wall or "V" pass (see figure 2-10).

Low Hard Serve

The first discussion concerns a low hard serve that, after contacting the back wall, stays close to the side wall (less than 4 inches) and must be returned from deep court. Because of the ball's close proximity to the side wall, stroking the ball side arm (with fingers pointing to side wall) becomes impractical considering the limited striking surface of the hand. Therefore, the stroke should be executed in an underhand fashion. The receiver benefits two ways: (1) more hand striking surface which will assist control, and (2) better vision because you will be looking down on the ball and will be able to determine its true distance from the side wall better. The visual aspect of the underhand stroke is particularly important when playing on courts with glass side walls to the floor, as depth perception is more of a problem than on plaster side walls.

The intended direction of the return is what we refer to as a Big "V." When returned from the left side, it will contact the front wall (head to chest height) to the right of center and angle toward the right side wall (contacting it on the fly) two to three feet high in the vicinity of the short line. *(Fig. 2-10)*

It must be stroked with solid power and the ball must hit at the right side wall on the fly. If the ball rebounds from the front wall to the floor before contacting the side wall, it provides the server with an opportunity to end the volley. *(Fig. 2-11)*

The basic problem most players have in executing a Big "V" is consistent control. It must be emphasized that it cannot be "wished" toward its intended direction. When stroking the ball, open up the front foot, pointing the toes toward the right of center. *(Fig. 2-12)* This will permit a greater range of motion with the upper part of the body which is essential. Control can only be gained through practice.

If the served ball is actually sliding along the wall, you have a genuine dilemma. Fortunately, it is the exception rather than the rule. Patience is needed when confronted with a wall slider. In many instances the ball will frequently move away from the wall an inch or two, permitting better hand contact. However, if such is not the case, then attempt to flip the ball (underhanded) up along the same course of its flight. A slider for a slider.

Lob Serves

The receiver has several concerns in returning lob serves; however, before discussing them I might mention that when the server sets up for a lob serve, I suggest the receiver stand as deep as possible, a hand's touch off the back wall (staying equidistant from the side walls). This will supply a little more reading time in order to determine the type of return.

In order to decide how to return a lob serve, the receiver must initially read how high and how hard the served ball contacts the front wall, how close to the side wall the ball is traveling, does it contact the side wall before touching the floor, and how close to the short line the ball strikes the floor. Without reacting properly to all of the above, returning lob serves will only increase in difficulty. The height of a lob serve initially contacting the front wall as well as the force of contact will help in a preliminary way to determine if the ball will carry the back wall sufficiently to return it off the back wall. This will be further substantiated by observing where the ball contacts the floor relative to the short line. If a lob serve is hit with moderate speed sufficient to cross within a foot or two of the short line, the receiver can attempt to take the ball on the rise (off the floor) and return it to the ceiling or take it from deeper court on its downward arc with the same objective. It depends on your individual skill. If the combination of height and force of the lob serve will provide a back wall shot (but the ball stays close to the side wall) then a Big "V" is in order. If the lob serve touches the side wall before contacting the floor, the receiver can step inside the angle of reflection and return the ball with his natural hand. In some cases an opportunity to shoot the ball may arise. Finally, if a lob serve is poorly executed *(Fig. 2-13)* and does not stay close to the side wall but allows the receiver to get an outside position on the ball permitting him to return the ball with his natural hand, he must respond to the opportunity. The receiver should never return the serve with his off hand when he can do it with his natural hand.

Photo 2-14: **Vern Roberts, Jr. returning a lob serve from the deep, left corner. A ceiling shot is his best choice.**

I suggest when stroking overhand with the left that you avoid jamming yourself. Often players allow the ball to get too close on overhand strokes, more so with the off hand than the natural. Confidence, I suspect, has a great deal to do with it. It is difficult for anyone to prescribe how far away the ball should be on contact because it directly relates to an individual's physical structure and coordination.

I might also add that in order to go up (overhand) one must be down. In other words, you can't be standing up (legs 180°) when going overhand. You must bend the back leg, drop the tail, and slightly dip the shoulder of the striking hand just prior to contact. Facing the front wall (instead of the side wall) when stroking overhand is another no-no.

3-Wall Serve

There are two basic 3-wall returns of service, and they relate to the angle of reflection off the third wall. If the ball coming off the third wall rebounds at an angle toward the opposite side wall *(Fig. 2-14)*, a punch to the ceiling is recommended. If the ball rebounding off the third wall angles toward the wall *(Fig. 2-15)*, I suggest an open hand, wrap-around shot directed up into the left wall, front wall, right wall.

When the server sets up for a 3-wall serve, the receiver should align in the same floor position as recommended for the lob serve. The receiver can determine how the 3-wall serve will reflect off the third wall by observing how far away from the side wall the served ball contacts the front wall. Also, listen to how hard the ball is contacted. The closer the ball contacts the front wall to the side wall with power, the more radical the angle of reflection off the third wall, something close to a right angle, traveling toward the opposite side wall. Conversely, the farther away from the side wall the ball contacts the front wall, the more likely the angle of reflection off the third wall will equal the angle of incidence. In this situation the ball will travel in a direction toward the back wall.

When the server makes the mistake of not hitting the 3-wall serve with power, the receiver should step inside the angle of reflection from the second wall *(Fig. 2-16)*, and return the ball the way it originated with solid power. If the receiver does not cut off a slow 3-wall serve, there is a good chance the ball will die in the left corner after contacting the third wall.

Returning Hop Serves

If your opponent has the ability to put a good hop on his serve, the first suggestion is to stand somewhat deeper on the court. The purpose is to allow the hopped serve to occur a little more in front of your normal receiving position, providing a fraction more time to react to the ball's spin action off the floor.

As the ball is being served, the receiver must attempt to read the server's elbow in order to determine which way the ball will hop. As a rule, if the elbow is close to the body, the ball will take a natural hop; if extended, the ball will reverse. However, like all general statements, there are some exceptions. Consider the player who utilizes an underhand stroke or something closely resembling it. His elbow is always close to his body. Regardless of how a player strokes his hop serves, the most important read (and reaction) will occur when the ball crosses the short line and contacts the floor. The receiver must stay light on his feet and avoid crowding the ball.

Advance knowledge of the server's hopping abilities is obviously helpful. If you are not aware of his hop talent, it is crucial to discover what talent he has as quickly as possible. For example, does he only throw a natural? If he can throw a reverse, does it simply straighten out when executed from right to left (assuming he is right handed) or does it take a big reverse? The same would apply to a natural from left to right. Does his position in the service zone tip off how the ball will hop? The receiver's mental awareness and reaction to these situations, and any others that may occur, will be an invaluable asset in coping with hop serves.

Regardless of the type of serve the receiver must react to, he must still go back to basics and return the serve offensively or defensively, the choice in direct relationship to placement of the serve. The receiver must constantly remind himself that he cannot manufacture an offensive return! The opportunity must be provided by the server. By and large the majority of serves in a match will only present defensive options for the receiver. *(Photo 2-15)*

The movement after returning the serve is an integral part of the service return process. This movement is dictated by the nature of the return itself. If you inacted a good defensive return, you would maintain a deep court position, assuming you only provided the server with defensive options. If the serve was returned poorly, affording the server offensive options, you had best change the short line as the error has already been made and there is no reason for you to compound the mistake by staying in the back court. If you attempt an offensive return, you had best put it away because the server is in good position to dig it out, but again your movement should place you in the front court.

The return of service may be defined as "condition red," a period in which your mental processes must be coordinated with your physical reflexes. In order to improve this critical aspect of the game, I offer as a final suggestion a drill in which I place a great deal of faith. We simply refer to it as the 2-shot drill. Its purpose is to assist the receiver in proper returns of serve. One player will simply serve the ball any and every way he can and the receiver returns the ball accordingly. If the receiver is having difficulty with a particular serve, the server gives him a steady diet of it until he succeeds. The two players can alternate their roles and can even develop a game out of it by giving a point to each successful return, with each player having the same number of chances to return the serve.

In closing I remind you of the basic objective of the return of serve and that is NEVER PROVIDE THE SERVER WITH AN OPPORTUNITY TO END THE VOLLEY WITH YOUR RETURN OF SERVE. This must be the paramount thought in your approach to returning the serve.

Photo 2-15: **Naty Alvardo returning a low drive serve. Note that he is about to hit the ball with his underhand, fist stroke in his attempt to hit a ceiling shot return.**

RETURN OF SERVICE

PETE TYSON

You will remember that in the section entitled "The Serve" I mentioned in my article what I call the five situations of handball, i.e. the serve, return of service, defense, offense and shot anticipation. This article is devoted to Situation #2, or the return of service.

What happens when you are about to receive service? Your opponent, the server, is taking his time, getting relaxed and comfortable while he is analyzing your weaknesses. He is making a decision whether to hit the ball high or low, what kind of speed and angle, and what kind of spin to put on it; he is going to position himself where he chooses in the service zone and hit the ball when he chooses. He is attempting his placement from about 17 feet away from the front wall and will do so with his strong hand. *(Photo 2-16A)*

You, the receiver, are going to have to return this serve. You are not sure what type of serve is coming and you will have only one or two seconds to get into position. You will most likely have to attempt your return from approximately 38 feet away with your weak hand and probably from a difficult position very close to the side and/or back wall.

Photo 2-16A

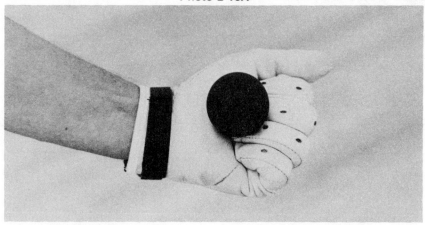

Photo 2-16A: Hand position for the fist shot. Note that ball contact is on cuticle area of middle two fingers.

Photo 2-16B

Photo 2-16C

Photo 2-16D

Photos 2-16B,C,D: Fred Lewis demonstrating the underhand fist shot to the ceiling. Note (1) the extended backswing, (2) the angle of arm at contact and that his back leg is bent and (3) the upward follow through motion of his arm after contact.

Does this sound like you are at a tremendous disadvantage? Does a duck go barefoot? Can Paul Haber hit ceiling shots? You better believe it! YOU ARE IN TROUBLE! What should you do?

These are your choices when attempting service return:

(1) Hit a kill shot.

(2) Hit a pass shot.

(3) Hit a defensive shot.

(4) Fail to return the ball.

(5) Give your opponent a "setup."

The first two choices (kill and pass) take tremendous accuracy. Considering your disadvantage, do you really think you can execute a kill or pass consistently? Consistently? (If your answer is yes, please call me when you are down Texas way as I need all the easy victories I can get!) If your opponent served ten serves, and you killed five and missed five, you are doing a pretty good job of shot execution. But is it good enough? The five times you killed the ball you gained the serve. The five times you missed, your opponent retained the serve and gained FIVE POINTS! You are demonstrating some exciting shots, but you are losing!

This is not "percentage handball." Attempting to kill or pass off a good serve is just too difficult. So what is left?

(3) Hit a defensive shot.

(4) Fail to return the ball.

(5) Give your opponent a setup.

Now do you know what your service return attempt should be? Right! You should be doing your best to neutralize the server's tremendous advantage by forcing him to retreat to rear court and by gaining for yourself a little time to assume a better position closer to the front wall. You do this by hitting defensive shots, primarily the ceiling shots or 3-wall returns. *(Fig. 2-17) (Photos 2-16B,C,D)*

Fortunately, there is a defensive counter to each of your opponent's good serves. Generally, serves will fall into three categories: low power, high lob, and crosscourt Z. Let's take these one at a time. *(Fig. 2-18)*

The best way to defend against the LOW POWER SERVE is to return it with the fist. You can either fist (punch) it to the ceiling *(Fig. 2-17)* or into the opposite side wall which will bring the ball "around the walls" and into rear court. *(Fig. 2-18)* Which is better—ceiling shot or 3-wall return? If you have a choice (sometimes you don't), I believe the ceiling shot is better because it will drive your opponent into the rear court, whereas the 3-wall return can be played directly after the floor bounce a few feet behind the short line, and it might even be taken out of the air. Paul Haber and Stuffy Singer, when returning the low power serve, will usually go to the ceiling, whereas Fred Lewis and Dennis Hofflander usually fist a 3-wall return. So which

125

is better? Let me make a suggestion. If you have difficulty getting good power when you fist the ball, you should attempt a ceiling shot because a good 3-wall return should be driven very hard.

There will be times when you have little choice, when the fist 3-wall shot is necessary, and this is when the ball "jams" you. You might have to play the ball very close to and slightly in front of your body. In this case you will find it easier to fist the ball into the opposite side wall. Is this shot really an important shot to have? Ask that big, jolly bear from Wisconsin named Ray Neveau. Ray is one of the finest left side doubles players ever to play the game. However, there was a time when I had no difficulty gaining weak returns when serving to Ray. All I had to do was serve a reverse hook that would start down

Figure 2-17

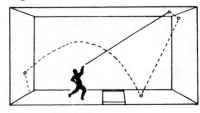

Figure 2-19

Figure 2-18

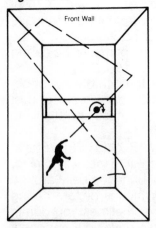

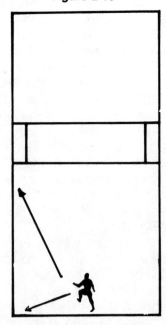

Figure 2-17: **Ceiling shot. Can be hit with underhand fist stroke or overhand open hand.**

Figure 2-18: **Left-handed fist 3-wall return.**

Figure 2-19: **Player moving into position to return lob serve. Note: 2 options.**

Figure 2-20

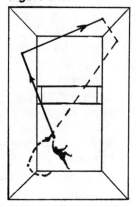

Figure 2-21

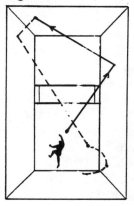

Figure 2-22

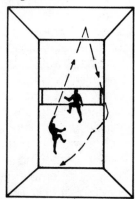

Figure 2-20: Player's return of Z-serve using left hand (open hand).

Figure 2-21: Player's return of Z-serve that comes off back wall.

Figure 2-22: Player's offensive, cross court, 2-wall angle "V" return.

the left wall and break back to the right, causing Ray to be "jammed." Result—set-up after set-up. Then Ray learned to fist a 3-wall shot, and suddenly instead of gaining dozens of setups, I WAS NOT GETTING ANY! That shot cost me two National Doubles Championships (finals of 1973 and 1974). Ask Ray if that shot is really important.

There are two schools of thought on how best to defend against the LOB SERVE. Stuffy Singer would rather move in and hit the ball as it is coming up off the floor, overhanding it to the ceiling. Fred Lewis moves into the rear corner and overhands it to the ceiling. There are advantages and disadvantages to both methods. Moving up on the ball as Singer does allows you to attempt your return from about 25 feet from the front wall, but it is more difficult to time a ball as it is coming up. Lewis must return the ball from 38 feet away which requires more strength, but he is hitting the ball as it is dropping which is easier to time. It will probably depend on the strength of your weak hand as to which method you should choose. However, I believe that with practice, Stuffy's method would be easier to master. *(Fig. 2-19)*

A good return of the Z-serve is the 3-wall return. Assuming the serve is hit to your left hand, you should back up very close to the back wall and about ten feet away from the side wall. Step toward the ball and attempt a left hand 3-wall return. This is an open-hand shot that first contacts the left side wall. *(Fig. 2-20)* It then hits the front wall and right side wall before bouncing on the floor and rebounding back towards the left rear corner, very much like the Z-serve that was served to you. If the Z-serve hits deep enough in the court to rebound off the back wall, you can pivot with the ball and hit a right hand 3-wall return. This is also an open-hand shot and it should contact the right side wall first. *(Fig. 2-21)*

Sometimes your opponent's serve may go into the rear corner and give you the opportunity for a back wall shot, but will be a difficult one if it is close to the side wall and doesn't rebound very far off the back wall. Lob serves will often do this as well as power serves hit slightly too high. When this occurs, it is usually best to attempt a cross court 2-wall angle (some players call this angle a "V"). The ball, after hitting the front wall, should contact the side wall slightly behind the short line so it will rebound back towards the corner from which it was hit. *(Fig. 2-22)*

The preceding are the types of "good percentage" shots you should be attempting whenever your opponent serves you a "good" serve (one that is very difficult to kill or pass). However, if your opponent is kind enough to serve you a ball "with a handle" such as one that comes off the back wall to your strong hand, by all means take the offense and attempt your good power kill or pass. Never assume that you are going to get a set-up. You should always assume that the serve is going to be a good one and THINK DEFENSE!

Photo 2-17: Former National Singles and National Doubles Champion, Stuffy Singer, blasting a kill shot in the finals of the 1979 National Doubles Championships. Singer is one of the most intelligent players in the game who would probably have won even more national titles if he had not suffered several major knee injuries.

MAKE DECISIONS
FOR VICTORY:
PLANNED REACTIONS

STUFFY SINGER

What did he hit? ... Where did he hit it? ... Where should I go? ... What shall I hit? ... Oh hell, I'll just end the volley!

You have just been witness to the thought pattern that goes on in every handball player's head during the course of almost every volley he plays. That thought process is called decision-making or the ability (or inability, in this case) to make up your mind. Let me give you a case study that will further demonstrate the futility of these exercises.

Your opposition is serving the ball, and he normally has a relatively good serve. You are standing back, getting ready to return serve and, as is normal, your mind is blank. Don't take that as an insult, but as a constructive evaluation of the circumstances involved. The following is a typical thought process of a player receiving service:

1. He served the ball.
2. It's going to the left.
3. I wonder which way it's going to hook?
4. Boy, that sure looks like a tough serve.
5. Should I play defense?
6. Should I punch the ball to the ceiling?
7. Should I hit it around three walls?
8. Should I just get it back any way I can?
9. It's not as tough as it looked.
10. Should I hit a killshot?
11. To the right?
12. To the left?
13. Straight ahead?

After all this, he still has to execute whatever shot it was he finally decided to hit.

In this instance our ball player makes the crucial mistake...he refuses to make a commitment! His refusal to commit puts him in the dubious position of always being 50% wrong. The only thing that could be right in this situation is for his opponent to make a mistake. Be prepared! Don't ever count on your opponent to make a mistake. If you prepare yourself for your opponent's good shots, you will also be able to handle mistakes.

Actually, it is asking too much of anybody to figure out where the serve is going, whether to play offense or defense, which offensive or defensive shot to hit and where to hit it. After figuring all that out and making all those decisions, it is improbable that anyone would still have enough time left to execute any shot properly.

My advice is to accept the fact that you are most vulnerable when returning the serve. By making this decision and accepting your problem before your opponent serves, you can make a full commitment to a good, effective, defensive return of serve and give yourself more time to concentrate on the pure execution of your defensive return.

Your thinking process prior to the serve might go something like this: I'm in trouble; I've got to play defense. My first choice is to fist the ball to the ceiling. If I can't do that, I must try to get the ball around three walls, and if all else fails, get the ball high and deep and preferably soft. The whole key to this theory is time. The more time you have, and the fewer decisions you have to make in that time, the better the results will be.

"Fence straddling," or the refusal to make commitments and decisions, is basically the fear of being embarrassed. By establishing a neutral posture, you are never totally wrong and therefore never embarrassed, but you will lose the volley anyway. Don't be afraid to commit; don't be afraid to be 100% wrong. I would rather be 100% wrong half the time and 100% right half the time and win, then be 50% wrong all the time and lose.

Photo 2-18: Johnny Sloan at his prime in the late 1950's. He was a 3-time National Singles Champion and 5-time National Doubles Champion.

SLOAN ON
FIST SHOT
JOHN SLOAN

When I first started playing handball I did not use a left hand—or "off hand"—fist shot, but upon advancing to top flight tournament play I soon found that those low, hop serves breaking to my left hand necessitated a change.

By fisting the ball on such serves, I can drive it down the left side or hit the ceiling and bring the opponent to the rear of the court without expending too much energy. Against a southpaw this could be varied with either an open hand or fist to front, right wall, or the fist to the ceiling.

There are many who frown upon the fist shot because they believe it to be too erratic for consistent use. However, practice will prove it to be a fine defensive weapon and on various occasions it can be used as an offensive shot.

Among the top flight tournament players, the only one who rarely uses a fist shot at any time is Vic Hershkowitz and he is as close to being completely ambidextrous as any player who ever got into a court.

Jimmy Jacobs uses either hand fist shots on a return of hop serves or difficult shots when he finds himself in back court—hitting the ball up to the ceiling. Jimmy will fist serves that are below his waist to the ceiling more than 80 percent of the time to get his opponent back from front court. Anyone who has played against him will admit this is one of his finest defensive weapons—and it was particularly noticeable in his finals match against Hershkowitz in the 1955 USHA National Singles Championships at the Los Angeles Athletic Club.

Various Types

Bob Brady uses a left fist shot for power passing shots as well as for ceiling shots from both the rear and front of the court. Of course, in the big courts (bigger than what we now call standard 20x40) the pass shot is more effective and on the 20x40 must be kept very low to be of value.

The ceiling shot is effective on any court, but on the 20x40 court it is better to hit it more softly to keep the ball from being a back wall setup. At all times I try to place my ceiling shots to either back corner.

They tell me Al Banuet used many unerringly accurate fist shots with either hand. However, he would be an exception to the general rule.

Phil Collins seldom uses a fist shot. He too, like Vic, hits just about everything open handed, but will occasionally fist when a ball is hit hard and in close to him—strictly a defensive return.

A lefthander, Morrie Singer uses a fist ball to the ceiling with his right hand to keep his opponent from maintaining a front court position. I believe this to be the main reason for his improvement.

If you analyze the game, a weak return on the serve puts you definitely behind that ol' "eight ball." By merely fisting to the ceiling you at once put your opponent away from front court and on the defensive.

Fist Below Waist

It must be remembered when the ball is above the waist it is most difficult to get any accuracy with the fist shot and it should be avoided. It is easier to return the ball to the ceiling or hit a well-placed shot along the side walls with an open hand shot. There is no difference in positioning yourself for a fist shot or an open hand shot. Your weight must still shift from your rear foot to the front foot, while lining yourself up to face the side wall. It is more difficult to hit any shot from a flat-footed position. Hitting the ball to the ceiling requires an uppercut motion of the arm swing, but in a pass shot more of a side arm motion is required to keep the ball low.

Basically, you have to build a game around your own physical attributes. You might very well find that by developing a couple of good defensive fist shots with your off hand you will give your opponent fewer set-ups and your game will improve tremendously.

BIBLIOGRAPHY

Dau, Mike. "Returning the Serve." *Handball,* 1977, Vol. 27, No. 3.
    "Specific Returns of Serve." *Handball,* 1977, Vol. 27, No. 3.
Singer, Stuffy. "Make Decisions for Victory: Planned Reactions." Excerpt from: *Handball,* 1977, Vol. 27, No. 3.
Sloan, John. "Sloan on Fist Shot." *Official U.S. Handball Association Membership Directory and Guide,* 1961-1962.
Tyson, Pete. "Return of Service." *Handball,* 1977, Vol. 27, No. 2.

PART III
DEFENSE

DEEE-FENSE

PETE TYSON

This is article #3 in my attempt to cover "The Five Situations of Handball." If you will remember in my previous article, the word, "situation," was defined "as anytime the ball is about to be hit." Articles #1 and #2 related to the first two situations, Serve and Return of Serve. This article is devoted to Situation #3, DEFENSE.

What is meant when we say you are on the defense? It means it is your turn to hit the ball, and you do not have a very good chance of hitting a kill or pass shot. Notice the words "good chance," because this is the idea behind these articles—attempting to make you aware of percentages in the game of handball and trying to convince you that your game will improve if you "play the percentages."

After the serve, there are two kinds of shots you should be attempting when it is your turn to hit the ball—(1) offensive kills or pass shots, or (2) defensive ceiling and three-wall returns. If you fail to hit one of these offensive or defensive shots, you will probably hit the ball into the floor or else give your opponent a setup (a high percentage chance of hitting an offensive shot).

The offensive kill and pass shots both require great accuracy. One of the biggest mistakes made in handball is attempting one of these offensive shots when chances of success are not good. A player who attempts offensive shots from defensive positions could be called, as the great Jim Jacobs once wrote, a "spectacular loser." Paul Haber was a much more spectacular player prior to 1966 than he was after. In 1966 at the National Championships in Salt Lake City, Paul showed up with a superb ceiling game. By emphasizing this defensive addition to his game, he became a much less spectacular player, but he became the National Champion and he remained Number One for a long time.

Alright, your next question should be—"How do I know when I'm on the offense or defense?" This is a very important question because (and I again quote from Jim Jacobs) "nothing, absolutely nothing, is as important to a great ballplayer as knowing when to go on 'offense' and when to go on 'defense.' Therein lies the secret of how to get all the 'easy shots' which makes winning such a simple accomplishment." Generally speaking, you are on the offense whenever you come to a complete stop before attempting your shot, make your attempt comfortably, and can make contact with the ball from below your waist.

It then follows you should consider yourself in a defensive position when you must attempt your shot while on the run, or from an uncomfortable position, perhaps too close to the body, or when you have to reach back to contact the ball; also when you attempt a shot from above the waist, and usually when you have to use your offhand from deep court.

The deceiving thing about this game is that even from these described "defensive positions," you can make a perfect kill or pass shot—sometimes. Another word for "sometimes" is "losing!" Attempting shots that you can make only "sometimes" is one of the mental errors that you can and must eliminate. The great thing about defensive shots is they do not require the pinpoint accuracy of an offensive shot, and even when you are in difficult defensive positions, you can execute defensive shots successfully a high percentage of the time.

Defensive Shots

The basic defensive shots are the CEILING SHOT and the THREE-WALL RETURN. Both of these shots can be hit either with the open hand or with the closed fist, but you must know which to use, because whenever the ball contacts another wall before striking the front wall (as both of these defensive shots do), the spin of the ball as it leaves your hand is of utmost importance. Whenever you contact the ball with the closed fist it will spin the opposite direction than it does when hit with the open hand.

Figure 2-23 shows the correct spin needed for the ceiling shot. This spin can be achieved by hitting the ball overhand with the open hand or underhand with the closed fist.

Figure 2-24 illustrates the correct clockwise spin needed for the three-wall return that first contacts the right side wall. This clockwise spin comes from hitting the ball with the open right hand or with the left hand fist (both strokes are sidearmed).

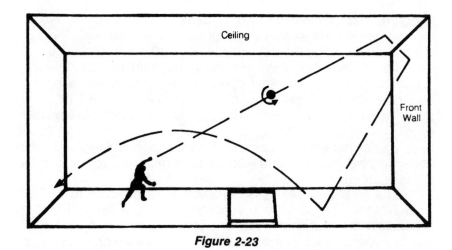

Figure 2-23

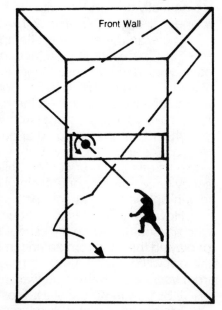

Figure 2-24   *Figure 2-25*

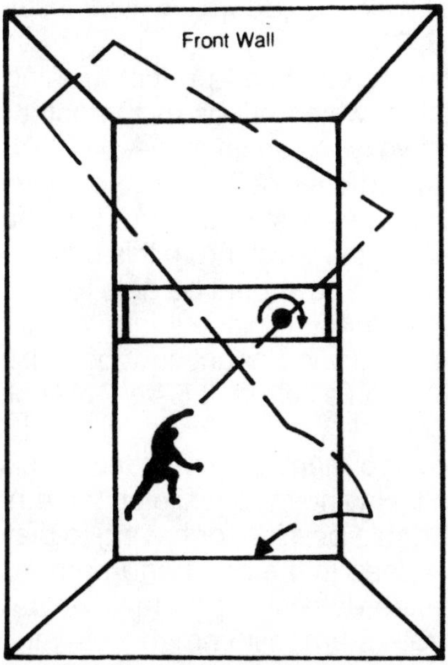

Figure 2-23: **The Ceiling Shot.**

Figure 2-24: **The three-wall shot hitting the right side wall first.**

Figure 2-25: **Three-wall shot hitting left side wall first.**

In **Figure 2-25** you see the correct counterclockwise spin necessary for the three-wall return that first contacts the left side wall. This spin is achieved by hitting the ball with the open left hand or with the right hand fist. Hitting these shots with the wrong spin will cause the ball to slow up and not carry into deep court. Ideally, both the ceiling shot and three-wall return should carry to the back wall and hit it about three feet high. This will force your opponent into a defensive position which is what you are trying to do. Your good defensive shots will keep your opponent from gaining offensive opportunities, and these shots will also give you a few seconds to recover and get back to a desirable court position.

A fist three-wall return is usually the correct shot to attempt whenever the ball "jams" you. And the open hand three-wall return is generally the best shot to attempt if you must reach back behind you to make contact with the ball. Try to hit these three-wall shots hard and make adjustments with your angle if the ball carries too deep (gives your opponent a back wall set-up) or doesn't carry deep enough.

Many players make the mistake of hitting their ceiling shots too hard which allows their opponents back wall offensive set-ups. Even many top players make the mistake of trying to hit their ceiling shots too perfectly and end up with the ball hitting a side wall, which usually spells disaster. **(Photos 2-19A,B,C)**

There are times when attempting to execute "perfect" ceiling shots are, percentage-wise, acceptable, which brings us to another point concerning defense. There are two types of defense—(1) CONTROLLED and (2) TROUBLE. "Controlled defense" means you have time to get set before hitting the ball with your strong hand, but you must make your shot attempt from above the waist. From this position you should not attempt to kill or pass, but you should be able to control your ceiling shot very well—well enough to place it into the opponent's off-hand rear corner. This is a very important shot because it may force your opponent into giving you a set-up. It is very difficult to win unless you get set-ups!

However, as I mentioned before, too many players attempt this kind of accuracy when they shouldn't. Having to hit while on the run, or playing the shot from an uncomfortable position, or having to play the ball with your off-hand from very deep in the court and perhaps from very close to the side wall, are the defensive positions we call TROUBLE (with a capital T). Most rallies are lost immediately after you attempt your shot from a "trouble" defensive position. Either you fail to return the ball or you give your opponent a set-up. You must get out of trouble with a defensive shot, but attempting to be too accurate from the "trouble" defensive position will often result in your ceiling shot hitting a side wall, which places your opponent on the

Photo 2-19A **Photo 2-19B** **Photo 2-19C**

Photo 2-19A,B,C: Fred Lewis demonstrating the overhand ceiling shot. Note the angle of his body as he leans back and the height at which the ball is about to be contacted. With the strong hand, a player can be very accurate in his attempt to make the ball rebound into the rear corners of the court.

Photo 2-20: Dennis Hofflander attempting a ceiling shot from a difficult position close to the sidewall. Naty Alvarado won this semi-final match of the 1981 Texas Pro Stop.

offense. When you are in "trouble," just try to get the ball into deep court close to the back wall. Don't try to stick it into the rear corner. Giving your opponent a shot in the middle of the court 38 feet away from the front wall is far better than taking the unnecessary risk of setting him up. Once again, the deceiving thing is that you can occasionally hit a superb defensive shot into the rear corner even when you are in trouble—occasionally. Is occasionally good enough for you? *(Photo 2-20)*

A player with a great defense can shut down his opponent's offensive opportunities. How is your opponent going to win if he has no offense? How are you going to lose if your opponent cannot score? The best "defensive" players in the last 22 years were Jim Jacobs, Johnny Sloan, Paul Haber and Fred Lewis. Between them they won the National Singles championship 18 times! These great champions were all "percentage" players who rarely hit the ball into the floor and gave very few opportunities for their opponent to take the offense. With their great defensive shots, they were able to control the rallies until their opponents gave them offensive opportunities, with their great DEFENSIVE SHOTS...

Photo 2-21: **Naty Alvarado about to hit an overhand ceiling shot from the right rear corner. Note that Lewis is stepping back to the rear court in anticipation of a deep return from Naty.**

WHATEVER THE LEVEL OF PLAY— GOOD HANDBALL REQUIRES DEFENSE

MORT LEVE

Stuffy Singer opines it appears reasonable that top pros (with the possible exception of "pure shooter" Dennis Hofflander) concentrate patiently on defense and wait for the percentage volley ending shot. It is the chess game for maneuvering and waiting for that vital breakthrough when the offensive shot presents itself.

"Yet," Stuffy tosses in, "I see the club type players invariably attempt shots that show no planning and have little or no chance of getting the point or handout." He adds, "These players should play with the same premise in mind as the very best national tournament players ... the main objective when that sure shot just isn't there is to keep the opponent from maintaining the offense. And that can't be done by trying to use the off-hand as an offensive weapon from deep court, rather than punching the ball to the ceiling or going around the walls."

Hofflander is an exception in that he can be very successful in shooting off the serve. His percentage is excellent and there's no one around who will argue with such a tactic when the player can propel the ball so strongly with either hand.

Fred Lewis is the personification of the instructional book ideal. His methodical, percentage game encompasses the patterns of Jim Jacobs and Paul Haber whom he has followed.

When watching the pros in action, it is noteworthy that so many volleying shots take full advantage of the wall or ceiling ... rarely are there any straight, front wall, defensive "alley" shots. And, this is where the "amateurs" miss the boat. They neglect to use the side walls enough and subsequently set up too many balls off the back wall ... or, in attempts to go to the ceiling, are not accurate enough— either missing the ceiling or hitting it too softly or too hard ... and when

Note: *This article was written several years ago after a Denver pro stop during which Stuffy Singer expressed some of his own thoughts and observations. At that time Dennis Hofflander was reaching his peak performance. Subsequent injuries have prevented him from staying on top along with Naty Alvarado and Fred Lewis.*

going around the walls, get it too low and allow the opponent at the short line area to pick the shot off, rather than having the ball carom behind him.

As Paul Haber will tell you, the last thing you should try to add to your repertoire is putting "stuff" on the serve. "Work on control of your straight serves and volleying shots, and offensive shots ... this is 100% more important than trying to toss a big hook at your opponent," Haber comments.

The player who has gained the advantages of being baptized in one-wall play knows well the values of the fly shot ... we don't just say fly kill because there are also the fly pass, fly ceiling, fly around the walls ... with the obvious advantages of precious time in not allowing the opponent to move into position or anticipate properly. Again, we would point to the basic difference between Hofflander and Lewis in fly kill attempts. Fred, with his one-wall beginnings, is much more potent ... Dennis has improved vastly over the last season in this department, and appears actually to kill with the fly better from the off-hand than with his natural hand.

What can be pointed out succinctly is: In carefully watching the pros on the Spalding tour it is clearly displayed how important it is to move quickly into position during the volley. The hardest thing to do in handball is to return and control a handball effectively while on the move. How much easier it is to move swiftly to the ball, be able to set and coordinate body movement for the shot.

The beginning handball player invariably finds himself floundering about the court, uncertain where to move, and then at the last moment flails awkwardly at the ball in an effort to return it to the front wall. He will not have that comfortable point of contact and as a result loses any possible coordinated power as well as all-important ball direction.

There is no way a player can get into proper position consistently without keeping his eyes on the ball—AT ALL TIMES. We emphasize that the use of the eye guard eliminates any "plate shyness," a fear of getting a hit in the eye by the ball. There is no reason why EVERY PLAYER should not wear an eye guard. It just takes a bit of getting used to, but from that point on you're home free.

LEARN TO
PLAY DEFENSE

TERRY MUCK

"The floor will beat you every time." This sage advice is repeated time after time in magazines and books on handball. What it means, in case you're wondering, is that continued use of low percentage kill shots will result in defeat.

"The floor will beat you every time," means more to the beginner. In fact, the more advanced you become, the more it means. At the highest levels of handball, shot execution begins to level out, and shot selection takes over as the determining factor in the winning and losing of games.

So call this an advanced bit of instructional advice if you want. You can read it if you are a beginner, but please realize that a higher priority for the beginner is shot technique; learn to hit the kill, pass, and serve. You can worry over the agony of shot selection later; right now play and enjoy your relative freedom from the subtleties of choosing offense and defense, kill and pass.

Since so many people talk about the importance of shot selection (handball experts such as Jacobs, Tyson, Singer, Leve, Lewis, etc.), there must be something to it. Further, if you have any doubts of its importance, watching a Pro Tournament will dispel them. The way handball is played today on the highest levels, shot selection *is* of paramount importance.

Although the problem is often raised, solutions are rarely given. Usually some vague advice recommends that you shoot good shots while on defense, and certain other good shots while on offense, or that you practice "percentage handball" whatever that means. The trouble with the advice most often given is that many of us don't know what "good" or "percentage" shots are, and no amount of explanation can teach us what is safe and what is risky.

Let's face it. Most of us learn handball by simply playing and finding out what works by trial and error. We form habits early in our handball playing careers, habits usually determined by our physical characteristics, so that a big strong person learns to hit hard pass shots, the short, quick person is usually a shooter, and the person with lots of stamina learns to play the "marathon" game. We have

Photo 2-22: **With his opponent controlling the front court, Terry Muck should be attempting a defensive ceiling shot with his fist.**

the habits reinforced because we win with these shots. They are our best shots.

So, when someone tells us to use percentage shots, our minds say "Yes, that sounds logical and right," but when we get back in the court our old habits take over, because the pressure of the game, and the good feeling we get from taking our best shots, removes the mental assent we gave to playing percentage handball.

How to break out of these self-defeating playing patterns? Try this. Determine before you start play that in every rally you will hit one defensive shot. When you are serving, begin counting after the serve, because the serve is an offensive shot. Don't worry about what kind of defensive shot you take: to begin with just don't kill the ball. Consider every shot except a kill shot defensive. After taking five defensive shots, then look for the rally ending kill.

Do not relax. Just because you are not killing the ball does not mean you are on vacation. You have to work just as hard to hit good defensive shots as you do to hit good offensive shots. Your opponent will soon catch on that you are not killing the ball much today and he will lay back for your passes and ceiling balls. Don't let this tempt you. Stick to your plan.

A couple of things will happen. You will find very few rallies last long enough for you to kill the ball. Someone will err. If you are hitting well-executed defensive shots, you will find your opponent hits the ball into the floor far more frequently than you ever imagined. You will also find there are a wide variety of defensive shots from which to choose.

This is one of the reasons this kind of game will improve your shot selection. You don't have to worry about choosing between many different shots; all you have to remember is not to kill the ball until you have hit five shots. The reason we recommend this game in the first place is that you can't learn shot selection until you learn the many shots there are at your disposal. This game will make you explore the uncharted regions of shot variety.

You may want to start out playing this game against an opponent you usually handle easily. At first it will even things up; later, as you begin to hit good defensive shots, you will beat him worse than ever. Then try it with better players or limit yourself to using just one defensive shot, say the ceiling ball. Make up your own games. By this time you will know what's best. The idea is to get you thinking about the shots you use. What you use will be determined by your physical capabilities. But you will find you have a much wider range of shots than you realized and you will learn to use them all more effectively.

OFFENSE, WITH NO DEFENSE

JIMMY JACOBS

There are a few top singles players in the United States today, most notably Stuffy Singer, who realize that EVERY TIME a singles player hits the ball an extremely important decision has to be made. IT HAS ABSOLUTELY NOTHING TO DO WITH THE PHYSICAL FUNCTION OF HITTING THE BALL. It is, chiefly, to decide whether you are on offense or defense.

I would say over 99% of the gallery is never aware such a choice is going on in the head of a top ball player! A gallery only measures a singles contestant by what they see with their eyes—the skill of his left hand—the speed he runs—the power in his arm—the accuracy of his kills—and the size of his hooks.

But nothing, absolutely nothing, is as important to a great ball player as knowing when to go on "offense" and when to go on "defense." Therein lies the secret of how to get all the "easy shots" which makes winning such a simple accomplishment.

Whenever you come to a COMPLETE STOP before you strike the ball, you are automatically on offense! This is the time when the great ball players choose to end the volley.

Whenever you are running at high speed when you contact the ball, you are on defense! Attempting to end a volley at a time like this is like buying a plane ticket back home. A ball player who goes for the kill during a peak running period is not courageous, he is simply uninformed. All of us have seen "spectacular kills" when a player runs madly for the ball, dives, and rekills the shot. There are numerous other situations which could be mentioned, all of them quite spectacular. We refer to these players as "Entertaining Losers."

When you are moving at a good speed after your opponent's shot, you must either punch it into the ceiling, or loft the ball, high, into a side wall first, so it hits three walls before hitting the ground. Both of these shots give you approximately 3 to 4 seconds to recover and get back to the desired center court position. Both of these defensive shots are quite unspectacular, but when done with consistency are worth AT LEAST 7 POINTS A GAME! They put you back in the volley on an equal basis, rather than putting you into a ridiculous situation where you are attempting to play offensive handball on the run.

Young ball players, who are willing to exchange some of their offensive enthusiasm for a small amount of defensive protection, will invariably be referred to by the delightful term "WINNERS."

Photo 2-23: Six-time National Singles Champion and five-time National Doubles Champion, Jim Jacobs, considered by most experts to be the greatest four-wall player ever.

THE CEILING SHOT

FRED LEWIS

A little over 20 years ago a young man named Jim Jacobs was trying to wrest the National Championship away from an older man named Vic Hershkowitz. Vic was one of the greatest offensive players in the game. His great power serve, catlike quickness, and ambidextrous play allowed him to dominate the front court against his opponents. After receiving several lessons from Vic, Jim realized he was going to have to move him out of the front court in order to win. Jim came up with an underhand fist ball to the ceiling and the rest was history.

The ceiling shot has revolutionized four-wall handball over the last 20 years. Handball has actually become a five-wall game. This shot is so important that one player was able to dominate the game for five years because he perfected the ceiling shot. Paul Haber was a spectacular player who never won a national championship until 1966. He was an all-out, two-handed shooter until he started to perfect the ceiling shot. Paul would play twenty games a day, hitting hundreds of ceiling shots. He literally was able to bury his opponents in the deep left-hand corner. The result was five national championships in six years.

It is extremely doubtful there ever will be another player with the ability to duplicate the control that Paul Haber exhibited with the ceiling shot. However, all handball players should strive to develop this shot. Even without the perfection of a Paul Haber, the ceiling shot is a valuable offensive, as well as a defensive, weapon for all players.

Basically there are two stroking motions used to propel the ball to the ceiling: the overhand stroke and the underhand fist. Depending upon the situation, each of these strokes may be used to go on offense or play defense.

As a general rule, the overhand stroke to the ceiling is used when the ball must be played above the head. Your physical court position will range from about three-quarters court to the back wall. Body position is similar to the sidearm stroke. The body is turned sideways so it is facing the side wall. One foot is in front of the other so you are able to step into the ball.

Photo 2-24: **Fred Lewis about to hit a defensive ceiling shot with his underhand fist stroke. In every sport, the player or team with the best defense is most often the winner.**

As you are about to step into the ball, the stroking arm is brought backward. As it moves forward, the elbow and wrist are bent slightly backward and the hand is facing the ceiling. As contact is made, the elbow and wrist snap forward. The ball should make contact initially with the center of the hand and then roll off the fingers.

The point of contact should be somewhere around the center of the body. The head is positioned so the eyes are watching the ball until contact is made. It is important when following through to get an upward trajectory on the ball, or the ball will never reach the ceiling. By bending your upper body backwards before you hit the ball, you may be able to get a consistent upward trajectory. It is similar to taking a popsicle stick, bending it backwards, and shooting a pea into the air.

As in the sidearm stroke, the free arm is used as a guide. When the stroking arm is brought backwards, the free arm pulls out of the way and leaves an unobstructed path. If the free arm is left to dangle at your side, much accuracy can be lost.

When you have the time to get into position, the ceiling shot becomes a tremendous offensive weapon. Your objective is to place the ball as close to the back corner as possible without coming too high off the back wall. At this point a little knowledge of geometry is helpful.

Let's say you're hitting the ball exactly in the middle of the court (ten feet from the side wall). In order to put the ball close to the corner, the ball should contact the ceiling about five feet from the side wall. In other words, try to hit the ceiling halfway between your court position and the side wall. It is important that you come straight overhand when employing this method. If you hit the ball with a three-quarter arm stroke, you will give the ball too much natural spin and it will hit the side wall. If you must hit with a three-quarter stroke, hit the ceiling closer in line with your court position.

One of Paul Haber's little tricks was to hit the ceiling shot with reverse spin. This allowed him to hit the ceiling very close to the side wall. The reverse spin caused the ball to run straight along the wall.

There has been much discussion about where the ceiling should be hit in relation to the front wall. Great control players such as Jim Jacobs, Paul Haber, and Stuffy Singer could hit the ceiling about one foot from the front wall. They possessed a "feather touch" and their shots would barely reach the backwall. Other players, such as Lou Russo, Gordy Pfeifer and Marty Decatur, hit the ball a little harder to the ceiling. They had just as much accuracy because they hit the ceiling further back from the front wall, about five feet. Therefore, we conclude the harder the ball is hit, the farther away from the front wall the ceiling should be contacted.

The underhand fist shot is the key to playing defensive handball. This shot may be used during the rally or on the return of serve. Because of the fist ball, players such as Jacobs, Haber, Sloan, and Singer were able to become percentage-control players. In Haber's case, the fist ball also became an offensive weapon.

The fist ball is approached just like any other shot. It is used mainly as a defensive weapon of the off-hand. The body is turned toward the sidewall so you can step into the ball. The stroking arm is brought straight backwards until it is almost at a 180 degree angle. As the arm moves forward to strike the ball, the elbow snaps forward and upward. The back should be erect. The legs play an important role in giving the ball an upward trajectory. As the arm begins its motion, the front foot steps toward the ball. The point of contact should be around the center of the body below the waist. As the ball drops below the waist, the back knee is bent. When contact is made, the back foot drives upward. This helps propel the ball towards the ceiling.

Once again we don't expect everyone to learn to play ceiling shots with the accuracy of a Paul Haber. However, a certain degree of proficiency can be attained by all players.

THE LOB

TERRY MUCK

The serve, the kill and the pass are the basic shots of handball, but your shot repertoire will be incomplete without the lob.

It sounds like some huge monster lumbering slowly out of the Okefenokee Swamp, blobs of flesh hanging from his jowls and belly, looking to steamroll anything in its path. The Lob is coming!

Or, it sounds like a premeditated act of sneaky violence, as in "lobbing a grenade" on some unsuspecting covey of enemy soldiers; a heavy, dangerous grenade, mind you. Even the dictionary's pronouncements on the "lob," a Middle English word, seem very anti-handball: "to move heavily and clumsily; heavy, hanging, thick." Despite all this, the "heavy, ponderous" lob is an integral part of "fast, quick" handball; as integral a part for some players as the kill, the drive and the punch.

Actually, the lob is more familiar as a tennis shot, where a player tries to drop the ball over the head of a net-rushing opponent, placing the high shot somewhere near the base line. In handball the lob has to be much more judiciously placed, because the back wall, the saviour of the aggressive ball player, protects against the tennis-like lob and demands more precision of the lobber.

Not every player uses the lob shot. Because of this selective use, it has been called the most sophisticated of all handball shots, sophisticated in the sense that it takes a great deal of thought, planning and discipline to use the lob effectively. Like the monster from the Okefenokee Swamp, the slow, heavy lob can be used for good, but make a mistake with it and those same properties that make it such a good shot (slow and tantilizing) turn it into a real mistake, a set-up for your opponent.

There are several important elements to the successful use of the lob shot. First, its use must be fitted into the overall strategy of a player's game style; the lob cannot be used indiscriminately or as the focal point of one's game. You cannot be a "lob ball player." You can only be a player who uses the lob well.

Second, the lob is used in two different situations, during the serve and the rally. The type of lob strategy differs for each of these situations and they must be clearly differentiated.

The lob calls for more discipline than any other shot, but it is a shot that can be used by any player, regardless of physical ability. All you have to do is think.

Lob Serve Checklist
1. Stand close to side wall.
2. Face front wall.
3. Drop ball and hit at head height.
4. Hit overhand with gentle, flipping motion.
5. Hit 15 feet high on front wall.
6. Don't hit side wall.

Overall Strategy
You can use the lob for three different reasons: to change the pace of the game, to take advantage of your opponent's weakness, or as a defensive maneuver to get yourself out of trouble.

Changing the pace of a game you are losing is vitally important; if you don't you're dead. If your opponent likes to play a fast tempo and he is having success at that tempo, the lob is one way of slowing him down, taking away his momentum. Without this change of pace you're likely to lose.

The trick is to be able to use the lob without ruining whatever momentum you might have. An inexperienced player often tries to hit lob shots without any understanding of what he hopes to accomplish through this shot. As a result, he hits a slow shot and moves slowly as well, not realizing that what he's looking for off the lob is the same thing he looks for off every other shot, namely a return with which he can go on the offensive.

For this very reason many inexperienced players become disenchanted with their attempts at hitting the lob. Think for a moment how you feel when you power a drive serve for the left crack. Now compare that with how you feel when you softly stroke an overhand lob serve down the left side wall. Your feelings are different. When you hit the drive serve, you feel aggressive, you want to push, to go on offense, to serve and shoot. Hitting it hard fires you up. On the other hand, when you hit the lob serve you move back deeper in the court, you relax a bit, you naturally look up expecting a high, soft return. Hitting it softly tends to make you think more defensively than offensively.

These are the normal reactions, you must realize these are the kind of reactions you are trying to elicit from your opponent, not from yourself. He's the one you're trying to slow down, not you. To be successful you must be able to hit the lob and still remain aggressive. It takes mental discipline.

A second reason for using the lob is to take advantage of your opponent's weakness. The lob is ideally suited for this, because the most universal weakness among all handball players is high on their off-hand side, exactly the place where the lob usually should go.

For some reason, striking a handball placed high above your head on your weak hand side is inordinately difficult. Most players compensate for this weakness by taking as few shots as possible from that position. Either they move way over and take the shot with their strong hand, or they let the ball drop low to a place where it is more manageable. Consequently, only the best placed lobs actually exploit an opponent's off-hand weakness. It takes a skillful feather touch to get the lob in precisely the right place.

A third reason for using the lob is as a defensive maneuver. When you find yourself so out of position you cannot stroke the ball with any power at all, a lob shot often comes to the rescue. Usually this shot is taken with an underhanded, scooping motion, lifting the ball out of that awkward position, high to deep court; but it can also be hit overhand, when you are off-balance, falling backward, for example.

This defensive use of the lob is often overlooked because it takes a great deal of presence of mind to hit such a finesse shot when you find yourself in a hopeless position. In this case, the lob really loses its finesse and is a last ditch effort to get yourself back in the rally; it takes very little physical effort and just may move your opponent to the back court long enough to allow you to establish some sort of center court position.

Oddly enough, the alternative to the defensive lob, when you have poor court position and are physically rushing your shot, is some kind of desperation kill shot, usually unsuccessful. So look more closely at the specifics of the lob and see if you can make a positive addition to your repertoire of shots.

BIBLIOGRAPHY

Jacobs, Jim. "Offense, with No Defense." *Official Program From U.S.H.A. National Contenders Tournament,* 1969.

Leve, Mort. "Whatever the Level of Play – Good Handball Requires Defense." *Handball,* 1980, Vol. 30, No. 4.

Lewis, Fred. "The Ceiling Shot." *Handball,* 1978, Vol. 28, No. 1.

Muck, Terry. "Learn to Play Defense." *Handball,* 1978, Vol. 28, No. 3.
    "The Lob." *Handball,* 1979, Vol. 29, No. 2.

Tyson, Pete. "DEEE-fense." *Handball,* 1977, Vol. 27, No. 3.

PART IV
OFFENSE

OFFENSIVE STRATEGIES
PETE TYSON

This is the fourth in my series of articles dealing with "The Five Situations of Handball." The subject under discussion is #4, or offense.

One of the most important decisions to be made by a top ballplayer as he moves into position to attempt a shot is whether to go on the "offense" or "defense." By making the correct decision he is "playing the percentages." This is the main theme in each of these articles—PLAYING THE PERCENTAGES!

Offense is that time when you have the opportunity to hit a rally-ending kill or pass shot. So, when is that time? As a rule, you should consider yourself to be "on the offense" whenever you have time to come to a complete stop before attempting your shot, you can stroke the ball from a comfortable position below your waist and, especially, when you can do so with your strong hand. The last part of the preceding statement brings up a much debated topic.

Offensive Off-Hand?

The question in the debate is, "Do you have to be able to hit kill shots with your off-hand?" I don't think so. I believe you must be able "to defense" with your off-hand. By that I mean you must hit the ball in such a manner that it will drive your opponent to a point very close to the back wall. From this court position, it will be very difficult for him to hit an offensive kill or pass.

Three of our greatest National Champions, Jim Jacobs, Paul Haber and Fred Lewis, played mostly "defense" with their off-hands. I recently re-read a letter Jim Jacobs wrote to me over 15 years ago. In it he said that prior to 1955 he was "left hand crazy"—that he attempted all kinds of spectacular kills with his off-hand; although he succeeded quite often, he lost the big important matches. He then decided to change his thinking and developed his "Sword and Shield Theory" in which he considered his off-hand to be his "shield," mainly defensive with no mistakes. His right hand became his "sword." When he decided to go on the offensive, it would be with his strong hand. Jimmy went on to say that when he defeated the great Vic Hershkowitz in the National Finals in 1955 (this was the first of his many National Championships), he scored NOT ONE POINT with his left hand, but he ONLY MISSED 4 SHOTS THE ENTIRE MATCH! In changing his game, Jacobs became a less spectacular player, but he also became the Number One player in the game for ten years!

Now I know you can counter this argument by asking, "What about Dennis Hofflander? Are you trying to tell me that Dennis should not be attempting kill shots with his left hand?" My answer is, "If you can hit kill shots like Dennis can as often as he can, then do it!" The great majority of us will never be able to hit the great offensive shots with our off-hands as often as Dennis can, but all of us can learn to "defense" with our off-hands and do it very well.

Court Percentages vs. Personal Percentages

When you start discussing the great offensive off-hands of players like Hofflander, Buzz Shumate, etc., you need to define what is meant by percentages in "offensive" handball. What these articles are attempting to relate is how to play the best percentage game according to your position on the court and the position of the ball in relation to the body (height, closeness to the body, strong or weak hand, etc.). For example, a kill shot attempt with your strong hand 20 feet away from the front wall should be a higher percentage shot than one hit with your off-hand from 30 feet away. The further you are from the front wall, the less your chances of hitting an accurate offensive shot; and keep in mind that offensive shots do require great accuracy. Also, if you must hit a ball from above the waist, you have less of a chance to make a good kill shot than if you had attempted your shot from around knee height.

Photo 2-25: **Even though Fred Lewis has a strong left hand, note in this photo how he crowds the left side wall in order to use his dominant right hand. Lewis' theory is to only use the weak hand when you cannot get into position to use the strong hand.**

When Paul Haber hits his favorite right corner kill from deep court with his off-hand, he is going against the "court percentages," but because he is so fantastically accurate with that particular shot, it is a percentage shot for him; this we refer to as PERSONAL PERCENTAGE. Many players have a shot or two that fits this "personal percentage" category. So if you can hit a kill shot with your off-hand from 35 feet away, and if you can make this shot 7 or 8 times out of 10 attempts, go ahead and use it. It is one of your personal percentage shots. You should recognize, however, that you will have days when you don't hit your shots as accurately as you would like, and on those days you should eliminate these higher risk "personal percentage" shots and start attempting the best percentage shot based on your court position—COURT PERCENTAGES.

You should also know that your percentages may change during a game. Spectacular shots that you can make a high percentage of the time when you are fresh can easily become low percentage shots when you are tired. Stuffy Singer, who is a fine teacher as well as a great ballplayer, says he will often play games after working out so he is tired when he starts playing. By doing this, he can analyze his game and discover which of his many great shots are still high percentage shots when he becomes tired and which are not. He then decides to eliminate the low percentage shots whenever he gets to a point in a match when he becomes tired. If you try this, it could mean you should eliminate over half of your shots when you are tired, especially if those shots begin finding the floor first instead of the bottom board. Remember, most of your really important matches will be won or lost when you are tired! It is no wonder the players who have really dominated this game were those with the great defensive shots they never missed. It is not easy to hit kill shots from 38 feet away when you are fresh, much less when you are tired at the end of a long, tough match. *(Photo 2-26)*

At the beginning of this article, I said that the most important decision you must make when attempting your shot is whether or not to go on offense. All right, let's say you are set and you can hit the ball from below the waist with your strong hand; now you make the correct decision to go on offense. What do you do? Should you attempt a kill? Straight or corner? Maybe a pass? Which kind of pass? A corner kill shot is a fine shot. Let's say you attempt it and hit a beautiful shot four inches high, but your opponent digs it up and passes you. Now what are your thoughts? Perhaps "If I hit it lower he won't get it next time!?" WRONG!! If you can hit that kill shot four inches high, you have done all that is necessary for success— PHYSICALLY. But to do what is necessary for success MENTALLY, you must understand percentages as they relate to offensive shot selections. Then you will understand why a "good" shot is not necessarily an "effective" shot.

In order for your offensive shot to be effective, the ball must hit the floor twice before your opponent can reach it. So the first question you need to ask yourself as you are about to attempt your shot is, "Where is my opponent?" How would you know where to angle your shot if you don't know where he is? Is he in front court, deep court, left court, left, right or center? You can't pass your opponent if he is in deep court, and it's very difficult to kill the ball into the corner if he is standing up close to the front wall. What happens if you don't execute perfectly? Jim Jacobs, who always had a unique way of getting your attention, said that ... "whenever you attempt a kill shot, assume you are going to miss it!" By this he meant you should assume your kill shot attempt will hit the front wall 12 inches high instead of 3 inches high. If this happens, will your shot still be a difficult one for your opponent to retrieve? If the answer is yes, then you are playing with your head as well as with your hands. This is percentage handball!

Photo 2-26: **Vern Roberts shooting a kill shot into the front left corner. This is a good percentage shot since his opponent is in the rear court.**

Toward the end of this article are diagrams showing a player and his opponent in various court positions and the good percentage shots to attempt for each positioning.

Another question you need to answer is where are you when you attempt your shot? Are you in center court or close to a side wall? Are you close to the front wall or close to the back wall? Your court position will also be a determining factor as to the shot you choose, because certain shots are just too difficult to make when the ball is in deep court, especially when the ball is very close to a side wall. The closer you are to the front wall and center of the court, the better your chances of greater accuracy with a wider selection of good shot possibilities. A left corner kill shot may be a good, intelligent shot according to your opponent's position, but from your position it may be too difficult to hit a high percentage of the time; so you should select another good shot you have a better chance of making.

Another important question that must be answered is what shot did you attempt last time when you and your opponent's court positions were similar? Don't attempt the same offensive shot every time from the same place. Give your opponent credit for a memory. He will start "over-playing" your shot which will allow him to retrieve a well hit ball. You should, as you have no doubt heard someone say, MIX 'EM UP! For every possible positioning of the players, there are two, three and sometimes four good, high percentage shot selections.

This "mixing 'em up" was one of the things that made players like Singer, Jacobs, Lewis, Johnny Sloan and Ken Schneider so very effective. Once you gave them the offensive opportunity, you did not know where they were going to hit it, which made their opponents hesitate. This hesitation allowed these great players to score with shots that weren't perfectly hit. This is also playing the percentages. It allows you to hit winners even when you are not executing your best. If you have to hit a perfect shot to score, you are making the wrong shot selection.

Still another very important question to be answered is, who are you playing? What are the strengths and weaknesses of that particular opponent? If possible, this should be answered before you begin the game. Sometimes watch your opponents play and attempt to discover their "favorite" shot while picking out weaknesses. Have a game plan before you start the game. Would you try to out-kill a Hofflander or out-volley a Lewis or Haber? You might try, but don't expect to get many points! Attempt to play with your "strengths" and force your opponent to play with his particular "weaknesses."

Kill Shot Strategy

As a general rule, when attempting kill shots, try to hit the front corners when your opponent is in rear court. *(Figure 2-26)* You should usually attempt to hit the side wall first so if the shot is hit a little high, it will rebound to the opposite side wall, and may still be a difficult shot to retrieve. Corner kill shot attempts that hit the front wall first will rebound to center court if hit too high, and this is what you want to avoid. Keep your shots from rebounding down the middle!

When your opponent is in front court, try to hit straight front wall kill shots angled so they will rebound close to a side wall. *(Figure 2-27)* Hit these shots very hard and even if you hit these shots a little high, they may still be effective.

Of course there will always be exceptions to these general rules. Fred Lewis often attempts corner kills that contact the front wall first, and he is successful a high percentage of the time because that particular shot happens to be one of his high "personal percentage" shots. *(Photo 2-27)*

Pass Shot Strategy

Sometimes when watching good young players it seems all they ever do is attempt kill shots on the offense. Passing shots are accidental or only used occasionally in very obvious situations. Don't be misled by the "box score" of the top Pro matches. For example, the box score of a typical game played by Fred Lewis might read: KILL SHOTS - 15 and PASS SHOTS - 4.

By looking at this you might believe the pass shot is not as important as the kill; but what this box score shows is how the rallies were won, not how many kills and passes were attempted. If it showed attempts, it might read: KILL SHOTS - 20 and PASS SHOTS - 50!!!

You will not score as often with the pass shot—directly; but indirectly, they wear your opponent down, force him into giving you setups, and keep him off-balance which allows you to score easier with your kill shot attempts.

There are three types of pass shots. *Figure 2-28* shows the one-wall or straight pass. This is a rather obvious shot that can be attempted whenever your opponent gives you a set-up in center court. It should (as all pass shots should) be hit very hard and low enough so it will not be playable off the back wall. Of course just how high will depend on your own particular power.

The two-wall or "V" pass is an excellent shot because it is more deceptive. As illustrated in *Figure 2-29,* the ball should rebound from the front wall and contact the side wall slightly behind your opponent before hitting the floor. This shot is usually hit higher than the one-wall pass, because it will lose speed after hitting the side wall. Again, just how high you hit these shots will depend on the height you contact the ball and your power. If Steve August were to hit a

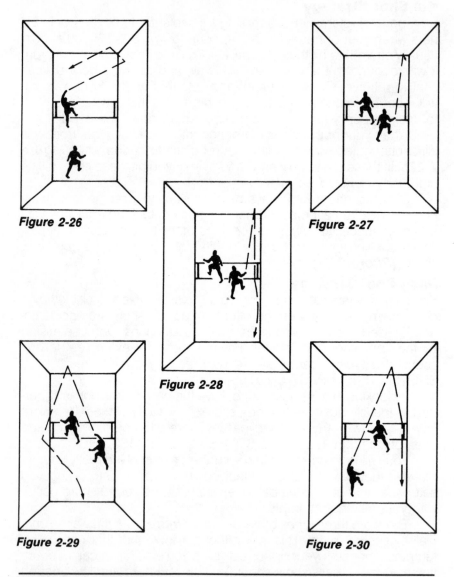

Figure 2-26

Figure 2-27

Figure 2-28

Figure 2-29

Figure 2-30

Figure 2-26: Corner kill shot with opponent in rear court.

Figure 2-27: Straight kill shot.

Figure 2-28: Straight pass shot: note that player hitting ball is between opponent and rebounding shot.

Figure 2-29: Two-wall pass shot: note that ball contacts the side wall just behind the opponent.

Figure 2-30: The "slider pass": This particular shot would have to be hit with reverse english, since it is hit down the right wall with the left hand.

one-wall pass that contacted the front wall two feet high, it would pro- bably come off the back wall for a setup!

The third type of pass is the "slider." As seen in **Figure 2-30**, this is a one-wall pass that rebounds from the front wall and strikes the floor very close to a side wall; because of the "English" imparted to the ball when you hit it, the shot "straightens out" and runs down the side wall. This shot can be hit down the same side wall as the hand with which you contact the ball if you put "natural English" on the ball—right hand down the right side wall and left hand down the left side wall. You can also hit these "sliders" down the opposite side wall if you are able to put "reverse English" on the ball.

It's very important to be able to execute these offensive shots; anyone can learn them with enough concentrated practice. And, it is just as important to make the correct shot selection—PLAY THE PERCENTAGES!

Photo 2-27: **Fred Lewis showing perfect follow through form as he drives a kill shot into the front right corner in this semi-final match of the 1981 National Championships.**

THE KILL SHOT

TERRY MUCK

Everybody wants to see the bomb in football, the home run in baseball, and a goal in hockey or soccer.

In handball, the shot that is the apple of the fan's eye is the kill shot, the ball that strikes the front wall so close to the floor it is unreturnable.

All galleries immediately respond to the kill shooter. They like the flash, the finality of this rally-ending stroke.

The kill shot is either good or bad, a point or an error. It is black and white, fair or foul, the white hats versus the black hats, American versus un-American. Abe Lincoln is a good kill shot, Adolph Hitler a missed kill shot.

Photo 2-28: Lewis is probably attempting a kill shot down the right side wall in this finals match of the 1981 Texas pro stop.

But, like all apparently simple phenomena, the successful kill shot is deeper than it looks. Many factors determine the rollout more than the final sweeping stroke that puts an end to the chase.

Jim Jacobs has said so much preparation goes into a kill shot that the final stroke is no more difficult than kicking the extra point after scoring a touchdown in football.

All these preparatory factors can be broken down and examined under three categories that are reflected in the three most commonly asked questions regarding the kill shot: How do I hit it? Where do I hit it? When do I hit it? **(Photo 2-29A,B)**

Photo 2-29A

Photo 2-29B

Photos 2-29A,B: **Naty Alvarado demonstrating the kill shot stroke. Note how he is about to contact the ball with his forearm parallel to the floor. Also note his long stride and how he stays low on his follow through.**

How do I hit it?

The technique of hitting a kill shot in many ways resembles hitting other shots. The most universal factor of all handball strokes, watching the ball, applies to the kill shot as well. The ball must be watched all the way into the hand as the hitting motion proceeds. Top players vary somewhat in other techniques of hitting the kill, but they are all together on the point of watching the ball intently.

Kill shot success depends a great deal on the amount of work one puts into getting the body in proper position to hit the ball. This means leg work, setting the body so it is facing the side wall, and striking the ball approximately in the center of the body. *(Fig. 2-31)*

This point of contact may vary from player to player; some hit the ball off the front foot, some a little closer to the back foot. But most hit it at, or near, the midline of their bodies, and chances are good this is your best point of contact. You can find out very easily by practicing the shot at different points; the place where the ball jumps off your hand with very little effort and with good control is your personal point of contact. The reason the ball behaves this way at the proper point of contact is timing. The wrist and arm snap occur at precisely the right moment as ball meets hand, and the ball takes off. *(Photo 2-30)*

Side Wall

Figure 2-31: **Hit the kill facing the side wall, with the ball at the midline of your body.**

170

Photo 2-30: Paul Haber attempting a kill shot. Note how he stays low on his follow through.

Photo 2-31: John Sabo attempting a kill shot against Dennis Hofflander. Note how far from his body the ball is as contact is made.

Determining the point of contact can get a little tricky because of one additional factor. You have to step into the kill shot. This means the midline of the body moves slightly forward; thus the old adage that you need to set up behind the ball and step into it. This move is not difficult, but takes some practice to get used to; it is essential that you step into the ball in order to generate the power necessary for a crisp shot.

To hit the kill shot effectively, you have to let it drop fairly low to the ground before you strike it. How low? It depends on several factors: your height, the kind of spin with which you naturally hit the ball, and the comfort with which you can bend over.

Ideally, the ball should be hit a foot from the floor with a flat stroke (forearm parallel to the floor) that gives natural rotation to the ball. With this stroke the ball goes into the front wall with the same trajectory you wish it to have as it comes off the front wall: low. A player who hits with this stroke has kill shots that "stay down"; that is, they don't bounce up high, making them retrievable for your opponent. *(Photo 2-31)*

It is impractical, however, for some players to let the ball drop as low as one foot from the floor before hitting it. Tall men find it difficult to bend over that far, as do people with bad backs and knees. This needn't be a fatal flaw, because quite acceptable, consistent kills can be hit from knee high or even a little higher. But some bending is still required in order to hit with a flat swing. If you find it necessary, for whatever reason, to hit your kills from this height, you may have to come over the top of the ball a little in order to make it "stay down." This doesn't mean a pronounced reverse hop, but just reverse rotation to help the ball bounce low.

One of the biggest errors a player can make in attempting the kill is to alter his natural swing just because he is "going for it." The kill shot stroke needs to be as smooth and relaxed as any other shot, perhaps more so because the margin of error is greatly reduced. Don't try to hit the ball harder, don't swing more quickly, don't jerk the ball, don't shorten your follow through. Any of these will sharply diminish your consistency and accuracy.

If your kill shots start going bad, there are several points of technique you can examine to try and remedy the situation.

If the ball is not hitting in the center of your hand so you can control it, the first thing to do is make sure you're watching the ball. Then try consciously to cup your hand so you feel as though you are caressing the ball as you strike it. This conscious "fondling" of the ball will also help you delay your wrist snap, and thus improve your timing.

If your kills are hitting too high on the front wall, the problem probably is not that you don't bend enough (although that is a question worth asking), but more likely you aren't staying low enough at the waist and knees. The hard work in kill shooting is not the initial bending at the waist and knees, but staying low as you carry out the swing. This is when the pressure is put on the back and knees. One hint that might be helpful in cajoling your body to stay low is to try and imagine your hand a foot from the floor (or whatever height your point of contact is) not only when you hit the ball, but on the follow through a foot in front of the ball. This will force you to keep your head and body down through the completion of the stroke.

Where do I hit it?

There are basically two kinds of kills; the straight kills and the corner kills.

Straight kills can either be hit down the side walls or on a diagonal across the court. *(Fig. 2-34)*

The other variety of corner kill is the cross court, corner kill, hit with your right hand to the left corner or with your left hand to the right corner. *(Figure 2-32)*

Photo 2-32: **Fred Lewis hitting his favorite kill shot into the front left corner as he defeats Naty Alvarado for the 1978 National Championship at the Tucson Athletic Club.**

Again, the standard shot here is side wall-front wall, but it can also be hit front wall-side wall for the same reasons as the other corner kills.

The cross court corner kill is a good surprise kill. Ordinarily a player hits it with natural "English" so it bites into the side wall and takes a very flat, soft angle into the front wall; this means it dies quite close to the front and is difficult to retrieve.

The danger of the shot is once you commit yourself to shoot it, you have almost no alternative but to carry it out; and your opponent, seeing your body angle, can learn to anticipate it rather well. The only alternative you have is to hit a high, reverse three-wall which your opponent can probably return even after committing himself to the kill.

When do I hit it?

Once you have mastered the technique of hitting the kill shot, and explored the varieties of kill shots available, you naturally wonder how to use the shot in the overall strategy of your game.

Perhaps a good maxim to keep in mind is no one wins with just a kill shot, but nobody wins without one.

Because it is such a popular shot, the kill shot's biggest danger, especially for younger players, is overuse. To these players, every shot is a potential kill. Generally, older players tend towards the opposite extreme; keep the ball in play at all costs and don't take a chance on a kill.

Of course, the optimum position is the one in between. Shoot at the right time and pass at the right time.

How do you decide the right time to kill? By position: your opponent's position, your position, and the ball's position. If your opponent is in front of you, don't kill the ball. Like all rules this one may occasionally be broken profitably. Usually, however, you should follow it. Don't give your opponent a chance to pick up an easy rekill off your own slightly missed kill. *(Photo 2-33)*

If your opponent is behind you, it is a good time to attempt a kill, provided two other factors are present; you have good position and the ball is in good position.

There are two facets to your own position: your position on the court and the position of your body. There are certain areas of the court close enough to the front wall to be considered good killing areas. There are also marginal areas, and, of course, poor areas.

These areas vary somewhat from player to player, but normally they can be located as follows: twenty-five feet from the front wall or closer is good; twenty-five to thirty feet from the front wall is marginal; and over thirty feet from the front wall is poor. *(Fig. 2-33)*

Even within the good area, a kill shot should not be attempted if your body position is poor. Good body position means you have time to set your feet, let the ball drop low, and you can move into the ball. Because the kill shot has such a low margin of error, you must have total control of your body and the ball before you can attempt the shot.

If your opponent is behind you, and you are in good position yourself, one final factor is necessary for a high percentage kill attempt; the ball's position. You can't kill a ball that is shoulder high or moving so fast it can't be controlled. The ball must be in such a position that it can be allowed to drop close to the floor and handled easily.

This can include balls in the air. The fly is one of the most effective offensive weapons in handball. It fits the criteria for a good kill shot because it drops low to the floor in prime killing position. Also, your opponent is frequently out of position (behind you) when you take the shot. Conversely, a kill off the serve is usually foolhardy because the ball is in poor position and your opponent is in front of you.

Photo 2-33: **Terry Muck hitting a left corner kill shot against Lewis in the finals of the Coral Gables, Florida Pro Stop.**

Practice your kill game. Think about it. When you start using the kill properly, you will find you don't have to roll the ball out. Three or four inches high will do because you will have your opponent out of position and he will not be able to retrieve it anyway. When you start scoring on these "high kills," you will know you have mastered the kill shot.

Straight kills down the side walls are most effective when your opponent is in the front court. A straight kill in this situation demands that your opponent move directly to the side wall to retrieve it; and if the kill is a little high, it has the same effect as a pass shot, running down the wall beyond your opponent's reach. *(Fig. 2-34,35)*

The other form of the straight kill, the diagonal, is best used from deep court or off the back wall when the threat of the hard V-pass has your opponent slightly on his heels *(Fig. 2-36)*. When alternating properly with the V-pass, this shot is effective; otherwise it is more dangerous than the shot down the side walls.

The other basic class of kills, the corner kills, are best used when your opponent is in the back court or he is slow afoot, because retrieving a corner kill demands a hard forward run. The corner kill can be hit in a variety of ways. The most common is the side wall-front wall kill hit with the right hand to the right corner and the left hand to the left corner. *(Fig. 2-37,38)* A variation of this shot is to hit the front wall first and then the side wall. *(Fig. 2-38)* This is a more dangerous shot because if missed, it bounces up high to the center of the court and is a setup. It is sometimes worth the risk for two reasons: 1) It changes the angle of the kill just enough so your opponent can't afford to overplay the standard side wall-front wall corner kill; and 2) it looks just enough like it might slide down the side wall that it momentarily freezes your opponent in his return attempt.

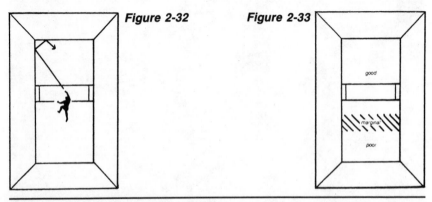

Figure 2-32   **Figure 2-33**

good

marginal

poor

Figure 2-32: **Corner, cross-court kill.**

Figure 2-33: **Various areas of a handball court and their merits for attempting kills.**

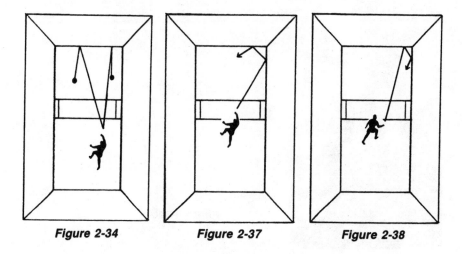

Figure 2-34   **Figure 2-37**   **Figure 2-38**

Figure 2-35   **Figure 2-36**

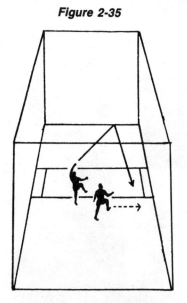

Figure 2-34: Straight kills down the side wall and the diagonal.

Figure 2-35: Straight kill or pass. Your opponent must move to side wall to retrieve.

Figure 2-36: Straight, diagonal kill alternated with hard V-pass.

Figure 2-37: Corner kill, side wall-front wall.

Figure 2-38: Corner kill, front wall-side wall.

Photo 2-34A

Photo 2-34B

Photo 2-34C

Photos 2-34A,B,C: Fred Lewis demonstrating how to hit a pass shot. Note that he lets the ball drop low so that his opponent might think he is attempting a kill shot. Also note how Lewis rises up on his follow through.

THE PASS SHOT

TERRY MUCK

An old adage on the professional handball tour maintains that you "kill for show and pass for dough" (golfers recently borrowed this concept, as in "drive for show and putt for dough").

Question the pro handballers further and they'll tell you flat out the majority of the points scored in a game of handball come from pass shots.

This answer flies in the face of what most people would expect. Most players would anticipate the kill shot or the ace serve as the single largest point-getting maneuver. But it's that little ol' down-home-folks pass shot that gives you the consistent winners.

A pass shot is just what the name implies; a ball that travels past your opponent (instead of right at him or in front of him) as it rebounds off the front wall. Players use many different methods to hit the ball past opponents; different strokes, different angles, different speeds, different spins. All aim at one purpose—forcing an opponent who is entrenched in front or middle court to the back court.

Good players simply adore the pass shot, and for good reason. The pass shot holds none of the dangers of the high-risk kill shot. The pass has a much wider margin of error; even if you don't hit it in precisely the spot you want, the shot still demands a well-executed return by your opponent.

Furthermore, you can execute the pass shot easily. You don't have to hit it hard, you don't have to bend low or reach high, and you don't have to worry about hitting it into the floor.

Players use several different varieties of pass shots: the straight pass, the two wall pass, and the volley pass.

Several verities or principles of use, if followed, make the pass shot the heart and soul of every handball rally. The value of the pass shot becomes clear when you look at all the good things that happen through its use. Once you become convinced of its value, you'll want to practice the pass shot constantly. It will make you a winner.

Varieties

Even beginning players, probably without realizing it, constantly hit the straight pass shot. They usually mis-hit it, mis-direct it, or flub it, but they attempt it all the same. Just hitting the ball back to the front wall is a variety of the straight pass, because most players don't try and hit it back at their opponent; they try to hit to one side of him.

However, systematic, conscious use of the straight pass is another story. The one thing that marks the passage of a player from the beginning stage of handball to the intermediate stage is the conscious placement of shots. The intermediate player tries to do something with the ball, and when he reaches this stage, the straight pass shot becomes his bread and butter.

Successful straight pass shots travel right down one of two side walls, as close as possible without touching one of them, or as one wag put it, "as close as a skinflint sticks to his money." *(Fig. 2-39,40,41)* Placement of the ball that close to a side wall forces the opponent to move out of the center court to retrieve the ball, and, it is hoped, all the way to one of the back corners.

The straight pass can be hit from any place on the court with either hand, as well as down either side wall. Advanced players put "English" on the ball to make it hug the wall, or as handball author Dick Robertson put it, "fade away along the side wall."

A straight pass hits the front wall and then hits the floor before touching any side wall. It then bounces into one of the rear corners. Only then, on the downward trajectory of the first bounce, might it strike one of the side walls.

In contrast to the straight pass, the two-wall pass hits the front wall and then the side wall on the fly (two walls) before striking the floor, ideally in middle court somewhere behind the short line. Because the angle at which the two-wall pass strikes the front wall resembles the letter V, it is often called a V-pass. *(Figs. 2-42,43)*

Many players call the two-wall pass the most devastating shot in handball. Whether we would go so far as to call it more devastating than the flat kill or the ace serve is questionable, but the two-wall pass certainly ranks as the most insidious shot in handball because of the cumulative damage it does to your opponent. It literally wears him down.

Thinking ballplayers use the V-pass to score points occasionally when they catch their opponent overplaying the front court, but more often to set up a winning shot two or three exchanges down the line. Constant use of the two-wall pass can be very damaging to a less disciplined player's psyche.

A third type of pass shot, the volley pass, can be either the straight or the two-wall variety. Volley, of course, means the ball is hit out of the air. Usually the volley in handball surprises the opponent; it startles

Figure 2-39

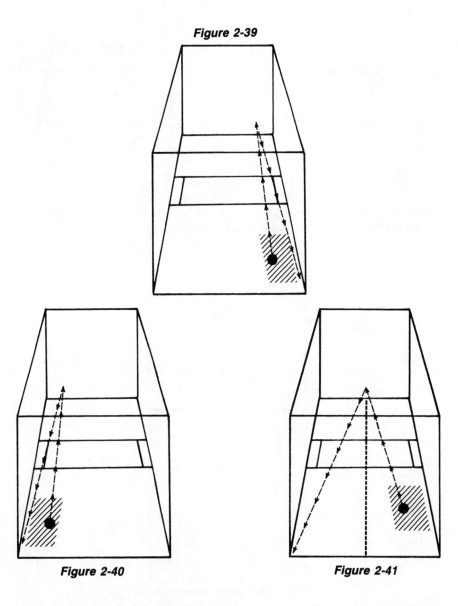

Figure 2-40

Figure 2-41

Figure 2-39: The straight pass shot.

Figure 2-40: The straight pass shot.

Figure 2-41: The straight pass shot, cross court variety. Note it doesn't hit the side wall.

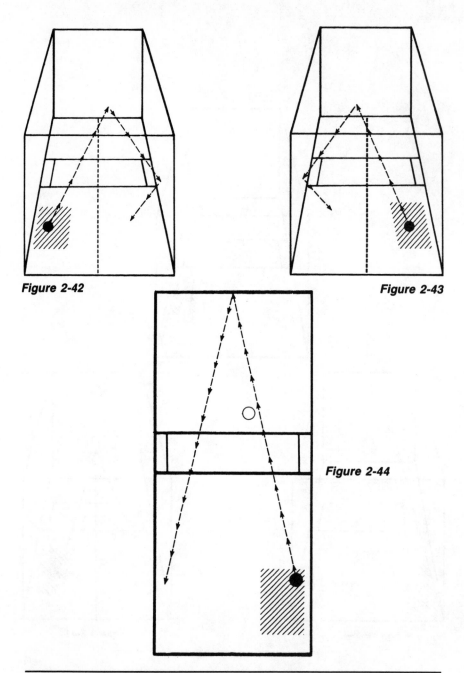

Figure 2-42

Figure 2-43

Figure 2-44

Figure 2-42: The two wall pass shot.

Figure 2-43: The two wall pass shot.

Figure 2-44: Hit the straight cross court pass when your opponent is in front court.

him when the ball comes back so quickly. In addition, the player who uses the volley shot usually attempts a kill shot off it; a pass attempt off the volley has tremendous effect. Frequently a player, seeing his opponent take the ball out of the air, starts an uncontrolled rush to the front court anticipating a kill attempt. A drive pass shot will catch such a player totally out of position.

Because of the increased tempo of the volley pass shot, the margin of error is even greater than that of the regular pass shot. Sometimes you catch your opponent so badly out of position, you can literally hit the ball anywhere to score a point just as long as it doesn't go to the back wall.

The advantage of this wide margin of error is diminished somewhat by the difficulty beginning players have in hitting the ball out of the air. It takes more work to get in position for a volley, and it takes better timing to strike the ball on its downward path.

Verities

All three types of pass shots can be hit successfully with any one of the three basic strokes of handball (the overhand, the sidearm, and the underhand), although the time, place, and purpose of the shot almost always make one type of stroke preferable to another. For instance, to get the desired angle and spin for the two-wall pass, an openhanded, sidearm stroke is best ninety-nine percent of the time. On the other hand, a player standing near one side wall who wishes to hit a straight pass down that near wall will very often find the overhand stroke most effective in getting the ball to run down the wall without angling into it. Some situations might call for an underhand fist shot to pop the ball quickly down one of the side walls or cross court past an unsuspecting foe.

But by far the most commonly used stroke is the basic sidearm, the *sine qua non* of handball swings. This is what makes the pass so easy to hit: the simple sidearm stroke. You don't have to strain to hit the ball to the ceiling, nor do you have to bend excessively low to the floor for the kill. The ball should be struck somewhere between the knees and the waist with that smooth, sweet swing that has already made you famous on your home courts.

You don't even have to hit the ball hard. A very common error that plagues handballers of all levels is trying to hit the pass too hard. Overhitting the ball usually results in loss of control, and control is the essential factor for a well-executed straight pass or two-wall pass. *(Photo 2-35)*

A couple of hints on control. In trying to hit the straight pass down the far wall, most players hit the front wall too low and angle the ball into the side wall too quickly. To avoid this, overplay the ball to the center of the court, hit it smoothly, and aim a little higher than you think necessary.

On the other hand, in hitting the two-wall pass, most players err the other way: they hit the ball too high (sending it to the back wall), and they don't angle it enough towards the side wall (giving the opponent a fly opportunity). The remedy is to aim lower than you normally would and to risk overplaying the corner angle rather than underplaying it. This way, should you hit the ball too sharply into the corner, the ball will come out at your foe from the side wall at an acute angle and may handcuff him—it won't be an easy shot by any means.

A final hint: don't rush the pass shot. Like making all handball shots, you should wait until both you and the ball are in the correct hitting position before striking the ball. Rushing the ball means you lose control of it, tip your opponent off on the shot (instead of surprising him like you mistakenly imagine you're doing by rushing the shot), and leave yourself off balance for any return. Remember, the longer you wait, the longer your opponent must wait; and when you're on the offensive, the advantage in waiting is all yours. Winning players use the right pass shot at the right time. In deciding which pass to use, it helps immensely for you to recognize two things: whether you are on the offensive or the defensive, and the position of your opponent.

Photo 2-35: **Fred Lewis hitting a pass shot against Vern Roberts in the Semifinals of the 1981 National Championships in Chicago. Lewis won this match and the finals.**

Not every pass shot is an outright attempt to score a point; in fact, very few passes should be attempted with that in mind. Many pass shots are strictly defensive shots, efforts to get out of trouble or establish a lost front court position. On these shots where you find yourself too far off balance to take a really good swing, you should simply try to get the ball around your opponent with a pass down the wall or a cross court two wall pass; you're just buying time to get yourself out of the hole into which your poor shots or your opponent's good shots have buried you. Don't try to do too much on a defensive pass shot—just play defense.

There are times, however, when you will find yourself in good position, well balanced and able to set for your shot, while your opponent is out of position, either too far forward in the front court or off to one side of the court. *(Fig. 2-44)* This is the time to go on the offensive with the pass. Try to score a point.

There's middle ground. That's when both you and your opponent have good position. When this happens, you use what is called a modified offensive pass; you hit a good, hard pass that probably won't score a point but will begin to maneuver your opponent out of position so you can score somewhere down the line in the rally. These maneuvering shots are the guts of good handball. They take hard work and patience, but they pay off with wins.*(Photos 2-36A,B,C)*

Photo 2-36A

Photo 2-36B

Photo 2-36C

Photos 2-36A,B,C: Gordy Pfeifer (A), Vern Roberts (B) and Naty Alvarado (C) chasing after pass shots just hit by Fred Lewis. Lewis has the best passing shots in the game.

Values

All the flashy kills a handball player makes owe a hearty thank you to the pass. Also, the pass adds to your game in other ways:

- It helps you maintain that all-important front court position.
- It helps wear down your opponent. If you want to punish him, pass him.
- The volley pass can increase the tempo of the game even more, and contribute to the tiring of your foe.

The pass shot is one of the easiest shots in handball to practice. Just go in the court and hit pass after pass, as long as your arm will stand it. Concentrate on hitting each and every one of them in the right place. Rest assured the practice will pay off in your matches. You can practice the pass shot with another player by simply standing on opposite sides of the court and hitting the ball back and forth to one another; change sides periodically so you get a chance to practice hitting pass shots with either hand. *(Fig. 2-45)*

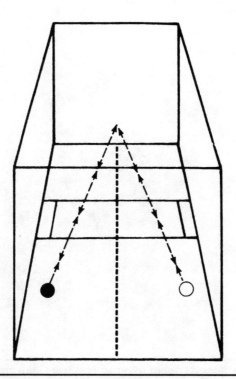

Figure 2-45: **A practice drill for hitting pass shots: stand on opposite sides of the court and hit pass shots at one another.**

THE PASS SHOTS

One of the most effective shots in handball is the pass, which is, as the nomenclature describes, the shot hit past the opponent that can result in the end of the volley, or can gain a weak return; at any rate it moves your opponent to deep court. The alluring phase of this shot use is it makes your opponent scurry in his effort to retrieve and can drain his energy. In trying to wear down the foe, the pass shot can be the best weapon to accomplish this strategy.

Photo 2-37: **Vern Roberts about to hit an offensive shot against Fred Lewis. Roberts' best shot selections in this situation are 1) kill down right wall, 2) pass down right wall and 3) 2-wall pass to the left.**

There is no one type of pass shot—it is dependent on the opponent's court position. If he is at the center short line area, you try to control the ball so it will hit into the side wall just behind him so he can't take it out of the air; at the same time, it is propelled with enough power and not so high that it will come off the back wall. The so-called "perfect pass" is one of the fascinating shots to see in this game of ours. It completely frustrates your foe, while at the same time taking a "piece of his guts." *(Figure 2-46)*

Many times the defensive man will try to anticipate a kill attempt and he moves in quickly; you have him at your mercy with a low hard pass shot.

From deep court you can attempt a pass down the wall if your opponent is positioned near an opposite wall. If he is in mid-court, you can go round the wall.

We invariably get back to the word "CONTROL" in handball tactics, and so it is with the pass shots. Controlled properly, the pass shot can be a most important part of your arsenal. The effectiveness is nullified, however, if the ball comes off that side or back wall.

When you are able to move into the ball and get your point of contact, the sidearmed stroke is best in making the pass attempt. This does not rule out the use of well-executed overhand power strokes down the walls or around the walls, or digging underhand strokes when you move to short court with your opponent in the near vicinity. When you attempt to "dump" a volley-ending shot to the front wall or either corner with your opponent breathing down your neck, it must be a good kill; however, if you flip it underhand past your man, your margin of error is greatly lessened. The worst that can happen usually is the ball will come off the back wall.

The offhand "shield" or predominantly defensive hand can be utilized in pass shots, fisting balls around the walls, or drilling the ball down the walls. Control of such strokes is not hard to master, as against attempts to shoot in volley-ending balls with your offhand.

Your defense against the pass shots is your ability to move fast. If the opponent's control is off, you might be able to pick the ball out of the air, but beware of getting yourself out of position, or hung up against a side wall. Your court coverage is your defense. If the pass shot is perfectly placed, then you're in trouble, no matter how quick you may be. If you have a "scouting report" on your opponent and he is prone to use a lot of pass shots, you might position yourself a step or two deeper than normally and then be better able to cover such pass shots.

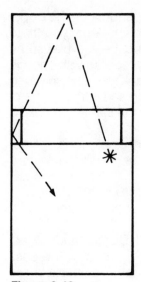

Figure 2-46

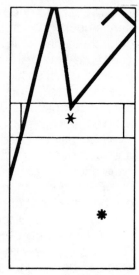

Figure 2-47

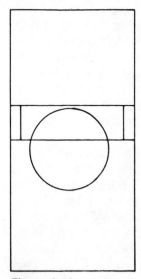

Figure 2-48

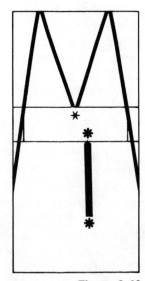

Figure 2-49

Figure 2-46: Basic two wall pass shot.

Figure 2-47: You ordinarily have two options on the fly—kill in the corner or pass down the wall. Both shots are away from your opponent in back court.

Figure 2-48: Most fly shots come from this center court area.

Figure 2-49: You can use the fly as an effective pass shot down either of the side walls past a charging opponent.

THE FLY SHOT

TERRY MUCK

If you want to apply pressure, use the fly.

In British slang, "fly" refers to a person who is knowing, sharp, smart, agile, or nimble-minded. In handball, the fly shot requires all of these things: a knowing, quick mind; a sharp stroke; smart positioning; and agile, fast feet. To use another slang expression, a player must really be "on his toes" to use the fly shot to good advantage.

In four-wall handball, the fly shot is a specialty shot that is used a small percentage of the time. A good defensive handball player hits his shots in such a way that he rarely gives you an opportunity to hit a shot out of the air. He hits the ceiling ball or tough angled three-wall shots that rarely intersect the prime center court position from which you would ordinarily hit most of your volley attempts.

Photo 2-38: One of the best at the fly shot, Naty Alvarado, moving in to hit a fly kill before Dennis Hofflander has a chance to move up to front court.

191

Yet the fly shot is a very advanced shot. Only the best players hit it well with any consistency, and even they use it sparingly, recognizing its difficulty. With little time to set for such a shot, and a limited number of places to hit it effectively, the fly is used much more rarely than the bread and butter shots of handball such as the pass, the kill, and the ceiling.

We're left with a paradoxical situation: the fly is a shot hit well by only the best players, and yet they get very little opportunity to use it.

A game where the fly shot is used much more frequently is one-wall handball. In that game, there are no side walls or ceiling which allow the defensive player to move the ball up and around the centrally located offensive player; the ball necessarily comes right back at a player on the fly many, many times during the course of a match, and he must be able to execute the fly shot successfully and often, probably as often as a four-wall player must use the ceiling shot in his game.

Most of the best fly shooters in four-wall handball are players who have played a great deal of one-wall handball sometime during their careers, and learned the movements of the shot in that game out of sheer necessity. Four-wallers can play a pretty good game of handball without using the fly shot, although the addition of the shot to one's game is a decided plus. It will round out your game with an offensive tactic that can be extremely explosive.

Fly Way

The key to hitting good fly shots is to get yourself in position to hit the ball well. The difficulty of getting good position for a fly shot is a reflection of the difficulty of taking a fly shot. You have to move very quickly and be able to adjust your body at the last moment in order to hit the ball at the correct height and with the proper weight shift.

The crucial step in hitting the fly comes before the stroke begins. It starts with anticipating your opponent's shot. Without this anticipation of his shot, your chances of taking a good fly shot are slim. Several clues can aid you in anticipating upcoming shots. First, watch your opponent as he hits the ball. It is a rare player indeed who does not give away somehow the kind of shot he is about to hit before he hits it. Work at picking up these subtle keys; a shift of the feet, the position of his arm, the way he looks at the ball, can all be a signal of what he intends to do with the ball.

Second, remember what shots he has taken in the past from similar positions on the court. If you have had a chance to watch him play, you know his tendencies. You also know very well what he has been doing in the particular match you are playing. Most players fall into shooting patterns that are very consistent and can really aid you in anticipating shots.

Third, maintain good court position yourself so you can move quickly for any shot your opponent might choose to hit. It does you very little good to know your opponent is going to hit a kill shot if you are standing next to the back wall because you were too lazy to run into center court position. Part of anticipation is to be in a position to retrieve all but the best of your opponent's shots.

Once you know where the ball is going, you have to move your feet to get there. One thing that makes the fly shot impossible to hit well is a failure to get in good hitting position. The fly is coming down from the front wall at a sharp angle and at a fast speed, which means your feet must adjust very quickly so you can move into the ball as you would for any other shot. If you see you don't have time to do this work with your feet, quickly back off and don't take the fly shot. Failure on the fly comes from poor position or a player taking the shot while back on his heels, falling away from the shot.

Once you get into position to hit the ball out of the air, take a full, normal swing as you would on any other shot. The tendency is to baby the ball with a short, half swing; players do this because of a lack of confidence that they will hit the ball out of the air well. When they try to take a "safe" short swing, the result is poor contact and the shot is wild, reinforcing their lack of confidence in the fly. The cure is to make yourself hit the ball with your regular swing. Don't try to hit the ball too hard, but don't try and baby it either. If you've done the work of getting into position, you can't help but hit the ball well if you take a smooth swing at it. *(Fig. 2-47)*

One way to increase your chances of success on the fly shot is to have a good plan of where you want to hit the ball. Having an idea of what you want to do with it helps in the execution of the shot, because your body naturally adjusts itself to the correct position if it knows the shot's purpose. Usually you have two choices with the fly: a kill or a pass. Because of the difficult position from which the fly is taken, you don't usually have many choices about location of the shot. One corner for the kill, one angle for the pass is about all you have. That's okay. Don't be too subtle with the location of the fly. You don't need to be, because you already have your opponent off step simply because you are forcing the tempo by taking a fly shot. In the case of the fly shot, shoot the obvious shot and concentrate on shooting it well. *(Fig. 2-47)*

(Photo 2-39)

Photo 2-39: **Naty Alvarado hitting a fly shot against Fred Lewis in the finals of the 1978 Nationals. Lewis has been in the finals in nine out of the last ten years, winning six and losing three.**

Fly Low

The most common use of the fly is offensive—killing in one of the front corners. The reason this is so effective is obvious: you are forcing the front court action on your opponent's shots from the back court. He is naturally out of position for a quick, well-placed kill shot in the front corner.

In many cases the kill shot does not need to be flat; a semi-kill will catch many an unsuspecting player flatfooted in the back court, off balance and too far from the corner to do anything about it other than watch. The key to this shot from the offensive player's point of view is to try not to be too fine with it. It doesn't have to be too fine. The danger is to hurry the shot. You must remember that because your opponent is so far out of the play, you need not rush the ball into the corner. Take your time and make a good firm shot. *(Fig. 2-48)*

Another positive factor in the fly kill is the amount of running it saves, not only on that particular shot, but in the prospect of cutting the rally short with the kill shot. Ironically, although the fly kill may save you a few steps, it probably won't save you very much in the way of energy. It takes very quick, fast reactions to get into proper striking position for a fly kill, far more energy than it takes to set for any other shot in handball. You will find yourself constantly shifting with tiny steps and shuffles right to the moment you finally commit yourself to the swing, and this constant readjustment takes a great deal of energy. The payoff is a rally-ending kill.

If you should find your opponent in the front court as you attempt a fly kill, the best choice of shots is not the corner kill but the straight kill down one of the side walls. That way, if your kill is a little bit high, you still have the advantage of a semi-pass shot, giving your opponent much more trouble than a missed corner kill would in that same situation.

A few technical hints on the fly kill. If you find the ball hurts your hand when you take the ball out of the air, the cause is poor timing which most likely comes from hitting the ball too far out in front of your body. Wait until the ball comes in to the normal hitting area close to your body, just as you wait and set up for other shots. If you find you're hitting the ball off the bottom of your hand into the floor, you're taking your eye off the ball. If you find you're hitting the ball much higher off the front wall than where you're aiming, you're not staying down low enough, long enough through the shot; that is, you're pulling up on the ball before you stroke through it.

Fly High

A more rare use of the fly shot is as a pass shot. This is rightly so, because the opportunity for a fly kill is usually present on any shot you have a chance to take out of the air. After you execute a few of these shots successfully, however, you will find your opponent charging headlong into the front court on any shot he realizes you might take out of the air. Because of the quickness of the shot, his charge to the front court will be fast and largely uncontrolled, and he is ripe for a pass shot. *(Fig. 2-49)*

You will find in trying this shot a few times that almost any kind of shot will be effective; you merely need to hit it to one side or the other of the court; even if your opponent does get his hand on the ball he will make a very weak, inaccurate return.

The fly pass can be used to speed up the tempo of a game. It forces your opponent to react much more quickly, and can be very tiring and upsetting to him. Meanwhile, you are saving energy because the fly pass is much easier to hit than the fly kill—you don't need to bend over for the shot and the precision footwork the kill demands is not quite as crucial to the pass.

The ideal result of the fly pass is your opponent scurrying back and forth and side to side in the court while you stand in the center sending weak return after weak return back down one of the side walls to one of the rear corners. A couple of lengthy rallies of this sort can be hopelessly demoralizing to an opponent, and can bring you far more long-term benefits than just the two or three actual points you might gain through the tactic.

In the fly shoot you have a specialty shot that can greatly speed up the tempo of a match and score you some fast points. It will help you control the center of the court and save a few steps. It is a difficult shot and the time you gain in taking the shot can easily be lost in accuracy if great care is not taken in its execution.

BIBLIOGRAPHY

Muck, Terry. "The Fly Shot." *Handball,* 1980, Vol. 30, No. 3.
    "The Kill Shot." *Handball,* 1978, Vol. 28, No. 4.
    "The Pass Shot." *Handball,* 1979, Vol. 29, No. 3.
"The Pass Shots." *Handball,* 1977, Vol. 27, No. 1.
Tyson, Pete. "Offensive Strategies." *Handball,* 1977, Vol. 27, No. 4.

PART V
SHOT ANTICIPATION

SHOT
ANTICIPATION
PETE TYSON

The fifth and final article in my series on "The Five Situations of Handball" deals with the subject of shot anticipation. *(Photo 2-40)* Many enthusiasts play pretty good handball when they are hitting the ball, but this is only 50% of the time involved in a game. The other 50%—when it is your opponent's turn to hit the ball—is the "situation" we call SHOT ANTICIPATION and it is just as important to play intelligent handball here as it is when you are hitting the ball.

Most people who "spectate" only watch the ball. They enjoy the game, but they do not really understand why certain plays work and others do not. To understand more fully, you should watch what is happening away from the ball. Take, as an example, professional basketball and watch a superstar like Rick Barry. Now everyone knows he is a great shooter, but there are a lot of great shooters in the pros. Watch Rick Barry when he is on defense, whether or not his man has the ball, and watch him when his team has the ball, especially when he doesn't have it. Never take your eyes off him; you will see great basketball played 100% of the time, and you will have an infinitely better understanding of how the game should be played.

The same is true for handball. It often appears the great players never have to move very far to hit the ball, but like most spectators, you are only watching them when they are hitting the ball. If you ever get the opportunity to watch a top handball player, do yourself a favor and take a lesson from him. No, you don't have to get into the court with him. Just watch him play ALL THE TIME! Don't take your eyes off him and you will learn a great deal about how to play the game—100% OF THE TIME! You will see by the various positions he takes why he is able to retrieve well-hit shots, and why he doesn't have to run very far to hit his shots.

So, what position should you be in when your opponent is about to hit the ball? There are two kinds of positioning—(1) PHYSICAL POSITION, meaning the position of the various body parts and (2) COURT POSITION.

Physical Position

First, in order to develop good shot anticipation, you should ALWAYS WATCH THE BALL. You have no doubt heard this phrase countless times, and yet, I often see an otherwise good player turn his back to the ball when his opponent is hitting the ball from rear court. How do you know what court position to be in if you don't watch your opponent hit the ball? Is he attempting a ceiling shot, or kill, left or right, or what? Should you be in front court, rear court, shaded to the left or right? You must watch the ball ALL THE TIME in order to answer these important questions.

Watch the ball but BE CAUTIOUS WHEN LOOKING BACK! Eye injuries can and do happen. WEAR EYE GUARDS! Unfortunately most players who wear the guard have already been hit in the eye previously. Don't make the excuse, "I can't see the ball well enough when I wear them." One of the finest pros in handball is Lou Russo. Louis has won National Championships in 1-wall, and 4-wall and he wears eye guards! There are several styles of eye guards now available; so pick one out and start getting used to it. I hope one day eye guards will be REQUIRED equipment as they already are in some clubs and for certain tournaments. If you wear glasses, they will work fine for eye protection. Just be sure they are shatterproof.

Photo 2-40: **Stuffy Singer about to hit against Naty Alvarado. Note that Naty is watching the ball and moving in anticipation of Stuffy's shot.**

If you don't wear glasses and you won't wear eye guards, at least raise your hand and look back through partially spread fingers. ALL top players watch the ball ALL THE TIME! You may have read where someone once asked Paul Haber if he always watches the ball. Paul's reply? "I even watch the ball during timeouts!" *(Photo 2-41)*

Second, don't be standing still when your opponent is hitting the ball. This does not mean you should be running. Definitely not! Just be moving slowly to that court area where you believe the ball is going to rebound, ready to change directions quickly should the ball be hit the other way. You can't make this change of direction to reach shots if you start from a flat-footed position. As soon as your opponent hits the ball, GET OFF YOUR MARK and take off fast! Even if the ball is hit where you have plenty of time to reach it, move as quickly as possible. Assuming you have time, move to a court position two or three steps deeper than you intend to be when you hit the ball. Get to this position quickly, stop, and then glide into your shot. Doing this will allow you to make adjustments as you move into the shot so you will always stroke the ball comfortably. It will also insure that your body momentum is going forward, allowing you to hit the ball harder with less effort and greatly reducing your chances of getting a sore arm.

Photo 2-41: **Lewis hitting against Alvarado. Note again that Alvarado is watching the ball and that he is wearing the protective eye guards.**

Most of your movement in the court is sidewards and backwards, so if you wish to train for handball you should run many short sprints. Run some forward but mostly moving to the left, right and backwards. Short distances of 10 to 20 yards will do. You will rarely have to run further than 15 feet when playing. Whenever you are training for a specific sport, attempt to duplicate the type of movement necessary for that sport. Again, in the case of handball, run short sprints, mostly sidewards and backwards.

After you hit the ball, glide, drift or walk toward your desired court position. Assuming you have hit an intelligent shot, you should have a few seconds to get into position and catch your breath. Don't lose this chance for wind recovery by sprinting to your position. You don't need to unless you hit a poor shot right at your opponent.

Third, try to stay on your feet. A great past National Champion, Gus Lewis, wrote a fine article a number of years ago in which he said "diving is wasted." He believed you could get to any shot on your feet that you might have reached by diving. Assuming you are anticipating properly and not standing flat-footed, this is probably true. I've watched Fred Lewis play many times, and I've never seen him leave his feet to retrieve a shot—and Fred is not classified as a fast player. He just anticipates very well and knows how to read his opponents' shots.

Photo 2-42: **Lewis watching and moving into front court as Vern Roberts is about to attempt a kill shot.**

Fourth, attempt to keep your feet lined up facing the front wall until your opponent hits his shot, especially if you have just "set him up." From this position you can move to the left or right equally quickly. Also, if you have set up your opponent, raise your forearms up parallel with the floor so you can cut down the time needed to stroke the ball, because in this case, with your opponent on the offense the ball will probably be moving very fast. *(Photo 2-42)*

Court Position

Where you position yourself on the court is dependent on the type of shot your opponent is going to attempt. There was a time when some handball veteran probably told you, "Get up to the short line after you hit your shot!" At one time this advice wasn't too bad, because the "fly-kill" game was very important. Then Jim Jacobs came along and "defensed" the ball so well that his opponents did not have "fly" opportunities, and today most top players also defend their "fist" shots so well that opportunities for fly kills don't come along very often. So, where should you go?

Let's first talk about the depth of your court position. This will depend on whether your opponent is:

• Serving
• Attempting an offensive shot
• Attempting a defensive shot from a controlled position, or
• Attempting a defensive shot from a "trouble" position (he will probably be attempting a defensive shot, but it is going to be difficult for him).

When Receiving Service

I believe too many players stand too far from the back wall when receiving service. Most service return attempts will be done within eight feet of the back wall. If you position yourself 6-8 feet from the back wall, you will usually have to move backwards to get into position for your attempt, *(Figures 2-50,51)* whereas if you assume a position just a step from the back wall, you will be behind the ball, moving forward into your shot. And if the ball comes off the back wall, you will be moving with it (as you should) instead of standing still, waiting for it to come to you. Waiting usually means you will have to reach back to hit the ball, resulting in little power, limited accuracy and a sore arm. It is especially important to assume the deepest position possible when receiving the "hook" serve. You will have more time to let the ball "break" before you attempt your shot. Don't rush the "hook" serve. Just move with the break and fist it to the ceiling if it breaks away from you, or attempt a fist 3-wall return if it breaks in and jams you.

The only way you might "get burned" playing this deep is if your opponent hits the crack just across the short line and the ball flattens out. But this doesn't happen often and even if it does, you should be able to make the return from your deep position unless the ball rolls out. *(Photo 2-43)*

Positions After Service

After the ball is put into play, your opponent will either be on the offense or defense (controlled or trouble) when hitting his shot. After hitting your shot, "drift" to a position about eight feet behind the short line as you watch the ball and your opponent. If it is apparent that he is on the defense, try to determine whether or not he is in a "controlled" defensive position or if he is in "trouble." If he is in control (able to set his feet before hitting the ball), he should be able to hit a good defensive shot most of the time; so you should retreat a few more steps, anticipating the deep return. I see many players standing at the short line when their opponents are obviously going to hit a ceiling shot. They have to do much more running than necessary.

However, if your opponent appears to be in trouble, hold your position and be ready to move in quickly for the fly-kill opportunity (this is about the only time you will get the chance). But also be ready to retreat in case he manages to execute a good defensive shot. Much depends on the skill level of your opponent. If he is weak in his ability to hit defensive "fist" shots, you should have a number of "fly" opportunities. But if he is a top player, he will more often than not make an adequate defensive shot even when he is in trouble, so you will be retreating still more.

Photo 2-43: Lewis is in back court because he thinks the shot that Roberts is attempting will not be a kill shot.

If you see you have made a mistake with your shot and have given your opponent the opportunity to take the offense, move up close to the short line. Don't move in front of this line or you will be passed too easily. Whether you stand just behind the short line or a couple of steps deeper might depend on your opponent's power. If he is a hard hitter, play off the farther line because even his low kill shots will carry, and you will be in better position to retrieve his hard pass shots. **Figures 2-52 and 2-53** show the proper "depth" positions.

Alright, now that you assume the proper depth, should you be in the center of the court or to the left or right? There are a number of variables here, but two places you should not get caught in are directly in front of, or directly behind your opponent. These two cases often occur whenever your opponent is hitting his shot from the middle of the court. Naturally, you don't want your shots to end up in that area, but sometimes it does happen.

Let's say you have given your opponent a back wall set-up right down the center of the court. Positioning yourself directly in front of him is illegal (can result in an avoidable hinder). If by chance the call (avoidable) is not made, what have you accomplished by getting hit standing in the center of the court? You have just blocked a shot that was going to come back to you in the middle of the court. Wrong! But you have to be somewhere, so in this case **(Fig. 2-54)** play at a slight angle, taking away one of his good corner opportunities.

If you give your opponent a set-up right in the middle of the court and up close, don't move in right behind him. You will not see the ball no matter where it is hit, but don't scream for a hinder because you created the block. No question about it, you are in trouble and your opponent has an excellent chance of winning the rally, but give yourself a chance! Play off slightly to one side as shown in **Figure 2-55**. Which side? Well, which side is his favorite shot? That might be the side to go to. Or you might bluff to one side and then break to the other side. But do something! You will be wrong sometimes! Waiting directly behind him is wrong all the time!

If your opponent is hitting the ball from the left or right side of the court (these are the usual cases), you must attempt to "read" his shot angle by watching the way his feet are lined up and where he makes contact with the ball (in front of, even with, or behind him). Then shade a step or two to the side where you think the ball is going to rebound, ready to move quickly the opposite way if you have "read" the shot wrong.

Another factor in good shot anticipation is your memory. Most players have favorite shots they like to attempt whenever the ball is in a certain position in the court.

Remember these shots so you can overplay these players and

dig up some of their best shots. Against most players you can overplay for certain shots. These "most players" do not include a Stuffy Singer or Fred Lewis who mix their offensive shots so well you never know what's coming next; but of course, these great ball players are two I have been referring to frequently—great handball players who know how to play great handball—100% of the time!

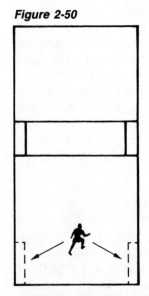

Figure 2-50

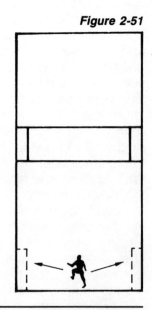

Figure 2-51

Figure 2-50: **Player receiving service will have to move backwards to attempt shot.**

Figure 2-51: **Receiver in better position to move into shot attempt.**

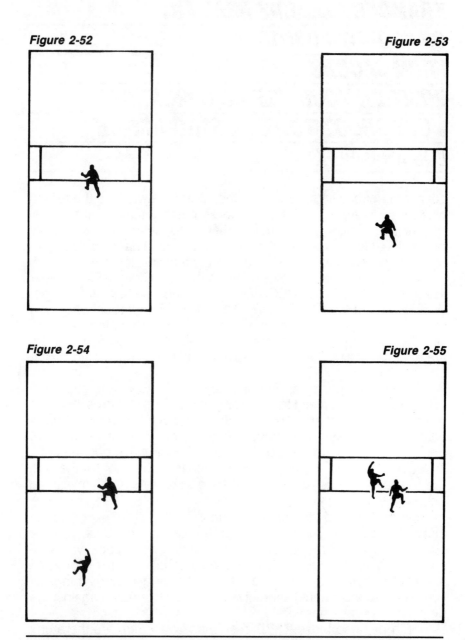

Figure 2-52

Figure 2-53

Figure 2-54

Figure 2-55

Figure 2-52: **Proper depth if opponent has an offensive opportunity.**

Figure 2-53: **Proper depth when opponent is hitting defensive shot.**

Figure 2-54: **Player is ''Taking Away'' the right front corner. Don't stand directly in front of opponent.**

Figure 2-55: **Position yourself at a slight angle. Don't stand directly behind opponent.**

KRAMBERG LEARNS REAL ART
OF "COURT POSITION"
FROM JACOBS ...
POSITION YOURSELF SO OPPONENT
MUST SHOOT TO YOUR STRONG SIDE

LOU KRAMBERG

"Jim, am I exposing too much of the court? I always get the feeling when I am playing with you that when it is my turn to hit the ball, my choice is limited. You, on the other hand, seem to have a multiple choice. I know you're not playing 'dirty,' yet, I have so little room and you have so much. What is the explanation for this?"

Jim Jacobs went on to explain in detail. "Okay, let's consider this a lesson in COURT POSITION. You used one very apt phrase, WHEN IT IS MY TURN TO HIT THE BALL. Remember, when you are playing singles, you get to hit the ball only 50% of the time. Obviously, your opponent gets the other 50%. Assuming both players are of equal ability, the one who plays better position should be the ultimate winner.

"I always try to give my opponent just ONE area to shoot for. I also prefer that he shoot to my strong hand. In other words, I expose more of the court to my STRONG SIDE and BLOCK out my WEAK SIDE. My theory is: I can move quicker to my strength. You know, Lou, for the rest of my handball career, if I could have but one wish, it would be—when my opponent shoots and does not kill the ball, I would be most satisfied to be allowed to hit his return with my strong hand.

"In response to your opening query. Yes! You are exposing too much of the court. But, I believe you are doing it because you are overly protective of me. Knowing that I have a weak back, you subconsciously are avoiding any chance of contact with me. For that I am most grateful, but I am afraid I have been taking advantage of you. You probably could score five more points a game against me by playing proper position."

"Big deal, so I lose 21-7!" responds Lou. "Jim, are there any rules for court position?"

"Yes, of course. For one, you must always give your opponent a clear, unobstructed swing at the ball. Two, you must never be in a straight line between your opponent, the ball, and the front wall. That is illegal. All you have to do is give him a clear shot at one part of the front wall. I'll let you in on one of my secrets. I purposely practiced a countless number of hours developing my game ABOVE THE

WAIST until it has become my strong suit. I found that when my front court position became 'intimidating,' my more knowledgeable opponents started to go overhead against me...ceiling, around-the walls.

"This is precisely what I want them to do. Anytime I can 'psyche' my opponent into going up or around me in lieu of shooting, I'm doing a good job out there. Mind you, now, in order to psyche your opponent, you must be prepared to CONVERT just about any ball he doesn't roll out. If you patsy the ball back, he's going to take batting practice against you.

"Lou, I would strongly advise you to play very strict court position against the 'A' players. Play less position against the 'Bs' and even less against the 'Cs'; they will then give you a better workout. Now, after we finish this match I expect to find at least 8 or 9 angry looking welts on your back and legs."

Photo 2-44: **Naty Alvarado is "taking away" the left front corner and forcing Lewis to shoot to his strong side. Again, note that Naty is watching the ball and moving as Lewis is about to hit his shot.**

MAKE DECISIONS FOR VICTORY: PLANNED REACTIONS

STUFFY SINGER

Picture a situation where you have just committed the unpardonable sin of hitting the ball front wall then back wall on the fly, giving your opponent a spectacularly easy set-up, better known as a "lollipop." The typical ball player, seeing the result of his generosity, makes a futile decision based on the following thoughts: "What will he do? Where will he hit it? Where should I go? How do I get there?" Suddenly, a light goes on in his head as he decides to make the one decision that will prove him to be wrong 99 times out of 100. He goes to the center court at the short line.

By placing yourself in the center court, you think you're doing the right thing. In actuality, your refusal to make a commitment means the only way you can possibly hope to win the volley is for your opponent to make a mistake. The percentages dictate he won't make that mistake unless you force him to. When is the last time you ever tried to hit a set-up like this down the center of the court? Well, neither will your opponent, so why go to the one place on the court where you know your opposition will never attempt to hit the ball?

Now, I can't tell you where to go; I'm no mind reader, but go somewhere. Fake running to the left front and then back up quickly to cover the pass shot. Back up to cover the pass shot, and then move forward to pick up the kill. Do something that will force your opponent to think twice about which shot he's going to hit, and where he's going to hit it. Don't straddle the fence; make some commitments, force things to happen, dictate.

The important thing to remember is you're going to lose most of this type of volley anyway, but if you can force a few extra errors or guess right a few extra times, you'll start winning a few more of those 21-20 games.

A PRO POINTER
ON POSITION
TERRY MUCK

I was sitting in the bar of the Mission Valley Inn the night before I was to play Naty Alvarado in the finals of the San Diego Pro Stop. As I sat sipping my ginger ale, Paul Haber came in, sat down next to me, and ordered something a little stronger than ginger ale. After we exchanged greetings, Paul dropped to a confidential tone and said, "I have a suggestion."

Paul has given me many suggestions over the years, and more than a few of them have paid off in spades. I can remember very well Paul's suggestion that I work on a small reverse serve to the right crack, because I didn't "waste myself enough" on the serve I had been using. That reverse serve has come in very handy for me, a guy who doesn't have the big power ace serve so many other players have. I also remember his advice to stand next to the back wall and hit ceiling balls (what else?) until I was ready to drop. I still wish I had taken this advice a little bit more seriously. Anyway, when Paul speaks, I listen.

He took out a napkin, and began to draw a diagram. "It's just a small point," he started, "but you never know what will help. You like to use the three-wall return of service, and Naty likes to take it out of the air whenever possible and kill it in the left front corner. I've watched you defend this shot against other players, and I think you're going about it wrong. You run up to the front court along the left side wall between the player and the wall. *(Fig. 2-56)* You've got to run around the right side of the player and come in from that side." *(Fig. 2-57)*

Now, picture the situation. You have just returned a shot from the back court using a three-wall shot (a very effective return, particularly against the serve). If you hit the three-wall a little too hard, you give your opponent a fly shot opportunity around the short line. Got the picture? Now consider the question Haber has raised: How do you run to the front court to position yourself to defend the possible fly kill? Do you run up the left side wall between the player and the left wall (Route One), or do you run around your opponent on the right side, anticipating the left front corner kill (Route Two)?

I agree with Haber that the best route in most situations is the

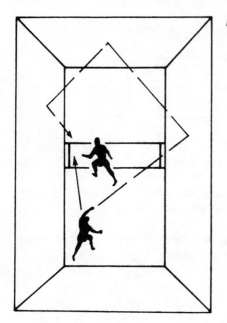

Figure 2-56

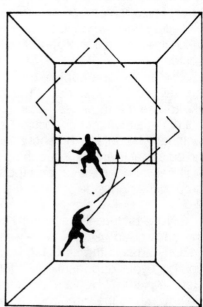

Figure 2-57

Figure 2-56: Route One

Figure 2-57: Route Two

second one. Run around your opponent on the right. This answer is based on the premise that most players take this fly shot with their right hand as it comes off the left wall. In this position, they stride towards the left front corner. Unless the ball comes off the side wall quite high, it is a difficult shot to execute. Route Two makes this difficult shot even harder.

In spite of its difficulty, there are several pro players who attempt this shot regularly, and make the left front corner kill consistently. Probably the two best are Stuffy Singer and Naty Alvarado. Stuffy takes the shot at the right time; if he sees the ball falling a little short, he steps back and hits it to the ceiling on the half volley. Naty tends to force the shot a little bit, but still makes a very good percentage of his attempts. By using this shot, both players tend to discourage the three-wall return of service.

Since the three-wall return of service is one of the best shots to use, it will not do to have this shot removed by the threat of the fly kill. Two suggestions: One, don't hit the ball so hard. Hit properly, the three-wall doesn't come off the side wall far enough to shoot. Two, use Route Two to the defensive front court position. There are several reasons why this is the best one to take.

Look at the situation. You've made a poor shot by hitting the three-wall too hard. Your objective after making a poor shot is to try to make the offensive player earn his point, that is, make a reasonably difficult shot to score. By taking Route One to the front court (the unacceptable route), you have left the offensive player too many easy scoring shots; the left corner kill, a straight pass down the right, or even a high, three-wall shot from the left front corner to the right rear corner. And to be effective, none of these shots need be precise. The side wall, front wall kill can be a little high yet still run away from the charging defenseman. The straight pass is easily hit down the right without hitting the right side wall. The high three-wall need only be hit fairly hard.

By taking Route Two you force the kill shot to be fine. If the kill is a little high, you are on top of it for the rekill or the pass. Route Two takes away the straight pass down the right, or at least forces a more finely executed pass. Route Two leaves the high three-wall shot, but that is retrievable.

Route Two does open up another possible shot for the offensive man; the hard pass straight down the left wall. But this is not an easy shot. As we said before, the offensive man is stepping towards the left front corner and taking the ball out of the air at a difficult angle. The straight hard pass is difficult to hit without catching the left side wall, or creating a hinder. *(Photo 2-45)*

Further, the run around approach makes the shot more difficult for the offensive player psychologically. He can see you easily. In Route One (straight up the side wall) the offensive player feels he has you blocked out of the play because his body shields you from the ball. Route Two removes this secure feeling and adds the visual element; as the player tries to hit the ball, he can see you out of the corner of his eye. Don't ever discount the importance of this. Paul Haber used this perfectly legal ploy for years; he called it "playing close."

One other comment; this recommended route is harder to take. You have to run all the way around your opponent, and you have to do it quickly. It takes hard work to get into this position properly, but it is worth it; winning handball takes work.

A final comment. I lost to Alvarado the next day, 21-9, 21-4. Paul came to watch and rooted for Naty the whole match. Naty killed everything so flat I could have run up and down the glass back wall and ceiling to get to the front court and it wouldn't have helped. So much for strategy.

Photo 2-45: Alvarado is attempting an offensive shot and Lewis must decide which way to go in to protect the front court. It makes a difference whether he goes to the right or left.

BIBLIOGRAPHY

Kramberg, Lou. "Kramberg Learns Real Art of 'Court Position' from Jacobs ... Position Yourself So Opponent Must Shoot to Your Strong Side." *Handball,* June 1976, Vol. 26, No. 3.

Muck, Terry. "A Pro Pointer on Position." *Handball,* Vol. 27, No. 4.

Singer, Stuffy. "Make Decisions for Victory: Planned Reactions." Excerpt from: *Handball,* 1977, Vol. 27, No. 3.

Tyson, Pete. "Shot Anticipation." *Handball,* 1977, Vol. 27, No. 5.

CHAPTER 3
DOUBLES

ASPECTS OF DOUBLES –
PHYSICAL, MENTAL,
PSYCHOLOGICAL
PETE TYSON

Some time ago I wrote a series of articles on the strategy of singles play, breaking the game down into five distinct areas that were called "situations" (the word, 'situation,' defined as "anytime the ball was about to be hit") and presenting the same strategy used by Jacobs, Haber, Lewis, etc., the greatest players of the last 25 years. These consistently superior players all played the same way, utilizing great control and defense to keep their opponents out of scoring position and patiently waiting for the inevitable mistake that would allow for the high percentage opportunity to end the rally.

However, doubles is a different story. It is far more complex because we are now talking about a TEAM SPORT. Success is not necessarily dependent on how well you can play singles, but rather on how well you can combine your talents with those of your partner. Success is highly dependent on your ability to recognize the particular 'situation' you are in and to understand the best percentage play for each of the SIX SITUATIONS. In the game of singles there are these five situations:
• Serving
• Returning service
• Defense (controlled and trouble)
• Offense
• Opponent is hitting the ball (shot anticipation).

These same situations exist in doubles, and there is also a sixth situation to consider—your partner is hitting the ball!

In addition, doubles is more complex because you are playing with a partner and you must learn how to blend your physical talents with his; unless you always play with the same partner, you will have some adjustments to make with each new player. Individual weaknesses can be covered up with proper teamwork, but this teamwork will vary depending on the strengths and weaknesses of that particular partner.

Another consideration in playing doubles is the different combinations of teams you face will cause you and your partner to make even further adjustments. These combinations cannot all be attacked

Photo 3-1: **Pete Tyson has taught and coached handball at the University of Texas at Austin for the past 22 years. His teams have won ten National Collegiate Doubles Champsionships. Pete won two National Collegiate Doubles Champsionships while a student at SMU, and in 1966 won the USHA National Open Doubles Championship with one of his students, Bob Lindsay. In 1979 he teamed with Dick Roberson to win the National Masters Doubles Championship. Another of his former students, Matt Kelly, was a member of the team that won the USHA National Doubles Championship in 1977.**

the same way. Different strategies must be employed depending on whether your opponents are two righthanders (the usual case), a righthander-lefthander combination or two lefthanders (God forbid!). You and your partner must determine how to best counter their strengths and exploit their weaknesses.

In addition, not only must you work with your partner physically and mentally, you must also understand what "makes him tick." What motivates him most? What words, if any, should you use to encourage him if he appears to have a letdown, or suddenly starts making errors, loses confidence or appears to be tired? How can you best communicate with him both during the rally and between rallies and during timeouts and between games? How can you suggest a change you would like him to make without appearing to criticize or appear too dominating and demanding?

Photo 3-2: **Stuffy Singer diving in and shooting with his left hand in the finals of the 1978 National Championships. That's his partner, Marty Decatur, urging him on while Matt Kelly is moving in fast. Singer and Decatur won this championship over Kelly and Skip McDowell.**

Stuffy Singer wrote an article in which he talked about Marty Decatur (many times National Doubles Champion) and mentioned how in their USHA finals match of 1978 things were not going particularly well for their team; at this point he (Stuffy) asked Marty to do something different with his return of serve. Now picture this. Here was Stuffy, a superb singles player but not especially known as a doubles player, telling perhaps the greatest doubles player of all time how to play the game! I'm sure Marty had his own ideas, ideas that had been successful for many years; and I'm not sure Marty was convinced his return of serve was the immediate problem. Nevertheless, Marty quickly made the requested adjustment. He made the adjustment because he knew the tremendous importance of the psychological aspect of doubles, and he wanted to show Stuffy that he had complete confidence in his judgment. This had to be a big psychological lift for Stuffy as he and Marty completely turned the match around and won the second and third games quite easily. As it turned out, the particular return of serve Marty started making did allow Stuffy to take better control of the offense. Stuffy was right (he usually is!), but I believe it was Marty's willingness and ability to adjust that made the difference.

This is the psychological aspect of doubles. It's a type of communication that encourages your partner and gives him confidence. One thing is certain, getting visibly upset with your partner will never help. It will only hinder his concentration and he will play worse; so don't ever put your partner down. Just the opposite, keep working on ways to bring him up!

Notice the above four aspects of doubles have nothing to do with your physical ability to execute the various shots, although the ability to place your shots accurately is obviously important. You need continually to spend time BY YOURSELF in regular practice sessions in order to improve physically. Remember, you only lose rallies when you make an error. This error might be (1) not returning the ball to the front wall or (2) returning the ball in such a manner that allows your opponent the opportunity to take the offense (in other words, you "set him up"). The only way you can improve your physical game, whether it is singles or doubles, is to reduce your errors. You can reduce your physical errors (skipping in kill shot attempts, hitting your ceiling shots too hard which allows your opponent a back wall setup, etc.) only by regular practice sessions.

However, just as many errors are made and just as many points and serves are given up because of MENTAL MISTAKES. These mental errors are often not obvious because the actual rally-ending mistake will be a physical one, but these mental errors CAUSE the physical errors in far too many cases.

The Six Situations of Doubles

1. Serving
2. Returning service
3. Defense
4. Offense
5. Opponent is hitting the ball
6. Partner is hitting the ball

EXAMPLE: One of your opponents serves to you, and the result is a setup off the back wall, but somehow you don't quite get into your best position to hit your shot with good power, although you do have a fair chance of hitting it low. Your opponents have control of the front court, and you go ahead and attempt your kill shot which, not hit with much power, contacts the front wall eight inches high; one of your opponents steps in and easily "puts it away" in the corner while you and your partner look on helplessly from back court. The error ended up being a physical one, because you did not hit your kill shot attempt low enough and your thinking might be, "I have to hit it lower next time." Right? Wrong (Or as Lou Russo would say, WRRROOONNNGGGG!). What caused the physical mistake of giving your opponents a setup was the mental error of attempting that shot in the first place. Right here is where you must understand the difference between a GOOD shot and an EFFECTIVE shot. That eight inch high shot was a 'good' shot but it was not 'effective' under the circumstances. If you and your opponents are in the court positions just described, and you are not in a hitting position that will allow you to really "power" the ball, you should have attempted a good 2-wall (sometimes called a "V") passing angle. You probably would not have won the rally by hitting that particular shot, since it did not have sufficient power to completely elude your opponents, but it would have caused them to retreat to rear court and would not have resulted in a setup. In other words, you wouldn't have won the rally, BUT YOU WOULDN'T HAVE LOST THE RALLY either. It's just as important not to lose rallies as it is to win them. (Maybe more important!)

The above example was to show that choosing the correct shot to hit according to the "situation" is just as important as executing the shot. Choosing correctly means you don't lose points by mental errors. You should play the percentages and, as I mentioned earlier, recognizing the situation and understanding the best percentage play for that particular situation is all important if you are to eliminate your mental errors. This will be the main emphasis of the future articles dealing specifically with doubles' SIX SITUATIONS.

Two good players who understand the mental and psychological aspects of doubles and really get "on the same wavelength" so their team is composed of two bodies, four arms and four legs but only ONE MIND can really be a great team. One mind controlling two bodies! That's why two players such as these can often defeat two other players who are superior in singles to either one of them. Witness the finals of the 1957 USHA National Doubles Championship in Dallas when the two top ranked singles players of that time, Jim Jacobs and Vic Hershkowitz, were playing a couple of youngsters from Chicago by the names of Johnny Sloan and Phil Collins. Jacobs and Hershkowitz were the Number 1 and 2 ranked players in the country and had been for the previous three years; nobody gave Sloan and Collins a chance. The result? Sloan and Collins with superior teamwork, being "on the same wavelength," upset Jacobs and Hershkowitz who, in this match, played as two great singles players playing together instead of as a team being controlled by the same thoughts.

Please don't think I am criticizing Jim Jacobs and Vic Hershkowitz. For the record, Vic was the finest all-around (1-wall, 3-wall and 4-wall) handball player who ever lived, and Jimmy is considered by most (and especially me!) as the greatest 4-wall champion of all time. Jacobs later became one of the all time great doubles players also. He teamed with Marty Decatur and FOR TEN YEARS THEY WERE NEVER DEFEATED—practice, exhibition, or tournament—NEVER DEFEATED. No, it was just to illustrate there is much, much more to effective doubles play than just being good singles players.

Every good player has his own ideas about how the game should be played, and they will, naturally, be based on what works best for him. There is nothing wrong with this kind of logic, especially when playing doubles, although you will get many different opinions. There are so many variables in doubles that it is very difficult to say for certain, "This is the best method."

I've had the great pleasure of teaching with and playing doubles with Fred Lewis at many of our handball camps for the past five years. Fred was a top ranked doubles player before he ever won his first of five National Singles Championships. The first day we ever played doubles together, we played very smoothly as a team with absolutely no mixups or misunderstandings. (Of course, playing with Fred can be even easier. All you have to do is yell "Yours" and then get out of the way!) It was very easy to play with him because he plays the "left side" the way I attempt to teach it to be played. I was also fortunate to have the opportunity of playing with Stuffy Singer at the 1974 National Championships but I had great difficulty coordinating with him. He played the left side differently than anyone I had ever teamed with, and I needed to make major adjustments which I was unable to do. Not that Stuffy's method was wrong (he has won the National Doubles Championship the last 2 years). It was just different, and I did not adjust, especially psychologically, in that one week we played together. Some of Stuffy's theories were more intricate than mine. He does things HE has the ability to do. It's a talent involving incredible reflexes and reactions most of us will never have.

Yet, I believe if players understand the basic principles of the "six situations of doubles" and especially the area involving proper court coverage, any two players can play well together with only minor adjustments.

The theories that will be presented in the upcoming series of doubles articles will be based on strategies proven successful for many of the top ranked doubles teams in the country.

Photo 3-3: **Jim Vandenbos on his knee shooting in the finals of the 1981 Doubles Championship in Chicago against Tom Kopaytic (2nd from left) and Jack Roberts (in back court). Vendenbos' partner was Jim Barnett (far left).**

DOUBLES –
SHOT ANTICIPATION AND
COURT COVERAGE

PETE TYSON

This article will deal with the different kinds of court coverages and positionings when it is NOT your turn to hit the ball—the most important area of effective doubles teamwork. Approximately 60-80% of all the time you are playing a doubles game, someone other than you is hitting the ball; and the position you assume during this time is just as important as the position you take when it is your turn to hit the ball. Many players play very well once it is their turn to hit; but as just pointed out, this is only 20-40% of the game.

Before we get into the various court positionings involved in doubles play, I believe it is important to review PHYSICAL POSITION-ING, that is, what the various parts of the body should be doing.

The actual court position you take is dependent on where your opponent is when he is getting ready to hit his shot, and the type of shot (offensive, defensive) he is apparently going to attempt. Thus, the FIRST and most important aspect of "physical positioning" is to ALWAYS WATCH THE BALL. If you don't watch the ball, how will you know where to position yourself? YOU WON'T! You will be blind as to what is about to take place—a ceiling shot, three-wall return, kill, or pass shot attempt. You will have to wait until the ball hits the front wall before moving into position. Good doubles (and singles) players move before the ball is even hit by the opponent because they can judge BY WATCHING where the ball is probably going to end up in the court.

This subject always brings up the very important area of SAFETY. PROTECT YOUR EYES! It is especially important in doubles because you are playing in a more narrow and confined court area, and you will be hit with the ball more often than in singles. Serious eye injuries can and have happened. I strongly urge you to wear eye guards. They will take some getting used to, but YOU CAN DO IT! There are many top players who wear them obviously without difficulty.

SECOND, don't be standing still when your opponent is hitting the ball. You will be able to "take off" much faster if you are already moving—moving into position for your shot and moving into the proper court position when your opponent or your partner is getting set to hit. Doubles play is faster than singles play. If you are constantly striving for the proper court positioning, you will get a good workout even if you never hit the ball (sometimes when playing the right side, you think you never will hit the ball). Speed in doubles play is reaction time and quickness. You will react faster and move quicker if you are not standing still when the ball is about to be hit.

THIRD, in my earlier article on "Shot Anticipation" in the game of singles, I talked about trying not to "dive" for shots. However, in doubles play, although you would still rather not dive, you will have to occasionally "hit the floor with your body." The ball is moving faster, and it is much more difficult to hit the ball out of your opponents' reach in doubles than it is in singles. Consequently, there will be many times when you must react very quickly, and you just do not have the time to anticipate your opponents' shots. You will be caught "on your heels" or leaning the wrong way and will not be able to get your feet moving. It is not unusual to see good doubles players "all over the floor," diving and striving to get up quickly before the ball is hit again. *(Photo 3-4)* There was a great action picture in *Handball* taken at the national doubles finals. It showed Stuffy Singer pushing himself up off the floor at the same time both his opponents, Vern Roberts and Dave Dohman, were in midair diving for the return. More often

Photo 3-4: **Action at the 1977 National 3-wall Doubles Championship. Vern Robert (far left) and partner, Dave Dohman (right) won this championship.**

than not, when time out is called to wipe the floor in a tough doubles match, it is blood that is being wiped up as a result of the bloody knees that occur by so much diving. You can avoid the painful and bloody knees by wearing knee pads as several of the top doubles players do.

FOURTH, draw your forearms up parallel with the floor and keep them there most of the time. Be ready for faster play and more hard hit shots in doubles than in singles. Because your opponents have less court to cover, they will more often be in set positions to really "power" the ball, and you must be able to react faster with your hands. Having your "arms up" will cut down the time you need to swing at the ball. If you ever had the pleasure (?) of playing against Ray Neveau and you didn't have your hands ready when he was hitting the ball, you would never return one of his "bullets." When big Ray really got set to hit the ball, you would say a silent prayer and hope that his shot was directed at your partner!

Court Division

Well, now that you are watching and moving and have your hands ready, where should your court position be? As in singles, this will depend on a number of things including where your opponent is and the type of shot he is attempting. It may also depend on where your partner is and if he is left-handed or right-handed. Your partner? That's right, don't forget about your partner. This is a TEAM sport. When it is your team's turn to make the return, which player should attempt the shot? In order to decide this, you must divide the court so each player knows the area for which he is responsible. NOTHING IN DOUBLES PLAY IS MORE IMPORTANT THAN THIS. You and your partner must have a clear understanding on court division, and then try your utmost to take only those shots which come into your specific court area. If a player moves in his partner's territory to attempt a shot, there will be confusion and a part of the court will usually be left unprotected. Naturally, you cannot always do this, and there are times when you must move over to "cover" for your partner, but for the most part, try to stay in "your court."

There are several acceptable methods of court division. A method used by many championship teams is shown in *Figure 3-1*. This court division assumes both partners are righthanded. Notice the court is divided right down the middle from the front wall to the short line. From the short line to the back wall, the dividing line veers slightly to the right and then goes straight to the back wall. In this court division, the right side player is responsible for the right half of the front court and the right third of the back court. The only difference between dividing the court in this manner and dividing the court down the middle all the way from front to back is the small alley (about 3 ' wide) just to the right of center in the rear half of the court. It's much

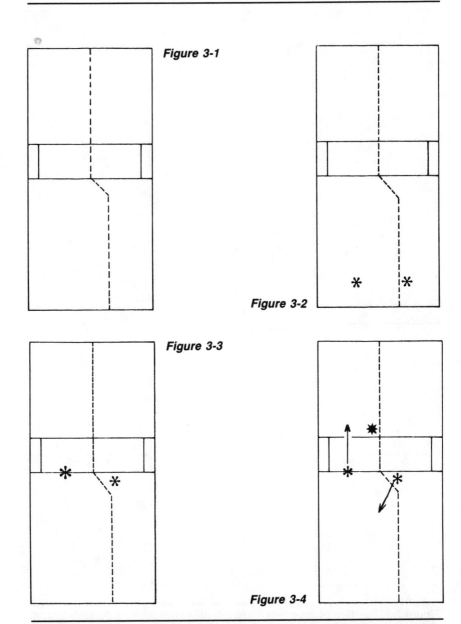

Figure 3-1

Figure 3-2

Figure 3-3

Figure 3-4

Figure 3-1: Court division for doubles team in which both partners are right-handed.

Figure 3-2: Position for team receiving service. Note: players are close to back wall and right side player is close to dividing line.

Figure 3-3: Position for team when opponent is set for offensive opportunity.

Figure 3-4: Opponent has easy front court offensive opportunity. Left side player moves in very close as right side partner retreats to back center court ready for anything that gets by his partner.

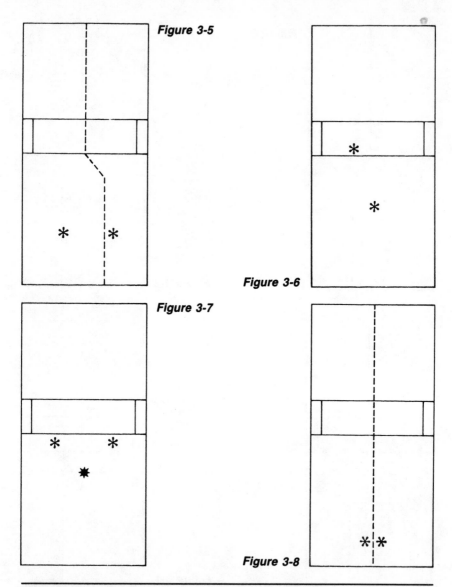

Figure 3-5

Figure 3-6

Figure 3-7

Figure 3-8

Figure 3-5: Position of team when opponent is attempting a defensive shot. Note again that right side player is close to dividing line.

Figures 3-6: Position of team when opponent is having trouble with shot attempt. Left side player is up close looking for fly kill opportunity while right side player covers back court.

Figure 3-7: Opponent has setup near center court. Both partners line up at angles attempting to block off front corners.

Figure 3-8: Court division for "lefty-righty" team. Note that partners' positions receiving service are both close to dividing line.

easier for the left side player with his dominant right hand to step over and play the shots in this area than it is for the right side player to back out of his territory in order to get his right hand on the shot; and he (right side player) certainly does not want to use his left hand on any shot that can be hit by his partner's right.

Depths of Court Positionings

The depth in the court that partners assume is based upon the kind of shot the opponent is attempting, which will be one of the following:

- Serving
- Attempting an offensive shot
- Attempting a defensive shot from a set and controlled position
- Attempting a shot from a "trouble" position in back court (reaching back or "jammed" or hitting while on the run)
- Diving for a low shot in front court

Figure 3-2 shows the team's position to receive service. Notice they are only two or three feet from the back wall. Too often players will play too far from the back wall, which will not only give them less time to position themselves for the return, but will also cause them to attempt their shots as they are retreating instead of the correct method of being behind the ball and stepping toward the front wall. Some positioning adjustments may have to be made against different kinds of serves (this will be discussed in more detail in the future article on "Return of Serve and Defense").

Figure 3-3 illustrates the players' positions when it appears the opponents have an offensive opportunity to hit a kill or pass shot. Whether this position is right on the short line or a step or two deeper depends on the opponent's power. If he tends to hit the ball very hard, the players should position a little deeper. If they play too close, many shots will be driven past them or through them—"Too hot to handle." Not many players have quick enough hands to play up closer against a power hitter. If, however, the opponent is a good "shooter" but doesn't have especially good power, one of the players might move up and actually take a position near the front service line because his opponent's kill shots are not going to rebound as far or as fast.

There will be times when an opponent will have a setup so easy and close to the front wall he should have little difficulty executing a very good kill shot. Here is a case when one player on your team should "over-commit" and attempt to intimidate the opponent by moving up very close to the front wall. By doing this, the player attempting the shot will see that his kill shot must be perfect or else it will be "dug" up. Quite often he will attempt a pass shot instead, or try to drive the ball through you, which is what you are trying to get him to do. On this particular play, your partner must retreat and move over to center court so he will have the opportunity to retrieve the power pass shot no matter in which direction it is hit. Notice in

Figure 3-4 this temporary court division is front and back instead of the usual side-by-side positioning. As soon as the return is made, the partners should hustle back to the side-by-side position because the "front-back" positioning is not very good most of the time when the opponents are hitting the ball.

Figure 3-5 shows the third "depth positioning" which the players should assume when the opponent is in a "controlled defensive" position and is apparently set to hit a ceiling shot or 3-wall shot. This is one area of doubles play where I have very often noticed positioning errors. Too often the right side player will remain near the shot line when the ball is obviously going to rear court and could easily end up in the right rear corner. He will have difficulty retreating fast enough to make the play, which will force his partner to cover for him. The result will be both players on the right side of the court, which will leave a large part of the left court unprotected. This mistake won't happen if the right side player will back up to a position halfway between the short line and the back wall. This will allow him to get into the proper position easily to play those defensive shots which sometimes turn out to be back wall setups. You might argue that if he played close to the short line, he would get fly kill opportunities; but really, this probably won't happen if the opponent is attempting his shot from a set position.

On the other hand, if the opponent is attempting a shot from a difficult ("trouble") position, this is the time "fly" shot opportunities most often occur and they should definitely be taken advantage of. This is another case for a temporary "front-back" type of court coverage. The partner who "fly shoots" the best should maintain his position around the short line, looking for that easy opportunity to pick one out of the air and end the rally, while his partner retreats to the middle of rear court in case the ball gets by **(see Figure 3-6)**.

As mentioned earlier, there will occasionally be some diving for shots in front court. When one of the opponents dives for a shot, the player on that side should follow closely, ready to move in quickly to retrieve the soft low shot that so often results in this specific situation. When this player moves in, his partner should retreat a little, ready to "cover" behind his partner in case the ball gets by him.

Angles of Court Positionings

Notice in most of the illustrations **(Figs. 3-2,3,5)** the right side player is very close to the imaginary dividing line. This positioning will allow him to play all shots in his court area with his dominant right hand; whereas, if he plays closer to the right side wall, he will be forced many times to use his left hand. Always remember you want your strong hand on the ball whenever possible. The right side player would like to be in such a position that if the ball were coming toward his left hand, he could simply step over to the right and let his partner play that shot with his right hand. When playing the right side, it is very important that you keep your left hand out of the way of your partner's strong right hand attempts. I promise you this is not easy to do. Playing the right side is much more difficult than playing the left (the author is obviously a right side player!). It is not more difficult physically, but mentally it is much tougher. There will be many shots that come within your reach that you must make the instant decision, "Should I hit it, or will my partner have a better shot?" And most of the time the left side player will have the better shot. The right side player must always be hustling into the proper position and assume every shot is being directed at him, knowing full well most of them won't be. He must submit to what seemingly is a lesser role on the team. There are many very fine players who just cannot do this. They cannot "keep their heads in the game" unless they are involved in hitting shots constantly.

Back to the subject of proper angles ... The ideal positioning of the right side player close to the imaginary dividing line is fine unless your team gives the opponents a shot opportunity along this same line. If this does happen (it usually means you have just hit a poor shot), you must slide over and attempt to line up between him and the front corner *(Figure 3-7)*. Be sure you don't stand directly in front of him (avoidable hinder!) or directly behind him where you would not be able to see the ball as it leaves his hand. Play at angles slightly to one side or the other. You will occasionally get pinned close to a side wall, but get away from it as soon as possible and keep trying to maintain a position at least six feet away from the right side wall.

Photo 3-5: Jack Roberts shooting in this doubles match. Note that all four players are watching the ball.

The left side player's positioning is similar to the right side player's as far as the various depths are concerned; and he should also play at angles with his opponent, trying to stay a step or two from the left side wall. He also is trying to get his right hand on the ball as much as possible, but he must not get caught so close to the side wall that he could not move to center court to hit those shots rebounding down the middle.

There is no question that the left side player is the workhorse of the team. He is going to play most of the shots and ideally would have a strong, hard-hitting left hand as well as good stamina as he will usually hit many more shots in a doubles game than he ever would in a singles game. He is going to be involved in most of the action, but he must not get so carried away he goes after his partner's shots. He must allow his partner in the game. Although he might hit some of these shots better than his right side partner, these advantages will be more than negated by the confusion it will cause, as well as causing the right side partner to really get "cold." If he does take his partner's shot, as will sometimes happen, as soon as the rally is over he should quickly tell his partner something like, "Hey, that was your shot I took—I'll let you have it next time." As earlier mentioned, "Nothing is more important than knowing which partner is supposed to make the return."

The Left-Hand Partner

When one of the partners is lefthanded, the court division is slightly different than it is for two righthanded partners. *Figure 3-8* shows the court division for a "lefty-righty" team to be straight down the center of the court. The same court depths apply when positioning for the opponents' shots as applied for the two righthanded partners. The angles are slightly different in that both partners should position themselves close to the imaginary center line (the lefthanded player should play left court). The weakness of the lefty-righty team is down the middle, so by both team members playing closer to the center, this area of weakness if made smaller. Each partner will have a better chance of getting his strong hand on the ball. Still, there may be confusion on shots that do come between these partners, so it is very important that the players quickly call "mine" or "yours" in order to avoid confusion. It would be well to decide beforehand which partner has the best "off-hand" and let him play those shots that come down the middle.

Positioning when Partner is Hitting

The main thing in this specific "situation" is to get out of the way and allow your partner a clear attempt at any shot he wants, especially when he is in an offensive position to try a kill or pass shot. *Figs. 3-9 and 3-10* illustrate that the player not hitting the ball should be off to the side and deep enough so the partner can direct his offen-

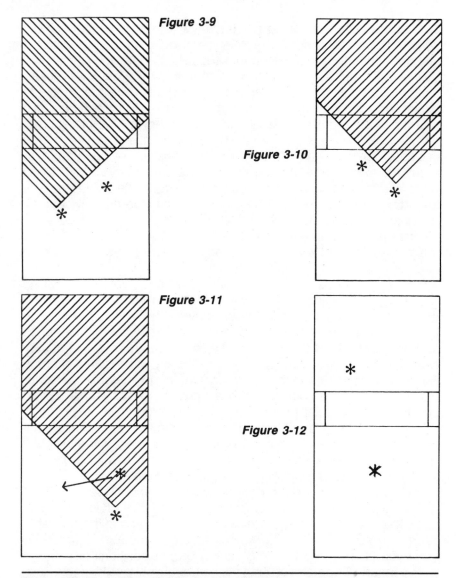

Figure 3-9

Figure 3-10

Figure 3-11

Figure 3-12

Figure 3-9: Illustration of players attempting shots while partner gets out of the way, allowing for all possible shot angles.

Figure 3-10: Illustration of players attempting shots while partner gets out of the way allowing for all possible shot angles.

Figure 3-11: Left side player is in partner's territory to attempt shot. Right side player must quickly move to left in order to give partner all angles to attempt his shot.

Figure 3-12: Left side player has moved up very close in front court to retrieve kill shot. Right side partner retreats to back center court to cover behind him in case he does not have time to get back to ideal position.

sive shot towards either corner (or anywhere in between) without worrying whether or not his partner might be in the path of his shot attempt. Once in a while a partner (usually the left side player) will be in a better position to play a deep shot, such as a back wall setup, even though it is in his partner's territory. In this case the right side player should quickly move to the left as shown in **Figure 3-11**, again making sure his partner has all possible angles in which to attempt his shot. This is another area where many mistakes are made, especially by the right side player. Occasionally, I've seen a player hit by his own partner's shot, and just as bad, I have many times witnessed a really tough shot directed at the right side opponent, only to end up in a "hinder" call because the right side partner couldn't get out of the way. SO GET OUT OF THE WAY and give your partner the opportunity to really "work on that right side opponent." There are several different ways he can attack that player if you will just give him the chance.

However, once your partner has hit his shot, you must quickly follow in, especially if it was a kill shot attempt from rear court. By moving in fast, you will be able to "cover" the front court in case the shot was not well executed and the opponents have the chance to drop in a quick kill shot. You must also be ready to move in quickly when it appears your partner is having difficulty with his shot attempt. Remember, this is when the opponents might get the opportunity for a quick fly kill before your partner has a chance to recover his desired position, so you must move in to cover front court.

If your partner is attempting his shot from a "controlled defensive" position, you should position yourself a few feet behind the short line, ready to move into the proper position which will be dictated by the type of shot your opponent next attempts.

Occasionally your partner will have to go in very close to the front wall to "dig" up a kill shot attempt. In this case you should drop back a few steps and be ready to cover behind him in case the next shot is driven past him before he has a chance to recover. **(Fig. 3-12)**

Even "knowing everything" about proper positioning, you and your partner will sometimes get "mixed up." Slight positioning adjustments will have to be made against different teams according to their particular strengths and weaknesses, and you need to know how best to communicate with your partner in order to solve these problems.

DOUBLES –
SERVICE AND OFFENSIVE
ATTACK STRATEGIES
PETE TYSON

Service Strategies

Serving in handball is much like pitching in baseball. If I were to ask you, "What is the best pitch in baseball?" what would your answer be? Although there are several good pitches (fast ball, slider, curve, screwball, changeup), your answer should be, "The one that works!" or "It depends on who you are pitching against." Both of these answers are correct, and the same is true for serving in handball. The best serve depends on the abilities of a particular opponent.

There are five things that can happen when your opponent(s) are returning your serve. They could:
- Hit a kill shot
- Hit a pass shot
- Hit a defensive ceiling or 3-wall shot
- Hit the ball into the floor
- Give you (your team) a "setup."

Above all, you want to place your serve in an area which eliminates your opponents' chances of hitting a kill shot or hitting a pass shot. What area is this?

Assuming both of your opponents are righthanded, this area is close to the left side wall and very deep in the rear corner. Also, the serve should be hit at such a height and speed that it is not playable off the back wall. This generally is the area against all righthanded players that is considered to be the "weakness," that area from which the receiver will not be able to hit a kill or pass shot successfully on his return attempt. Now, whether you hit your serve into this area fast and low, high and soft, at a sharp "Z" angle, or with natural or reverse spins depends on that particular opponent and his defensive abilities for those specific serves. If you place your serve into that area where your opponent cannot hit a kill or pass shot, you have hit a GOOD serve. However, in order for that "good" serve to be EFFECTIVE, it must also be one that is difficult for him to hit a defensive ceiling or 3-wall shot, and once again, it will depend on that particular opponent's defensive abilities.

EVERY PLAYER HAS THREE WEAK HANDS! These three weak hands are:
- Below the waist
- Above the shoulders
- Between the waist and the shoulders.

A player can be very strong in one of these stroke areas and very weak in another.

The LOW DRIVE SERVE *(Fig. 3-13)* will come to your opponent below his waist. When you hit this serve, you are trying to discover his ability or inability to "fist the ball" to the ceiling or around the walls.

The LOB SERVE *(Fig. 3-14)* will force your opponent to hit with his off hand from above the shoulders. Can he hit ceiling shots from this position? Consistently?

The HALF-LOB or CHANGEUP will force him to attempt his return from between the waist and shoulders. For many players (including some of the pros), this particular height is a very difficult one from which to execute a defensive shot.

When the "Z"-serve is properly executed *(Fig. 3-15)*, the opponent must attempt his return from an area so very close to the back wall that the ceiling shot or any kind of a "fist" return is nearly impossible. Can he make an effective 3-wall shot from that position?

Photo 3-6: **Jack Roberts shooting a back wall kill in the finals of the 1981 National Doubles Championships. Note that his opponent is giving him a clear shot to the front wall. Roberts and Tom Kopaytic won this championship.**

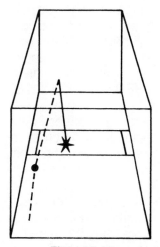

Figure 3-13

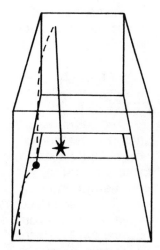

Figure 3-14

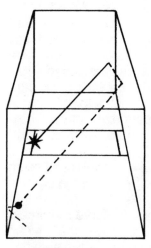

Figure 3-15

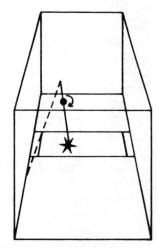

Figure 3-16

Figure 3-13: The low drive serve. Note that the ball strikes the floor close to the short line to keep it from rebounding off the back wall.

Figure 3-14: The lob serve. This serve can be very effective against an opponent who has difficulty hitting a ceiling shot with his off hand from above his shoulders.

Figure 3-15: The Z serve. This serve can be hit overhand, sidearm, underhand, or even with a closed fist.

Figure 3-16: The crotch serve. Natural (clockwise) spin is put on the ball and this will make it more likely to "flatten out."

Remember, you are trying to discover which of your "good" serves your opponent has the most difficulty defending. Then he can only hit the ball into the floor or give a setup. Although it is very nice when your opponent doesn't even return the serve, you should realize this will not happen very often, particularly as you advance into higher levels of competition. THE MAIN PURPOSE WHEN SERVING IS TO GET A SETUP!!

The setup will allow you the opportunity to take the offense and attempt a percentage rally-ending kill or pass shot. It doesn't matter how skilled you are at executing kill and pass shots, you cannot hit these shots unless you find some way to force your opponent to give you the opportunity!

You should direct your serves at the area of biggest weakness. Again, assuming you are playing against two righthanders, this area may very well be in that left rear corner. Notice I said may be. In many cases a doubles team is composed of two players whose abilities are NOT equal, and usually that weaker player is the right side partner. Even though serves directed at him can be played with his dominant right hand, his returns may not be as good as those played by his partner's left hand, especially if you are serving low hard "hooks" that are breaking both ways into the right rear corner. Indeed, this is very often the case, and it puts a lot of pressure on that right side player because he knows he is not as skilled as his partner and might really begin to "press." Not only may he begin to tighten up, his partner will often feel very frustrated because he cannot help out without abandoning his side. Eventually, the stronger partner may try to "help out" which can create confusion and even more frustration and pressure for the right side player.

If both opponents return service equally well, and you can't seem to find a serve that "works," you might decide to "go for the crack," that is, to serve your low power serve just across the short line into the crotch of the floor and side wall. Although this serve requires a certain element of luck, with practice you will discover that "luck" happens more often. This is a dangerous serve in singles because if you contact the side wall a little too high, your opponent can usually get set well enough to drive the ball past you. But in doubles, your partner is covering one side of the court so this is less likely to happen. Applying some "English" on the ball will make this particular serve more effective and more likely to "flatten out," even if it hits a few inches up on the side wall instead of directly in the crack. Fred Lewis and Marty Decatur are both very adept at putting a "natural" (clockwise) spin *(Fig. 3-16)* on the ball when directing their power serves to the left and they quite often hit the crotch which results in the flat "ACE."

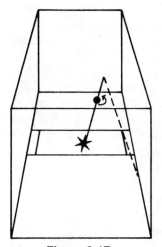

Figure 3-17

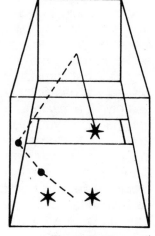

Figure 3-18

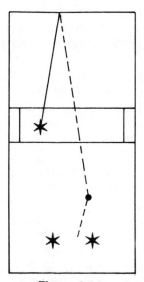

Figure 3-19

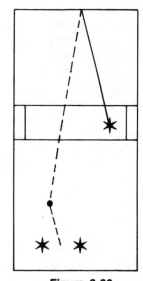

Figure 3-20

Figure 3-17: Crotch serve to the right. Reverse (counterclockwise) spin will make the ball more likely to "flatten out."

Figure 3-18: Good angle serve to hit to a "lefty-right" team.

Figure 3-19: Low drive serve with "natural" hook. Good serve against lefty-righty team.

Figure 3-20: Low drive serve with "reverse" hook. Good serve when weakness is down the middle.

Terry Muck is often effective at hitting a good "reverse" (counter-clockwise) spin *(Fig. 3-17)* on his low serve to the right and has picked up many points by catching that crack of the floor and right side wall just across the short line. I once witnessed Phil Collins hit 14 flat crotch serves in one game! You will often play several matches without hitting one, but sometimes you will be "in the groove" and you really will feel you can hit that crack; you won't ever know, however, unless you give it a few tries each time you play. You should hit this serve very hard so if you miss the crack it will not give your opponent time to get set and "tee off" on it. Also, make sure your partner is positioned in the forward part of the doubles box so as not to have a potential flat ACE serve hit him on the ankles before it crosses the short line.

Serving to the Lefthanded-Righthanded Team

As mentioned before, you must direct your serves to weakness in order to force a mistake which results in a setup for your team. The weakness of a team composed of a lefthanded left side player and a righthanded right side player is DOWN THE MIDDLE. Since both of their off hands are in the center, you need to develop some serves that will go into that area. They must be hit hard so one opponent will not have time to "run around the ball" and play it with his strong hand, and they too, like all other good serves, should not come off the back wall.

One such serve that will go into this weak middle area is an angle serve that hits the side wall near the short line. This serve *(Fig. 3-18)* is hit higher than the low power serve directed toward a rear corner. The ball should contact the side wall a foot or two high and rebound between the receivers. Again, make sure it is not hit so high it rebounds off the back wall high enough for the receiver to get good position on his return attempt. As with the "crotch serve," the server's partner should stand in the forward part of the doubles box in order to allow the ball to hit the side wall at the proper angle.

Another good way to attack this weak middle area is to hit a low power serve right down the middle of the court. This serve can be even more difficult for the receivers if "English" is put on the ball so it will "hook" back towards the center of the court. *Figure 3-19* illustrates the left side player hitting a NATURAL HOOK which is directed towards the right side receiver, but after contacting the floor, the ball hooks back into the weak center area. If the right side player can serve a REVERSE HOOK, he might have success by directing his serve at his left side opponent so the ball will break to the right and towards the middle *(Figure 3-20)*.

It would be very nice if you knew the weaknesses of your opponents before the match began, and you were able to direct a particular serve into those areas and achieve the desired results throughout the match. However, this is generally not the case. It will usually take some experimenting with your various "good" serves to determine where the weakness lies. And this "weakness" may change during the game. The receiver may adjust to a serve that was giving him difficulty so he begins to make good returns. Perhaps your serves that were effective in the beginning may begin to lose some of the necessary accuracy. Also, remember that a player's ability to hit shots accurately often changes when he is a little tired towards the end of a tough match. Sometimes just a subtle change in speed or slight difference in angle may cause your opponent to err or set you up. I doubt it was noticed by the spectators this year at the National Championships in Miami, but a slight change in the angle of a serve won the match point in both the semi-finals and finals of the Open Doubles Championship. Stuffy Singer moved just one short step to the right in the service zone from where he had been serving to hit his low drive serve with a good natural hook and achieved the CRUCIAL match ending ACE in BOTH MATCHES.

Alright, one more time: "What is the best serve in doubles?" Answer: "THE ONE THAT WORKS!"

Photo 3-7: **Stuffy Singer moving in to hit a fly shot as partner, Marty Decatur, watches from back court. That's Dennis Hofflander moving into front court. Hofflander's partner is Terry Muck in this Doubles Pro Tournament in Austin, Texas.**

Offensive Strategies

Just as in singles, the most important question you must ask yourself as you are preparing to hit the ball is "Am I on the OFFENSE or DEFENSE?" In other words, are you in good enough position to attempt a high percentage offensive kill or passing shot, or must you go on the defense? As a general rule, YOU SHOULD CONSIDER YOURSELF TO BE "ON THE OFFENSE" WHENEVER YOU HAVE TIME TO COME TO A COMPLETE STOP BEFORE HITTING THE BALL AND YOU CAN ATTEMPT YOUR SHOT FROM A COMFORTABLE POSITION BELOW THE WAIST. Attempting the accurate offensive shots when you are not well set is not "playing the percentages." The trouble with this game is you can go against the percentages and occasionally hit a perfect offensive shot from a defensive position. However, the handball definition of "occasionally" is LOSING. The definition of "consistent percentage shots" is WINNING! So play the percentages and only attempt those offensive shots (especially the kill shots) when you are set well enough to succeed at least seven or eight out of ten tries.

Now, once you are in a good position to hit the offensive shot, where do you hit it? Let's answer another question first: "How do you hit it?" Answer: HARD! Whereas in singles play you can sometimes succeed by dropping in a soft kill shot because your opponent is caught in deep court, this will rarely be the case in doubles. The court is too well covered. By the time your "soft" kill shot attempt reaches the front wall, one of your opponents will be very close to it. Because of this, you should DRIVE the ball very hard, even when attempting kill shots. Quite often, when your accuracy is slightly off, your shots may rebound right back to your opponents, but at least if you have really hit the ball hard, they won't have time to do anything but retrieve. They will not have time to get set well enough to "take the offense." About the only shot that should not really be "pounded" in doubles is the defensive ceiling shot.

Back to the question of "Where do you hit the offensive shot attempt?" As in serving, one good method is to "go to the weak man" if he is obviously weaker than his partner. Aim your kill shots in front of him, and when he comes in close to anticipate the kill, drive the ball past him or right at him. You can often have good success by hitting hooks where they will rebound and bounce on the floor directly in front of him *(Fig. 3-21)*. I've seen this particular tactic be highly successful even against very good players. The hard driving "hook" is definitely one of the offensive weapons that should be used. The team which has the ability to hit hooks, not only on the serves but also during the rally, has nearly twice the offensive potential as the team that cannot. I played a lot of doubles with Dick Robertson several years ago, and we defeated many good teams, many times only because we both had the ability to hook the ball both ways (natural and reverse) on any offensive attempt. The only bad thing about hooks is some players cannot hit them without hurting their arms. Indeed, I have had a sore arm at the end of every tournament I ever played. I can remember Jim Jacobs (Jim hit a lot of hooks) having to get shots in his arm before he could play in the finals of the 1965 National Championships, and he was unable to hit hooks in that final match. He won anyway, but Jacobs could do things most humans couldn't do!

So, one method of attacking a team is by "going at" the weaker man. But what if there is no apparent weakness? Well, one kind of successful strategy for several of the New York teams is the FREEZE OUT method. You and your partner decide before the match to direct every shot at the left side opponent, thereby "freezing out" the right side player. The right side player hits the ball only about 20% of the time under normal circumstances and, as was pointed out in an earlier article, it's difficult for him to "keep his head in the game" and not get "cold." When you employ the "freeze out" method, you give him even fewer chances to hit the ball; and when you accidentally hit the ball in his direction, he will have an extremely tough time making a good return. What you are attempting to do is play TWO AGAINST ONE; even if that one player is more skilled than either you or your partner, he will still find it most difficult to beat both of you at the same time. This is good strategy, especially if you feel their team is better than yours. See if one of them can beat both of you!

Notice I said to "freeze out" the right side player because it is generally impossible to freeze out the left side player. It is much easier to direct the ball to the left half of the court than to the right; and if you do play the right side opponent, he can hit all shots with his strong hand. When you direct all shots to the left side player, you can force him to play many shots with his off-hand. That's even better. You and your partner against the left side opponent's left hand! (Can you picture one player trying to defeat Jacobs and Decatur?!?) Every serve, kill shots, pass and drive shots, ceiling shots, all hit to the left can really wear down that opponent, and stamina is a very important factor in handball. When a player is tired, he doesn't execute as well, and it takes great execution to end rallies in doubles because the court is so well covered.

A THIRD way to "attack" your opponents offensively is to attempt the good, high percentage kills and passes based upon your opponents' court positions. In other words, "Shoot for the opening" or "Hit 'em where they ain't." Attempt your kill shots so they will rebound into the first half of the court in front of the opponent who is deeper. I've seen many teams, even good teams in the closing rounds of a National Championship, get one of their opponents in trouble in deep

Figure 3-21

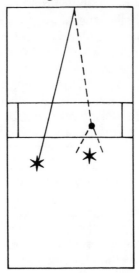

Figure 3-22

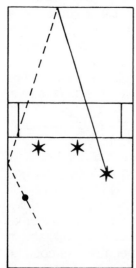

Figure 3-23

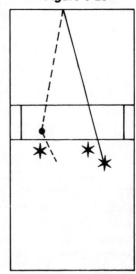

Figures 3-21: Ball is driven towards weaker right side opponent with "english" so that it will hook left or right after contacting floor directly in front of him.

Figure 3-22: Two wall pass angled so it will contact side wall just behind opponent. Good shot to attempt if both opponents are anticipating the kill shot.

Figure 3-23: Ball is hit with english so it will hook after hitting floor directly in front of opponent. Another good shot if both opponents are in front court.

Figure 3-24A

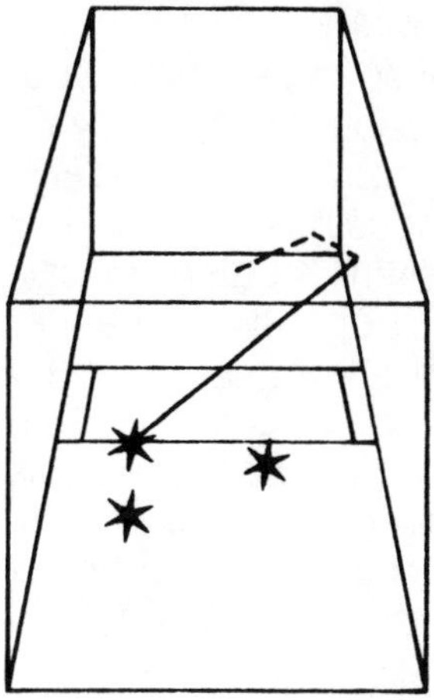

Figure 3-24B

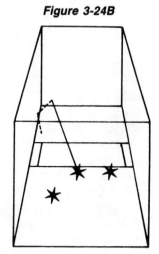

Figure 3-25A

Figure 3-25B

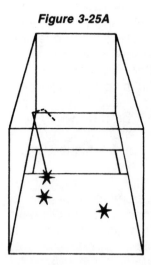

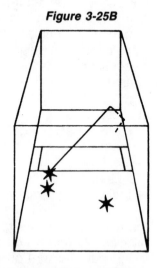

Figures 3-24A,B: Illustrate good corner kill shot angles to attempt if left side opponent is a little deep. Notice the shot rebounds into left front half of court.

Figures 3-25A,B: Illustrate good angles to attempt if right side opponent is a little deep. Notice that ball rebounds into front right half of court.

court, forcing him to return a fat setup. Then, they promptly hit a "good" shot six months high in front of the other opponent who was in good front court position to "dig" up the shot and keep the rally going. That same low shot directed to the other side (in front of the deeper opponent) would have won the rally easily.

To employ this kind of strategy, you must know where your opponents (both of them) are when you are about to attempt your shot. If both are in front court, you should drive a 2-WALL PASS *(Fig. 3-22)*. *Figures 3-24 and 3-25* illustrate the various INSIDE CORNER KILLS (front wall-side wall) and OUTSIDE CORNER KILLS (side wall-front wall) that can be effective when one of the opponents is deeper in the court. The other opponent (closest to the front wall) may try to "help out" by coming across to retrieve those kill shots; so you must "keep him honest" by occasionally driving the ball right at his position, even when there is an obvious opening to the other side. Mix up your offensive kills and passes with some drives and hooks so your opponents will not be able to anticipate your shots. Otherwise, the only way you'll score is when you execute your kill shot perfectly. Although you can do this sometimes, remember, another definition of "sometimes" is LOSING!

When "percentage" handball is discussed, it is necessary to mention "personal" percentages as well as "court" percentages. For example: If your left side opponent is in front court, and you attempt a kill shot in the left front corner, you have not attempted a "court percentage" shot; because if you hit the ball just slightly high, your opponent will not only be able to make the retrieve, but he is also close enough to the front wall to "re-kill" your shot easily. However, if your attempt "flattens out" and you can "flatten" that particular shot consistently (seven out of ten times), we call that a "personal percentage" shot; you should definitely keep hitting it as long as you are successful. Be aware, however, that there will be days when your "personal percentage" shots will not be that sharp. You must be prepared to abandon those shots and attempt the higher "court percentage" shots.

Generally speaking, the left side player is the partner who must hit the scoring shots. He will have many more opportunities and better angles to work with than his partner. His strong hand should have the ability to end the rally from all areas of the court. If he cannot hit kill shots with his off hand, he must be able to drive the ball with it and put pressure on the opponents, not giving them setups.

The right side player must either be able to hit good kill shots with his strong right hand or drive the ball at the opponent's weaknesses, thereby forcing setups for his partner. It would be nice if he could do both of these equally well, but this is usually not the case. Often, he will not be able to get "grooved in" on his kill shots because he doesn't have time to get set, and he doesn't have many good angles to work with. But he can still "POUND" the ball at the opponents' weaknesses. It's not enough for him to be just a good, steady retriever. He must do something offensively with the ball—again, either by "shooting" very well or by forcing setups for his partner.

Different teams will have different strategies based upon what works for them. For example, Fred Lewis and Gordie Pfeifer not only hit the ball very hard consistently, they also rarely miss. They don't give points away by hitting the floor. Their opponents must make every point themselves without the benefit of a Lewis or Pfeifer error.

On the other hand, you have a Ray Neveau who often skipped in kill shot attempts, but more often than not he "rolled them out" or hit the ball so hard at his opponents he forced many hand errors. He scored a lot of points for his opponents by his shooting errors but he scored more for his team. Ray's partner, Simie, killed the ball very well when he had the opportunity, but he let Big Ray take almost everything in the rear court because Ray was such an offensive threat—even from 38 feet away.

Doubles is a fascinating game. There are so many variables, so many different things to consider, including the strengths and weaknesses of four players who are competing at a very fast pace and whose positions are continually and rapidly changing. Still, your team must have an OFFENSIVE PLAN based not only upon your opponents' weaknesses, but also on your team's particular strengths. You would like to do what you can do best, but if it isn't working, be prepared to call time out, talk it over, and try a different attack.

DOUBLES–
RETURN OF SERVE
AND DEFENSE

PETE TYSON

The main emphasis in this series of articles is on the strategy of successful doubles play. When, why and where should a particular shot be hit or a position be taken? There is much more to this game than simply being able to hit the ball where you want it to go. If you are to learn to play intelligently, you must understand percentages as they relate to the various situations encountered during the course of a game.

Return Of Service Strategies

In the article on "service strategies," it was pointed out that the main purpose of serving was to get a setup, so the main purpose when returning service is not to give a setup! When returning service, you are not trying to win the rally. Rather, you are trying not to lose the rally!

Consider this particular situation carefully. The server has all of the advantages. He can take his time and think about your weaknesses, and he is going to hit his best shot with his strong hand only 17 feet away from the front wall. He can put whatever speed and spin on the ball he desires, and if he wins the rally, he scores a point and serves again with all of the same advantages.

If you win the rally, you only get the serve. You are going to have to start from a position as deep in the court as you could possibly be. You will have only one or two seconds to get into position to make the return. The ball is going to be in a difficult area, very close to the side wall and/or back wall when you contact it; plus you will probably have to attempt your return with your off-hand.

You are obviously at a tremendous disadvantage. In other words, YOU ARE IN TROUBLE! At this point, when your opponent is about to serve, the odds are about 80-20 he is going to win the rally. That means for every 100 times he serves, he will win the rally 80 times—unless you can make a return that will neutralize his advantages. You would like to get "into the rally" with at least a 50-50 chance of winning. The only way you can do this is by returning the serve in such a manner that your opponents will have to retreat to the rear court, while you and your partner have time to move up to a more desirable position closer to the front wall.

Attempting an offensive kill shot from the receiving position is the quickest way to lose the game. Your opponents have the front court so well covered that if you are just slightly off with your kill shot attempt, they will have a very easy opportunity to end the rally with a "rekill" before your team has a chance to move up. Of course, if the serve turns out to be a setup for which you have time to get set, and you can play with your strong hand, by all means take the "offense," but still be cautious with your kill shot attempts. Power passing shots would be better percentage shots.

However, you must not assume the serve is going to result in a setup. Just the opposite! You must believe the serve is going to be tough, and if it is, your only high percentage choice is to hit a defensive shot. Remember, your opponent (the server) wants to get a setup. In order not to oblige him, you must move him (them) off the short line and into the rear court.

So what specific returns should you be attempting? This, of course, depends on the type of serve that is hit to you. **(Fig. 3-26,27,28)**

Photo 3-8: **Marty Decatur attempting a back wall shot against Skip McDowell and Matt Kelly in the finals of the 1978 Nationals. Marty, considered by many to be the best doubles player ever, has won the National 4-wall Doubles Championship 8 times. He also has won many 1-wall and 3-wall National Championships.**

Figure 3-26

Figure 3-27

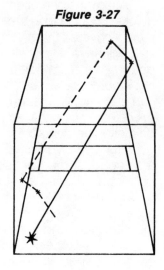

Figure 3-28

Figure 3-29

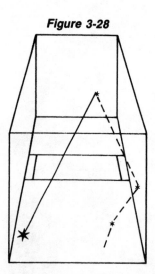

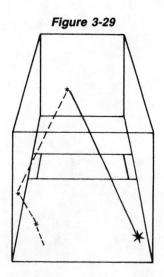

Figure 3-26: Returning the low drive serve by hitting a ceiling shot with the underhand fist.

Figure 3-27: Return of a low drive serve that "jams" you should be the three-wall return hit with a fist into the opposite side wall.

Figure 3-28: The two-wall passing angle return of the serve that comes off the back wall.

Figure 3-29: Right side player returning service by hitting a two-wall angle to the left.

Returning the Low Power Serve

The serve that will be hit to you often is the low power serve. There are four different returns you must be prepared to make, depending on where you and the ball are at the time.

These same returns apply if you are the right side doubles partner, even though the ball can be played with your strong hand. However, because it is your strong hand, you will be able to hit the ball harder, and you will occasionally have time to get set well enough to hit a hard two-wall return to the left *(Fig. 3-29)*. But if you are not getting the proper angle on that return in order to drive the ball out of your opponent's reach, get the ball up to the ceiling or around the walls—whatever it takes to get the serving team into the rear court without giving a back wall setup.

Returning the Lob Serve

If your opponents hit a lob serve, there are also several return possibilities, but unlike returning the low drive serve, you will have time to choose the position you wish to take in attempting the return.

Because you (the left side player) don't have to worry about serves hit towards the right rear corner, you can move over quickly to the left side wall before your opponent contacts the ball. Unless the serve is perfectly executed, you will be able to get your strong hand on the ball, and you can easily overhand the ball to the ceiling.

If the lob is so well directed that you must use your off hand, you can move up quickly and hit the ball on the "fly." Remember, you cannot reach across the short line to contact the ball—a violation that would result in a point for the server. One method to "fly" the ball is to use your underhand fist to hit a power passing shot. The two-wall pass would be a good choice; but just the fact that you drive the ball very hard (not so high that it will come off the back wall) will usually be effective because the server and his partner cannot leave the service zone until after the served ball passes the short line. Consequently, a hard drive will not give them much time to retreat and get set.

If, however, the lob serve bounces just across the short line, (this means you could not legally "fly" the ball) you should hit the ball after it contacts the floor, using your overhand stroke to hit the ball to the ceiling or perhaps a two-wall angle to the right.

The fourth possibility is to retreat to the rear corner to wait for the ball. If you do this, you should attempt the overhand ceiling shot, or if the ball comes off the back wall, the two-wall passing angle would be the best percentage choice. It takes a very strong off-hand to hit these returns from the deep rear court consistently. If you don't have this kind of necessary strength, you should learn to "run up" and play the ball either on the fly or just after the bounce. It's a little more difficult to time your shot when you charge forward, but once you

Figure 3-30

Figure 3-31

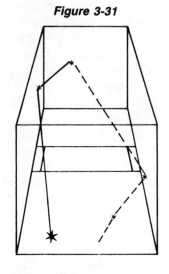

Figure 3-32

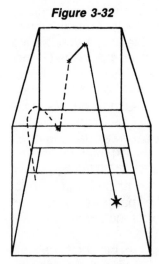

Figure 3-33

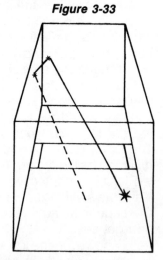

Figure 3-30: Left side player charging to return lob serve while right side player moves over to cover deep court in case ball gets by partner. Player could hit a ceiling shot as shown in Figure 1 or a two-wall angle as shown in Figure 3.

Figure 3-31: Player hitting an open hand three-wall shot on his return of the Z-serve.

Figure 3-32: Ceiling shot to attempt from a "controlled" defensive position.

Figure 3-33: Overhand drive angle from a "controlled" defensive position to attempt against the lefty-righty team. Note that rebound is through the middle of the court.

develop this timing, the lob serve will never again be an effective weapon against you.

As was previously mentioned, you can "over-commit" on returning this serve because of your partner, who in this case, should move over to center court ready to make the return in case the ball is not playable from the position to which you have committed. *(Fig. 3-30)*

The first possibility is that the serve contacts the floor just across the short line and does not hit the side wall or back wall after bouncing. In this case, you should move quickly to the side and attempt the underhand fist ceiling shot. Don't try to direct your ceiling shot so it will rebound and drop in a rear court, or too often you will catch a side which will result in an easy setup for your opponents. Rather, aim your shot so it will rebound right down the center of the court. By doing this, you allow a margin for error. If your shot contacts the ceiling several feet to either side of where you are aiming, your return will still end up in the rear court which is absolutely essential. You just do not have the time to position yourself properly for the accuracy it takes to drop that ceiling shot into the rear corner, so do not take the unnecessary risk.

If the serve hits the side wall crotch, or it has some "English" which causes the ball to "jam" you, your best return would be to hit a fist 3-wall return that contacts the opposite side wall first. As *Figure 3-27* illustrates, attempt to make the ball hit the side wall close to the front wall in order not to give the opportunity for a fly shot. *(Photo 3-9)*

Occasionally, the serve may be hit high enough so it will rebound off the back wall, but it will still be a difficult one if it is close to the side wall and doesn't rebound very far off the back wall. Your return should be a 2-wall or "V" shot. *(Figure 3-28)* Be sure to angle this shot so it will contact the side wall at or slightly behind the short line out of the opponents' reach.

Sometimes the low power serve will "hook" into the rear corner and hit the side wall before hitting the back wall very low. Again, this is not a setup because the ball is very low and close to the back wall as it rebounds. You should follow the ball "around the corner" in order to get your strong hand on the ball. You will probably have to reach back and contact the ball behind you which will make the open hand 3-wall return the easiest and best shot to attempt.

Again, these are the four things most likely to happen when the low drive serve is hit to you. You are not going to have time to think about these returns. The position of the ball will determine your choice, so you must be able to react with the proper return without thinking. Practice these returns until they become reflexive acts.

Returning the Z-Serve

Once again, you have options on where to position yourself for the return of this serve. As in returning the lob serve, you can "over-commit" because your partner can move over to deep center court to cover for you.

One option is to run up quickly just before the server contacts the ball and move into position to "fly" the ball with your strong hand. You should attempt to "power" the ball past your opponents before they have a chance to retreat. Remember, your partner must move over to center court in case the ball gets past you.

Another return possibility would be to let the ball hit the floor, then step in and overhand the ball to the ceiling, using your strong hand if you can or your off-hand if you must.

The third option would be to allow the ball to hit the side wall and then hit an open hand three-wall return with your off-hand. *(Fig. 3-31)* The main advantage in letting the ball get to this deep court position is it might come off the back wall and allow you the opportunity to take an offensive shot such as a power pass or a hard driving "hook" with your strong hand.

As was mentioned in an earlier article on "Court Coverage," it's important for the partner not hitting the ball to move up quickly in case the service return is weak. He has the chance to cover your mistake by possibly "digging up" a kill shot attempt hit quickly by the opponents.

Photo 3-9: Dave Dohman making a tough return in the finals of the 1977 National 3-wall Championships against John Sabo (left) and Fred Munsch (2nd from right), while partner Vern Roberts looks on.

Is the return of serve really that important? The top players in the game will tell you this is the most important of all the shots! In the game of singles, the player who returns service best is definitely the one who is going to get the most opportunities to win rallies. It's not quite as obvious in doubles because a partner can often "cover" for a mistake, but it is still of utmost importance.

Remember, you want to return each serve so you can get on equal footing with the serving team. You are not trying to win the rally on this shot. You are trying not to lose the rally!

One last point. Don't forget that doubles is a "team sport" and sometimes it may be necessary to sacrifice individual pride for the good of the team. If a serve is really getting to you so you are making a lot of return errors, be prepared to let your partner either trade sides with you or move to the middle of the court and take complete charge of returning service while you move back out of the way. I know and you know this is something you hope will not be necessary, but sometimes it might make the difference between winning and losing. Indeed, it has! On two different occasions, I have seen a team win the National Championship because one player on that winning team allowed his partner to take over service return completely. I've also seen a team lose the National Championship because the right side player had "too much pride" and did not let his partner know he had injured his right arm.

This maneuver should not be looked upon as degrading, but as a way to benefit the team. Anyone can have an off day, but don't let it defeat you if there is something that can be done about it. Don't be stubborn! Do what is necessary for success. *(Photo 3-10)*

Defense

"Defense" is the "situation" during the rally when it is your turn to hit the ball, but you are not in a position for the accuracy necessary to hit the offensive kill or pass shots. This situation can be further divided into Trouble Defense and Controlled Defense.

Trouble Defense

Returning service would be an example of "trouble defense"—also, during the rally when you have to hit the ball while on the run, or from an uncomfortable position (perhaps too close to the body) or having to reach back behind you to make contact, or perhaps you are having to play the ball with your off-hand from a difficult position deep in the court and close to the side wall. Again, these are examples of defensive positions that we would term "trouble defense," and the purpose of a shot hit from one of these positions is the same as when returning service—to get out of trouble!

The same kinds of ceiling shots, three-wall returns and two-wall passing angles described in returning service also apply during the rally when you are caught in one of these "trouble defensive" positions. You are trying not to give a setup. This is why certain teams are so difficult to defeat. The only way you can win a rally is for your opponents to make the mistake of hitting the ball into the floor or giving you a setup. Good teams will not "give" you anything! You must attempt to force these mistakes by making your opponents return the ball from a "trouble" defensive position. But the great teams are able to hit good defensive shots even when they are in trouble. So how do you win rallies against players with superb defensive abilities? Answer: you don't very often! That's why they win!

Because you have only half as much court to cover in doubles as in singles, you will not often have to hit the ball while on the run the way you sometimes must do in singles, especially when chasing down a pass shot. In doubles, more often than not, this so-called "trouble position" will occur when you are "jammed" by a ball that must be played very close to the body. In this case, two good returns would be to hit a fist three-wall shot into the opposite side wall or if possible, hit a fist drive towards the opponents' weakness, i.e. down the left wall against two righthanders or down the middle against a "lefty-righty" team.

Photo 3-10: Skip McDowell hitting from deep court in the quarterfinals of the 1981 National Doubles Championships. Skip's partner is Harry Robertson (left) and their opponents were Ken Ginty (right) and Don Robinson. The top players think that Robinson (2nd from left) is the hardest hitter in the game.

Controlled Defense

There will be many times during the game when you do have time to get set, time you do not have in returning service or in one of the other "trouble" defensive positions. But in this case, the ball must be played from a shoulder high or higher position which is just too high to execute an offensive shot successfully. We would term this position, "Controlled Defense." You are not trying "to get out of trouble" because you are not in trouble! The strategy in this situation is to attempt to force a mistake from your opponents. One way to do this is by hitting your ceiling shot so it will drop in the weak hand rear corner. *(Fig. 3-32)* This shot requires accuracy, and you can be accurate when you are hitting from the "controlled" set position. You might also drive the ball at the opponents' weakness, but because you are attempting your shot from a high position, be cautious and don't hit the front wall too high or you will give your opponents a back wall setup. If both of your opponents are righthanded, drive the ball down the left side wall, or down the middle against the "lefty-righty" team. *(Fig. 3-33)*

Figure 3-34	*Figure 3-35*

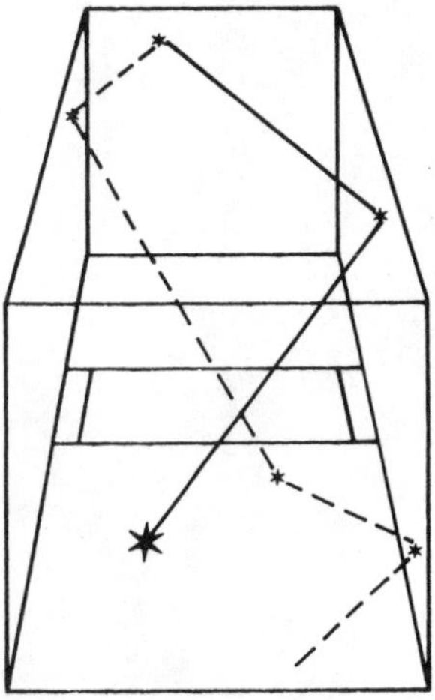

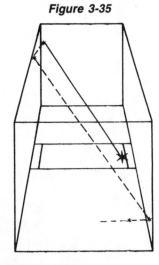

Figure 3-34: **Three-wall shot to use against the lefty-righty team. As in Figure 3-34, the rebound is back through the weak middle area of the court.**

Figures 3-35: **The "mystery shot." Another type of three-wall return to use against the lefty-righty team.**

Also, against the "lefty-righty" team, you should be hitting more three-wall shots than ceiling shots because the rebound of the three-wall shot *(Fig. 3-34)* is back through the middle of the court into their weak area. Notice this three-wall shot has a different angle than the one you should be hitting against two righthanders. *(Fig. 3-27)*

The right side player might sometimes be in a position to hit the "mystery shot" (it would take another article to explain the name given this shot). Notice in *Figure 3-35* that this shot contacts the front wall very high and close to the left front corner. It then hits the side wall and angles across court, where it hits the right side wall before hitting the floor.

Because of the spin imparted to the ball when it "wraps" the front left corner, the ball "straightens out" and parallels the back wall on its rebound towards the left rear corner. Confused? So might your opponents be. This shot will force the lefthanded opponent to return a difficult shot from deep court using his off-hand, and a setup for your team could very easily be the result.

The most consistent winners in any sport are the players and teams who have the best defense. What does having a great defense mean in the game of handball? The only way you can lose a rally is if you hit the ball into the floor or give your opponents a setup which permits them to hit the offensive kill or pass shot. Great defense means you do neither of these. How can you not win rallies if you don't lose them!?!

Photo 3-11: **Dave Dohman putting everything into his kill shot attempt in the finals of the 1979 National Doubles Championship as Stuffy Singer moves up. Singer and Marty Decatur won this match in a close tie-breaker over Dohman and Vern Roberts.**

COURT CLINIC
MORT LEVE

Question: What suggestions would you have for better doubles performance?

Answer: We have often written that the right side player in doubles has a much tougher assignment than would appear on the surface. Assuming that we have two righthanders as partners, the man on the right must discipline himself to act as "second fiddle" to his left side partner. In other words, the man on the left must dominate. Too often, especially with the less experienced players, we find the rightsider moving too far toward center court to take caroming shots off the right side wall, either hitting the ball in an awkward, off-balance position with his right or making the usually fatal mistake of "sticking in" his left hand. The man on the left has a much better angle on these shots, moving into the ball with full right hand control.

We also note that the "club" right side player has a tendency to "hang back" too much, finding himself out in "right field" when he should be in front court to dig and keep the ball in play. Ideally, the left sider should be given the job of roaming deep court and, if lines were drawn, he would be given approximately three-quarters of the 20x40 territory.

Through the years there have been varied types of champion doubles tandems. These stalwarts have not prescribed strictly to the letter of left/right strategy, but rather, have parlayed their strengths into getting 21 first.

Sam Haber-Ken Schneider ... won three open doubles titles in the early USHA tournament years. Sam, the bottom board shooting lefthander, superbly potent off the back wall, was more of a confined left portion of the court custodian, going up and back; this permitted Kenny to move a lot in the center court, retrieving strongly, and coupling volleying shots. Lefty Coyle would play the left side in this manner also, with emphasis on his quick handed corner kills from short court and, when performing with Billy Baier, would allow Billy to roam far and wide.

Johnny Sloan-Phil Collins ... actually, "The Wrist Kid" Collins, playing on the right, had the deft volley ending shot ability combined with the big serve and strength off the back wall. Sloan, ever the court general, unerringly moved the ball around with amazingly controlled left hand fist shots, and when taking center court shots, had the quickness to execute corner fly kills. Teamwork was a by-word with these national champions, never more emphasized than in their big 1957 Dallas USHA national victory over the so-called "Monster Team" of Vic Hershkowitz and Jim Jacobs. At that time Jacobs and Hershkowitz were ranked 1-2 in open singles, and it seemed the pair of them would run roughshod over any competition. However, this torrid three-game match was decided mainly on teamwork. Neither Jim nor Vic could play in a supporting role when one or the other was on the left side.

Jacobs finally found the answer when he enjoyed a championship ten-year reign with Marty Decatur. Both Jim and Marty could do it all, and they arrived at the right formula by dividing up left court participation. The continual switch-over kept them both fresher than their opponents. The combinations of the bombastic serves each of them had, and their full arsenal of offensive and defensive shots made them a truly super team.

Oscar Obert-Ruby Obert ... enjoyed tremendous success in all phases of the game—one-wall, three-wall, and four-wall. Oscar was the dominating left sider with Ruby patiently and deftly keeping the ball in play. Oscar, a "pure shooter," could end the volley from any portion of the court.

Ray Neveau-Simie Fein ... three-time national winners ... the perfect example of the "playing by the book" success. Perhaps we could say that Simie allows Ray even more leeway than is expected. He gives Ray free rein, knowing his power-packed shooting ability. It appears that Neveau covers even more than three-quarters of the court. Fein's difficult role in staying out of much of the action is to produce when he is needed, and this he does coolly and with fine execution. Invariably we will find Simie making key shots with those blue chips down. Neveau, one of the game's most exciting performers, moves superbly for a 220-plus pounder. In essence he's a "Big Cat," and we have said often he could have been a top-ranked singles' performer throughout his career had he been willing to pay the price of Spartan conditioning.

It has been shown that it is NOT necessary for two fine ball players to play together for years before achieving winning stature. A prime example would be the Fred Lewis-Gordy Pfeifer teamup. Steady Freddie, playing left side, with his known big serve, strong off hand overhead returns, and percentage volley ending shots ... Gordy, also with the big serve, outstanding digs, and deadly right hand shooting, either from deep or short court. Too bad we could not witness this team against an "in prime" opposition of Jacobs-Decatur.

We would be remiss if we left out Paul Haber in any top drawer doubles conversation. Whoever Paul teamed with it spelled strength, although his experience with Lou Russo was a bit frustrating in the domination department. Paul has always liked to get a Paul Morlos partner and then take charge completely. This was okay until two big guns like a Lewis and Pfeifer provided the competition. Haber won a big national invitational doubles with Don Ardito, who displays fine doubles ability. In essence a team up of a Haber with a strictly right sider like Pfeifer or August would be a most potent combine.

Photo 3-12: Lou Russo drives from deep court in the finals of the 1977 National 3-wall Championships. No one is more qualified to write an instructional article on doubles than Russo. In 1969, Lou achieved one of the enviable records in handball by winning the one-, three-, and four-wall national doubles titles with three different partners.

LOU RUSSO
ON DOUBLES
LOU RUSSO
WITH MORT LEVE

In playing doubles, emphasis must be put on teamwork and an understanding of doubles strategy. There have been many different types of doubles champions, but always prevalent has been the element of teamwork.

In one-wall doubles, a southpaw should play on the right side, directly opposite to his position in four-wall handball. The reason for this is that in one-wall, there are no side walls. The 20-foot playing court is more or less a central corridor. Players can move out to the 6-or-more foot "apron" area on either side of the 20-foot confines. Thus the left-hander can maneuver to take most balls with his strong hand, while at the same time protect that inside central area. So it is with the righthander playing left side. *(Fig. 3-36)*

In four-wall if the team is comprised of a lefthander and a righthander, the lefthander would take over the left side. *(Fig. 3-37)* There is an element of vulnerability right down the middle, and it is the teamwork that decides which player will take charge of shots in this area. The court is divided more or less in two equal portions for the left-righthand combine, with coverup necessary in some back court returns. There must be a piston-like movement to cover the court well. *(Fig. 3-38)* In a serve to one partner, the other moves forward to protect front court; then, as play ensues, the covering teamwork takes over.

Most of the time we find the doubles team consists of two righthanders and the pattern calls for domination by the partner taking over the left side. This is not a matter of dividing the court in two. The man on the left should take his half and then the middle corridor with his strong hand. *(Fig. 3-39)* The big mistake usually is that the right side player tries to move quickly toward center court to take balls caroming off the right side wall. To move to the left and then try to coordinate a right hand shot is a very difficult maneuver and usually results in a weak return.

It is much easier for the left side player to move to his right and take that ball bouncing off the right side wall, gaining good position and point of contact.

Figure 3-36

right-hander   left-hander

Figure 3-37

left-hander   right-hander

Figure 3-38

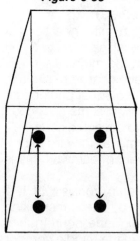

Figure 3-39

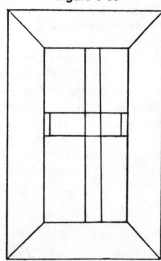

Figure 3-36: **Positioning of right- and left-handers in one-wall doubles.**

Figure 3-37: **Positioning of right- and left-handers in four-wall doubles.**

Figures 3-38: **A good doubles team moves like the complementing pistons of a car engine. When one player is in front the other is in back and vice versa.**

Figures 3-39: **When two right-handers play four-wall doubles the player on the left dominates and takes balls down the central corridor of the court.**

The player on the right side, subjugating himself to his partner, has the responsibility of keeping the ball in play, not leaving his front court vacant, and when the good shot does present itself, being ready to put it away. The big serve is, of course, an invaluable asset for such a doubles team.

Certain basic "don'ts" of doubles are:

- Don't get hung up on a side wall. Stay away from those walls so you have ample room to maneuver and stroke the ball.
- Don't stick out your weak hand to return any ball that can better be handled by your left side partner with his strong hand.
- Don't let yourself get out of position during the rally. Keep moving and be ready to back up your partner.
- Don't hang back in deep court and leave front court wide open for the opponents.
- Don't try to shoot from behind your opponents. In singles you can shoot if your opponent is positioned to one side, or you can go for the pass; but in doubles you must realize that, with your opponents in front court, you would have to pin-point or bottom board the ball to end the rally, and if you don't accomplish this you will find your team to be sitting ducks.
- Defensive shots are all-important in doubles, and the use of ceiling shots and around the walls shots are safe usually. Again, they must be controlled.
- Don't be abusive toward your partner. Be encouraging and be compassionate of any errors he might make. Use simple "Yours" and "Mine" to indicate who should take certain shots. Give this signal in ample time to avoid any confusion.
- Don't hesitate to communicate with your partner. Discuss your strategy before the match, at time outs, and in between games.

In winning national one-wall and three-wall doubles, the aggressive shooting game and big serve were the prime factors in success. Good fly shooting is necessary in the outdoor games of one-wall and three-wall—together with strong service. The latter is even more important in one-wall where the serve can gain quick points. In three-wall, the effective serve into deep court can often set up the front court fly kill.

Doubles in handball offers a fine change of pace from singles, and a challenge of the teamwork and strategy. There is little margin for uncontrolled shots in doubles; you can get away with some shots in singles that lack definite pinpointing, but against good doubles competition this is tantamount to committing suicide.

Handball doubles is fun. It keeps many older players in the courts after they find they can no longer handle spirited singles play. And, simply, there is no way you can get in a court if you have played the game for any length of time and not give it that full effort. This is a highly competitive pastime and seldom will you find any true hand-baller content to taper off into a slow-down pace. But doubles can give the enjoyment and continuation of that competition. *(Photo 3-13)*

In racquetball the majority of players seem to "shy away" from doubles because of those four "lethal" racquet weapons in the cozy confines of the 20′x40′ court. We think some entrepreneur will come along one of these days and build a larger court for racquetball. It makes sense as squash has a larger court for its doubles competition.

One thing you do want to avoid is getting into a regular doubles play clique that will confine your efforts to competing against the same players time after time. There's no way your play will progress unless you gain a variety of good playing opposition. "Variety is the spice of life," and "Variety of handball competition leads to improved play."

The interspersing of some doubles play with your singles will prove beneficial. It will teach you court discipline and make you work on better control of your shots. You might tend to be somewhat sloppy if you are constantly victorious in singles, getting away with shots that are not well controlled. But, you will find in doubles those same shots will backfire emphatically.

I personally find the year-long combination of four-wall, three-wall and one-wall tend to give me a real feel for handball. As a businessman, my prime drawback is the inability to indulge myself more than a couple of times a week in court play. To the youngster coming up in handball, I would prescribe everyday play if at all possible.

Photo 3-13: **Finals of the National Masters Doubles tournament in 1965 at The University of Texas. Ken Schneider and Gus Lewis (in back court) defeated Raleigh Blakely and Alvis Grant for the title.**

Photo 3-14: **Oscar, Carl and Ruby Obert accepting more of their many National Champsionship awards.**

CHAMPIONSHIP DOUBLES PLAY

RUBY OBERT

General Hints and Strategy

Get into, and stay in shape! Learn to pace yourself and to take time-outs at the right time. The stars of the first game (usually younger players) wilt under the physical and mental exhaustion of competitive play. This doesn't mean you should play cool and leisurely. Show your opponent you mean business, but use only enough energy to get to 21 points. Gordy Pfeifer and Dennis Hofflander power the ball continuously, but if you don't possess the rubber-armed endurance of an Oscar Obert, few survive. Johnny Sloan, Naty Alvarado and Carl Obert are great examples of men who use court know-how rather than raw power to win.

Develop teamwork which can only be polished by continuous play with teams of different caliber and shot-making ability.

Discuss beforehand the known strengths and weaknesses of your opponents. Usually the right side player of an all righthanded team is the weaker player. Play him continually. Even if he looks good for a while, the payoff will come. Remember though, it may be an advantage to serve to the stronger player. The theory here is that by keeping him in the back court, a kill or drive at his weak partner may be the key to victory.

In a lefty-righty combination, play the know weakness of the weaker player.

With regard to your own team, keep in mind there can be only one dominant player. If both of you are trying to set up the play and end it with kills, etc., you'll find the percentage of success decreases. This is probably the reason that two very successful singles players don't necessarily do well in doubles. Each is thinking of an individual game plan which doesn't account for his partner's position.

The essence of teamwork is to realize that with two righthanders, the left side man is the dominant player, his partner is the supporting player, and each has a different role. The dominant player covers the center court with his strong hand, and his better left hand protects the vulnerable and difficult left wall. He should control the pace of the game and is the shotmaker. His job is to keep his team on the offensive.

The supporting player many times holds the key to victory. In theory your opponents will play the weaker man. So he must be alert and never miss. Most right side players admit they get the junk over there, and yet they must be consistent. This is where the real challenge lies.

It takes tremendous self-discipline not to take shots which you probably could take, but which would be better taken by your partner. Sometimes three or more years of practice together is required to learn the oft forgotten fundamental—the supporting player's role is to keep the opponents on the defensive. This is achieved with a variety of shots discussed separately later. Many times it is this ability to change the speed of the ball, coupled with the partner's power, which throws off the timing of the opponents.

Voice signals play an important part in the doubles game. Not only do they warn a partner of trouble near the back wall, but also tell him that a better shot may be had by his not hitting the ball. Voice signals also have a role in encouraging your partner to better play.

Choice of service is very important. Your partner may be able to help you choose because he observes the positions of the receiving team. In general, the serve should either get an ace (which is difficult in doubles) or get a weak return.

Return of service is equally important. Returning the ball high in one-wall and to the ceiling and around the walls in three- and four-wall will buy time for your team to get into position.

Avoid playing in a pattern. Change your choice of serves and volleys to alter the rhythm of the game when necessary.

Don't hesitate to change a losing game plan; no matter what the score, keep playing, for many a lost cause has turned around.

Know the rules, i.e., order of service, staying in box, etc.

A key factor, often overlooked, is to cheer for your partner and to encourage him even if he misses a few.

Four-Wall

Serve: The server's strategy in four-wall is to get an ace or a weak return that can be turned into a quick point.

If the receiver returns the service well, the server's next shot may be a pass shot that doesn't reach the back wall.

Left side server usually hits a serve that either catches part of one or more walls before or after the service zone. He usually hits a hop between himself and the left wall, or a "Z" serve. Sometimes a hop to the right side receiver is also used. Most players do not have the skill to hit a high lofting serve to the left.

The right side server should hit the left wall midway between the short line and the back wall, or a hop over the short line to the left.

Enough can't be said about changing the speed and placement of your serve.

I don't believe there's any classic return for a given serve so I suggest you discover where you strengths and weaknesses are, and develop skill to put your opponent on the defensive.

Most times the left side retriever tries to hit the ceiling, or catch the front and side walls high, to buy time. The right side receiver usually tries to hit front and side walls on the fly about shoulder high to drive the server back or to make him take a poor shot. I've rarely seen a kill off the service unless it was a real hanger. After all, if you miss, it is a point against you.

Know the different shots and practice them continually in different directions and at different speeds. This will help you gain confidence and choose the right shot during the ensuing volley.

If you find that you are missing a certain shot change it for a while.

Always work on your weak hand because that is where the game is won or lost, especially on the volley.

BIBLIOGRAPHY

Leve, Mort. "Court Clinic." *Handball,* 1976, Vol. 26, No. 4.

Obert, Ruby. "Championship Doubles Play." *Handball,* 1981, Vol. 31, No. 2.

Russo, Lou and Mort Leve. "Lou Russo On Doubles." *Handball,* 1978, Vol. 28, No. 5.

Tyson, Pete. "Aspects of Doubles – Physical, Mental, Psychological." *Handball,* 1979, Vol. 29, No. 4.

"Doubles – Return of Serve and Defense." *Handball,* 1980, Vol. 30, No. 1.

"Doubles – Service and Offensive Attack Strategies." *Handball,* 1979, Vol. 29, No. 6.

"Doubles – Shot Anticipation and Court Coverage." *Handball,* 1979, Vol. 29, No. 5.

CHAPTER 4
A SENSE OF HANDBALL

PART I
MENTAL PREPAREDNESS

STUFFY SINGER'S
3 C'S OF HANDBALL
STUFFY SINGER

Almost everyone, whether teaching or learning the game of handball, tends to emphasize the physical aspect of the game, and rightly so, since the execution of the various shots is the most important single part of the ol' ball game.

Anybody will tell you "He's got a great left, that's why he wins," or "He wasn't in shape, that's why he lost," and then there's that world renowned statement, "You gotta shoot more" ... Bob Davidson.

These are all well and good, but we all have different physical abilities. Some are strong, others not so strong. Some can hit the ball well with their off-hands, others cannot. Most can bend over, but some can't. The reason I bring this up is because in my opinion, these varying physical abilities make it almost impossible to discuss anything but generalities with regard to the physical portion of the game. After that, you must set out on your own to discover what type of game suits you best.

What I'd like to bring out in this article are three of the numerous intangible items which, when everything else is equal, will make the difference between winning and losing. It doesn't matter whether you're a national caliber ball player, or a class double z in your own club—the intangibles make the difference. I like to call these three intangibles THE THREE C's OF HANDBALL.

Concentration: You must have heard this word at least a thousand times. Usually, however, it's in the sentence: "You must concentrate on the ball." If by chance you don't realize the full importance of this statement, I suggest you look at some old *ACE* magazines and notice how the ball players who win the tournaments seem almost to swallow the ball with their eyes. Someone once asked Paul Haber exactly when he watches the ball. The unbelievable reply was, "I even watch it during time outs." There's got to be a reason.

By concentration I don't mean just watching the ball. I mean concentrate on whether to play offense or defense on a particular shot. I mean concentrate on getting into position early enough so as not to be forced to hit the ball while you are on the run. Concentrate on hitting the ball, at all times, to an area which is predicated not on where the ball is, but where your opponent is. In other words, try to have some basis of thought, some reason for doing whatever it is you are doing.

Confidence: This one's a little tougher to master because success is what breeds confidence.

You must have confidence in your ability to make correct decisions—confidence that you can make your particular repertoire of shots—confidence that you can win the game. Unfortunately, it's easier said than done.

One of the ways I used to develop confidence in my shots was to practice hitting certain shots in a court by myself. During an hour's practice session I would probably hit hundreds of the same shots over and over again until I could make them consistently. Needless to say, this is very unlike game conditions where, if you get 10 or 20 chances to make the same shot during the course of a match, it's a lot. The concentrated practice also serves another purpose. Since during a game you are penalized by means of points if you miss, the result is usually a slight loss of confidence. Conversely, the mind, during practice, seems to reject the errors and record only the successful attempts.

Photo 4-1: **Stuffy Singer playing Jimmy Jacobs in the Semi-finals of the 1965 National Championships at the University of Texas, Austin. Jacobs went on to defeat Dave Graybill in the finals to win his sixth and last National Singles Title. Stuffy took third over Oscar Obert.**

With regard to confidence in your ability to win games, I think the words of Vince Lombardi pretty well sum it up: "Winning is a habit." There's only one way to acquire this habit and that's to WIN. No matter how many points you allow your opponent, or whether it's practice or a tournament, you must win every game possible. If you do this, pretty soon you start to get the feeling of being a winner; even though it may not be true, you think it's true, and that is what's important!

Courage: This last one is the toughest because it has many intangibles wrapped up in one. I think you might as well call it the courage of your convictions. The best way I can explain it is to relate my feelings regarding percentages. I think there is always a right and a wrong thing to do with all shots. I do not feel circumstances change the percentages. It is my opinion that if a shot is the correct one to take at 0-0 in the first game, it's the correct one to take at 20-20 in the third!

Photo 4-2: **"Coach" Tyson demonstrating underhand punching shot to the ceiling.**

TYSON'S 3 H'S—
HAND ... HEAD ... HEART

PETE TYSON

Borrowing from Stuffy Singer's idea for an article, "The Three C's of Handball," I would like to talk about Handball's Three H's.

I read an article in a tennis magazine a number of years ago in which appeared the following quote which is especially appropriate for the game of handball. "A man who uses his hand only is called a laborer, and a man who uses his head only is called an apprentice, but a man who uses his hand, head, and heart is an artist." It is these three H's—Hand, Head and Heart that I want to discuss.

Hand

This refers to shot execution, being able to hit the ball where you want to. The mastery of the various serves and the several offensive and defensive shots is obviously essential to any player. Hitting a particular shot is a specific motor skill that can be learned by repetition. You can learn to hit the ball anywhere you want with either hand—if you are willing to work enough. If there is a secret to the mastery of any particular shot, it is concentrated practice. The proper execution of just one new shot can really improve your game. Often a player will go into the court to work on improving his game, hitting 15 or 20 back wall shots, lob serves, etc. This is fine if you are just trying to keep the shot accuracy you already possess, but there must be much more emphasis on a particular shot if you are really looking for improvement. What I suggest is that you should decide to learn one new shot and then go into the court and hit that shot until you learn it. It could mean hitting the same shot 200 times a day for a month. You might ask, "Does anybody ever spend that much time just practicing one shot?"

Ask Jim Jacobs or Paul Haber. Anyone who has witnessed the USHA National tournaments for the last 15 years knows how much they have been dominated by these two fantastic players. Jacobs and Haber excel in many aspects of the game, but the one shot they hit better than any other player is the ceiling shot, both from above the waist with the overhand open hand stroke and from below the waist with the underarm fist stroke. Do you want to be able to hit the ceiling shot the way they do? Then do what they did. Someone tells the story about how Jacobs perfected his ceiling shot. Jimmy is reported to have said, "I went into the court at 8 o'clock in the morning and I hit ceiling shots until noon." Take a look at Paul Haber's hand sometime and notice that heavy calloused ridge. A reporter once told Paul the only other person he ever saw with a callous like that was golf's fabulous Ben Hogan, and you know what a perfectionist that man was.

Maybe it's the fly kill you want to learn first. If you've ever seen Lou Russo or Marty Decatur hit this shot, you know what an asset this spectacular shot can be for your game. Ask them how they learned it to the perfection they both now possess. Watch Bill Yambrick, or Buzz Shumate or Bob Lindsay hit the ball with their "off" hand and you will see great natural left hands. Sometime ask these players how they developed their off-hands. Yambrick did it by the "amputation" method. Buzz's dad, Les Shumate, only let Buzz hit left handed the first year he started playing. He told Buzz handball was strictly a left handed game (probably the only lie Les ever told). I personally watched Bob Lindsay spend countless hours at the University of Texas working on his great left hand.

So pick your shot—just one—and practice it until you learn it. Then pick another shot. With the addition of each shot to your repertoire, you will see the improvement to your game.

Head

This refers to shot choice—choosing the correct shot to hit according to the situation. The "situation" can involve quite a number of things. What is your sequence of thoughts as you are lining up a shot? In discussing this subject with some of our leading players, I found that most of them put their thoughts in this order:

• What is my opponent's position in the court?
• Where is my position?
• What is the height of the ball when I hit my shot (which might determine if I am on the offense or if I must attempt a defensive shot)?
• What are the best shots to attempt according to the answers to the first three questions?
• Which of these shots can I execute and which of these are my best "percentage" shots? (Right here it might become evident that there is a shot you don't know how to hit which would be useful to your game—learn it!)
• What shot did I attempt last time in this same situation? (I don't want to hit the same shot each time in this particular situation, allowing my opponent to anticipate my shot.)

Also very important in shot choice is your opponent. Who is he? What are his particular strengths and weaknesses? Every opponent you play is different, and you should have a game plan for each one, designed to take advantage of your strength and his weaknesses. This involves analyzing not only his style of game, but also things such as his speed and endurance. Are you going to try to wear him down with pass shots and ceiling shots? Maybe if his name is Pete Tyson, but certainly not if he's a Dave Graybill. Don't ever be so hard-headed that you won't change your game plan if it is not working. You have nothing further to lose by changing and you might find the answer to his game.

Will just thinking really mean that much to your game? Talk to some young strong player who has just been beaten badly by a man at least 30 years older. The younger player was stronger, faster, had better stamina, hit the ball harder and may even have had better shot execution. So why did he lose? Use your head!

Heart

The third "H" is heart. This is the intangible. What does it mean? It's been called several other names, such as desire, guts, drive, the will to win. You see it in the player who fights you tooth and toenail for every point—also in players who never give up no matter what the odds. You hate to run up against one of these players in a tournament because you know you've really got a fight on your hands. He can never be taken lightly even if he doesn't have the skill you do. He doesn't understand the word "quit." He is the creator of "upsets." He's the player who gets the most out of his ability. Someone once said that performance in any sport is about 20% ability and 80% what is done with that ability. You rarely see a national or world champion who doesn't possess this ingredient we call "heart." But you also see it in players who don't have the physical ability of the best, but nevertheless occasionally rise to "super status" because of their overwhelming desire.

The best example of "heart" I've ever witnessed is Alvis Grant from Dallas. This true Texas gentleman fits all the above descriptions and several top players (the great Jimmy Jacobs among others) can attest to that. I love to play with Alvis, but oh, how I hate to play against him. I'm sure you can think of other players who also fit this description, and I'm sure you admire them as much as I do Alvis.

It is my firm belief that this "heart" is found within everyone, only some people never get it to the surface. Every coach in the world would like to know how to bring this out in their players. Who knows what magic was possessed by Knute Rockne or Vince Lombardi? They somehow seemed to obtain great, almost superhuman, efforts from their players. You've perhaps read some coaches' favorite quotes such as "Winning is the only thing," "There is no substitute for victory," and "Show me a good loser and I'll show you a loser." But what about the other half, the players who don't win? Are they to hang their heads in disgrace?

You might think that one of the above quotes on winning belonged to Lombardi. Not according to his great quarterback Bart

Starr. Starr was quoted in a sports column as saying: "The most important thing I learned from Coach Lombardi was that winning is not the most important thing, but making the effort to win is." This is the philosophy I would recommend for every game player. Make your best effort to win, and if you are defeated in spite of this, you don't have to apologize to anyone—especially yourself.

Photo 4-3: **Ageless Ken Schneider unleashes his wide arc, left handed swing as Stan Clawson and Bud Perelman get in position during 1978 National Golden Masters Doubles Finals at Tucson Athletic Club. This was Schneider's ninth National Masters Doubles titles.**

THE FIVE SITUATIONS OF HANDBALL

PETE TYSON

The player who gets to 21 first does so because he makes fewer mistakes than his opponent. These mistakes can be classified into two categories—(1) PHYSICAL and (2) MENTAL. "Physical" refers to shot execution, the ability to place your shot accurately. "Mental" refers to playing the percentages—choosing the correct shot to hit according to the situation.

To recapitulate what I've written in previous articles, there are five situations in the game of handball. My definition of the word "situation" is ANYTIME THE BALL IS ABOUT TO BE HIT. Whenever the ball is about to be hit, you are either: (1) the server ... (2) the receiver of the service ... (3) on the offense (a good chance to end the rally) ... (4) on the defense, or ... (5) your opponent is about to hit the ball.

In each situation it is important to have good execution. It is also necessary to know what you should be attempting to execute. Knowing what to do is just as important as knowing how to do. This is the strategy of handball—recognizing what the situation is and understanding the percentage play for the specific situation.

Each time you lose a rally, it's because you made either a physical mistake or a mental mistake. Physical mistakes will always be with us—a kill shot attempt hit too low, a ceiling shot hit too hard allowing the opponent a back wall setup, a hand error, etc. These physical errors can be greatly reduced by practice. Now I know it is much more fun to play a couple of games than it is to spend that same time practicing by yourself. I imagine Jacobs, Haber, Lewis and all the other great players you always read and hear about felt the same way. It all depends on your goals. How much desire do you have to be a good player? How good a player do you wish to be? It is entirely up to YOU! You must learn to execute—consistently. This consistency is gained by many hours of specific practice. This is the secret—PRACTICE!

If you learn to execute well, you have a chance of being a really good player. The reason I say "chance" is because there are many players with excellent execution but who never win an important match. Eliminating physical mistakes is essential, but this alone will not produce a championship brand of handball. What defeats these fine physical players most often are mental mistakes, but unlike physical mistakes, these mental errors NEED NEVER OCCUR.

Mental mistakes occur when you play against the percentages, choosing the wrong shot according to that particular "situation." One of the main reasons a mental error is not as obvious as a physical one is because occasionally you can win a rally with a shot that was not the best percentage shot to attempt, and all you remember is that you won the volley. Do you ever remember all the times when that particular shot hit in that specific situation lost the volley for you? Are you really thinking, or are you just hoping you'll have perfect execution every time, probably remembering a glorious day in the past when you rolled out everything? If you are waiting for that kind of day to occur again, expect a long drought between victories.

Stuffy Singer is a very intelligent player as well as a marvelous physical player. I've seen Stuffy execute a great shot to win a point yet wear a very disgusted look on his face. The reason for Stuffy's disgust is that although perfectly executed, the shot should not have been attempted in the first place. It was a poor percentage shot to attempt in that situation. Stuffy knew he was lucky and no good player wants to place victory or defeat into the hands of luck. Stuffy knows better than anyone that good execution without good choice will not defeat a good player.

Percentages, Positioning And Conditioning

How often have we used the term "percentage handball?" Invariably this comes up in any instructional discussions. The Fred Lewis type of consistent winning is based on percentage handball. To the average spectator, it was never electrifying to watch Jim Jacobs methodically grind out win after win with his percentage handball, nor is it that exciting with Lewis, but the handball "purist" can thoroughly appreciate the talents involved.

It is one thing to play percentage handball, but in so doing you must have the ability to retrieve the ball, not set up the return and control returns with both hands. Then, to perch yourself on the top rung of "handballdom," you must couple this with a strong serve, kill and pass, and possess the stamina to keep up a steady tempo throughout the match. And, one could add, the composure to maintain a sort of coolness during tournament play that will not permit you to become nettled should your opponent "get a hot streak," though he may not necessarily be playing the percentage game.

At the Storm Meadows A.C. Summer Junior Instructional Camp, both Pete Tyson and Ken Schneider pointed the following factors out. Pete made the remark, "You can keep from losing with your off-hand, but you won't win with your off-hand." Ken added, "You must be able to have an offensive/defensive return with your off-hand." To make sense that means you do not set the ball up with your off-hand.

The fist punch to the ceiling and around the walls is a basic weapon that is a "must" with the off-hand.

Pete further pointed out that there are two kinds of mistakes in the court—physical and mental. The physical mistakes can only be corrected through practice, practice and more practice; then, that all-important exposure in competition. The mental phase of the game can be handled by players of any class; meaning that with some thought and study on any player's part, he can make decisions during a game to avoid shots that have a small percentage of ultimate success.

Right away we have the glaring exception in the person of Dennis Hofflander. Dennis can roll out a startling number of returns off the serve, either to his right or left hands, and he does it with confident abandon. For the last two seasons he had been second only to one player, Fred Lewis. We have talked with Dennis about his game several times, who recounted two specific occasions during unhappy air trips home after losing to Fred in the finals of a Pro Tour Stop. Two factors came into the conversation ... (1) where Dennis had gone through a grueling, semi-final, three gamer and just did not have the leg spring left for the finals and thus could not return the Lewis serve effectively ... (2) where he battled "Numero Uno" Lewis down to the wire and lost because of a couple of key miscues; flooring the ball off the serve or coming up high on a kill attempt from three-quarters court and then becoming a sitting duck when Lewis "re-killed." Dennis wants to incorporate more percentage handball into his game and work on a better serve. With this as a goal he honestly feels no one could beat him. It is most difficult to get out of set patterns of play that have been developed over some years of tournament experience.

The 1975 Pro Finals at Las Vegas between Lewis and Hofflander was a classic match that will go down in handball history with the best of them. Pete Tyson has scanned the video tape of the match countless times and has come up with this interesting observation: total points on the three games—Lewis 61, Hofflander 58! Only three points differentiated these two from the pay-off match. Both went into the pay-off finals with two previous Pro Tour wins each. The amazing statistic that Pete throws out is that Fred lost the serve or point only four times in those three games by hitting the ball into the floor; Dennis had a staggering total of 26 "in the floor" shots. If he had shaved off half a dozen of these errors, the match no doubt would have been his. Spectacular-wise, Hofflander has it ... the crowd "oohs and aahs" when he blasts in a flat, straight, front wall kill or corner kill with his off-hand from out in left field, some 35 feet away ... but consistency is the key.

POSITIONING...As in baseball, either throwing or batting, you must coordinate eye-hand and body movement to get the maximum power and control of your shots. We noted at the camp that the junior neophytes invariably would be lunging for the ball, waiting too long to move to position. Tyson: "Don't just stand where you think the ball is going to come, run to a point a couple of steps behind the ball in case it takes a tricky bounce; also, this keeps you in balance and prevents you from hitting the ball flat-footed." In other words, you move quickly, face the side wall of whatever hand you are using and then address the ball properly. We know there are times when you cannot reach the area where you can position in this fashion and that is where you must learn to defense, while moving directly to the ball and not into it. The fist to the ceiling or around the walls while on such a pattern is effective and can keep you out of trouble.

CONDITIONING...Work at exercises, duplicating what you do in the court. In any running, remember that most of the court movements are sidewards or backwards, and use this in your training. Ken Schneider notes that stamina plays such an important part in handball and with this everyone is in agreement. You can gain stamina through interval training...you can gain most of the needed stamina through everyday play, if you are able to schedule such a program. Paul Haber certainly gained his stamina through strict hours and hours in the court as did Vic Hershkowitz in his prime years. I know Dennis Hofflander does a lot of jogging and sprinting combined with light weight-lifting, stair climbing and lots of play. Fred Lewis will combine some jogging and light weight-lifting. We remember both Stuffy Singer and Jim Jacobs highly recommending reverse curl, light weight-lifting after playing as a counter muscle exercise to alleviate any elbow or shoulder soreness.

As we all know back troubles seem to be a part and parcel of handball. There are some good stretching exercises in "Stretching" by Bob Anderson, P.O. Box 1002, Englewood, CO 80110 (illustrated by Jean Anderson). Some of the following notes are taken from "A Series of Stretching for the Back," a section in Anderson's booklet.

It is best to work out on a firm but not hard surface. Lying on the back, pull left leg toward chest, keeping back of head on mat, but don't strain if you can't come up a bit. Keep the other leg straight as possible, again without straining. Do this with both legs...this helps to slowly loosen up the back and hamstring muscles.

In the sitting position, hold knees with hands and pull them to chest, gently roll up and down your spine, keeping chin down toward chest further stretching the muscles along the spine. Do not rush, try to roll as evenly and controlled as possible...back and forth four to eight times or until you feel your back start to limber up.

Spinal roll from sitting position with alternating lower leg cross and pull down. After you have pulled your feet toward your chest, release your feet as you roll up to a sitting position with your feet together and uncrossed. (Always commence each roll with the legs uncrossed). On each repetition alternate the crossing of your lower legs, so with the pull down phase of the roll the lower back will be stretched evenly on both sides. Six to eight repetitions. Take your time, do not work too hard at the beginning and concentrate on relaxing in every stretch that you do. Find a stretch that feels good and do not torture yourself. There are good back stretching exercises contained in this booklet.

Invariably, when showing a player the right execution of strokes and positioning, that player will have difficulty executing at the onset. Again, it is a matter of taking lessons home and dedicating oneself religiously to practice. The practice need not be done alone as we realize that often it is next to impossible to get the needed court time. The house game will then have to suffice...however, if at all possible, work on your own.

Photo 4-4: **"Steady" Fred Lewis gets set to shoot against Terry Muck in the semi-finals of the 1978 National Open Singles at the Tucson Athletic Club. Lewis won 14,13.**

APPLY PRESSURE
TO WIN

TERRY MUCK

Players dread playing certain other players. "He really takes it out of me," is usually how they express that dread. Perhaps you have noticed how some matches against certain people tire you much more than others. Forget winning or losing for a minute. Against some opponents you come out of the court gassed, win or lose. Against others you come out relatively fresh, win or lose. Pressure makes the difference; some players apply it, others don't.

Pressure comes in two forms, physical and mental. You apply physical pressure by the kinds of shots you use, where you hit those shots, and your overall physical condition. You apply mental pressure through your concentration, your confidence, and the tempo which you establish. Pressure comes from making your opponent work as hard as possible for each and every shot. The more pressure you apply, the better chance you have of winning. Some ways of applying physical pressure include:

Shotmaking. Very few of us have the complete repertoire of shots which bless the champions, Platek, Jacobs, Banuet. We all, however, have our good shots which we control effectively; these shots score points. The trouble most players run into is not using their good shots enough. Instead of hitting shots they have mastered, they try to take shots beyond their level of competence. For example, it takes a great deal of power and practice to kill from deep court, yet many players who have not developed power nor practiced this skill shoot ball after ball into the floor from deep court. Instead of applying pressure to their opponent, they heap it on themselves. Solution? Practice a wide variety of shots and use them intelligently in matches. Determine which shots score points and which shots consistently cost you points. Don't relieve the pressure you can apply on your opponent by taking poor shots.

Maneuvering. A good rule of thumb in shot selection is to select that shot which makes your opponent move the longest distance. It may not end the volley, but in the long run you will gain more points than by attempting a shot which gives your opponent a chance to setup. Every club or Y has an older player who gives all the younger players fits, not because he hits the ball hard or hits the bottom board so often, but because he maneuvers the young bucks all over the court while he calmly stands in the center, cutting off shots and putting them down the walls or into the corners. His opponents come out gasping for the breath, and he barely breaks a sweat. This is physical pressure through maneuvering.

Outlasting. Stamina wins games. Anyone who has ever played handball knows this. The pressure of physical fatigue is the greatest of all pressures. If your opponent tires, you should be in good enough shape to take advantage. Watch for signs of fatigue in your opponent and get yourself in shape.

Physical pressure is essential, but mental pressure can spell the difference between two evenly matched players. Under mental pressure we include the intangibles, concentration and confidence, and also the important factor called tempo. You can apply mental pressure through gamesmanship, but this is such a controversial and wide-ranging topic we will not do more than mention it here and make it the subject of a future instructional article. Some ways of applying mental pressure include:

Concentration. Handball's instructional cliche. Everyone talks about it, few practice it, no one can teach it. Concentration is many things: energy, will, desire, single-mindedness. Concentration is hard work, so you must have physical condition in order to practice it. You must want to win badly enough to expend the energy to concentrate, so desire is an essential ingredient of concentration. All outside thoughts must be blocked from your mind; think of nothing else but the match you are playing. How can I win this match? How can I score a point? Concentration means total devotion to playing good handball and nothing else.

Tempo. You can exert pressure on your opponent by speeding up or decreasing the tempo of a match. If he feels comfortable playing a slow game, play a fast tempo. If he feels comfortable playing a fast game, play a slow tempo. You will feel comfortable playing either, because you are the one determining the tempo of the match. It is hoped your opponent will begin to feel manipulated, which is exactly what is happening. Playing a game to which he is unaccustomed, he will feel the pressure mount.

Cutting-off balls in the air and playing a front court game increases the tempo of a match. It takes a lot of quick side-to-side front court movement, so you will have to be in good condition to play a fast tempo. Naty Alvarado, a star of the Pro Tour, is the perfect example of a fast tempo player. Stuffy Singer also plays a fast tempo very well, when he chooses to.

Paul Haber invariably establishes a slow tempo with his deep court control, using the ceiling and deep pass shots to force his opponent into errors. All good players learn to play fast and slow tempos, but all prefer one or the other in the average situation. In developing your game, experiment with speeding games up and slowing them down. The talent will be invaluable in tournament play.

Confidence. Your opponent knows when you have confidence in your game, and your confidence plants seeds of doubt in his mind. Display your confidence, not through outright cockiness, but in the subtle ways open to you: dress like a champion with the right clothes always freshly laundered; don't express anger at your missed shots or calls that go against you; give the impression that you can win despite bad breaks. Remember, your opponent builds his confidence on your lack of confidence. Don't do anything that will indicate your confidence is cracking. If you miss a good percentage shot, don't rant and rave, but be sure you make the next similar shot. Everyone will be convinced it must have been a mistake that you missed the one before. You can build your confidence through practicing shots.

Photo 4-5: **Dennis Hofflander shows his form and concentration. Dennis is the #4 ranking pro on the 1981 Pro Tour.**

HOW TO WIN
11-POINT TIE-BREAKERS

TERRY MUCK

Players are devising new game plans to win these short nail-biters, realizing that they differ markedly from the standard 21 point game. Winning tie-breakers depends on many factors. There are five to consider.

Let's start with a preliminary. Why be in a tie-breaker at all? Too often false security is the culprit. Winning the first game of a match soothes and calms the nervous energy which enabled us to perform well in the first place, and we wallow in the advantage gained by winning the first game. Although a first game win is an advantage, the shortness of the tie-breaker decreases that advantage because the loser no longer has two long, hard games to look at in order to win. He now figures he has one hard game to play, and then one glorious burst of energy in the tie-breaker will win it all. The tie-breaker not only changes third game strategy, it changes second game strategy. It makes the two game win the only safe way to go.

When the tie-breaker was first proposed, not all players felt it would work. One pro thought this might happen: One player, clearly superior to his opponent, decides to save himself some court time. He wins the first game in short fashion, and then, instead of playing the long second game, he simply lets his opponent serve out 21 points and resumes his all-out play in the short third game. He has saved himself a half game's hard play. This has not happened due to the shortness of the tie-breaker and the importance of momentum. Eleven points goes too quickly; the player who scores first in the tie-breaker can gain an advantage very hard to make up. To use this tactic, it would take a very controlled player who could turn it on and off with enough effectiveness to be assured of a win. In the highly competitive atmosphere of the professional tournaments, where the margin of victory is very fine, this play would be foolhardy.

Factor two starts in the second game. Play in the second game determines who starts serving in the tie-breaker. The man who scores the most combined points in the first two games serves first in the tie-breaker. The smart handballer keeps this in mind as he plays the second game of the match. By playing a little harder in a losing effort, he can gain that all-important edge the first serve gives: jumping out on top in the tie-breaker is twice as important as jumping out on top in the normal 21 point game. This sustained effort will provide an extra benefit: you will find yourself winning many games you formerly thought were lost causes, simply because you stuck in there and played each point as if it meant the match.

Factor three: having the serve is important, but having a good serve spells the difference between winning and losing the tie-breaker. An 11 point game leaves no time to search around for an effective serve, or to waste a couple of service opportunities with poorly executed serves. Make sure as you begin the tie-breaker that you know exactly how you are going to serve, and that you concentrate on making whatever serve you choose a good one. It pays to use a serve that has been successful in the first two games (it is hoped there has been at least one that has produced a few points). By doing this you at least are relying on a serve you know you are hitting properly in this particular match. If none of your serves have been doing well, don't hesitate to begin the tie-breaker with a new serve that might catch your opponent off guard; just make sure it's a serve you have mastered, because this is no time to experiment.

Factor four: time-outs. The rules allow two time-outs in the tie-breaker; use them. Use them when the score reads 0-3, 3-6. Use them when your opponent scores more than three points in a row. Use them when you tire. Remember that tie-breakers start at the equivalent of 10-10, and 21 is not far away. Players make a mistake in saving their time-outs; they usually don't use them. Each player has his own time-out psychology; adapt this thinking to the shorter tie-breaker.

Finally, get excited and forget about pacing yourself. Go into the court psyched up, ready to score points in any way possible. Victory is close, and a little positive emotion can carry you there. You don't have to worry about running out of gas 15-15; just keep telling yourself that anyone can play 11 points and go all out.

These five factors will help you win tie-breakers. They can fit in with any style of play: a killing game, a passing game, a ceiling game, a control game, a running game. Think about them as you prepare for this new experience; and if you think about them now, you will have the jump on your competitors who have not taken the time to learn how to play them effectively.

THE GAME PLAN

"Arthur Ashe Game Plan Upsets Conners at Wimbledon ... included meditation, concentration, motivation and some of the neatest, softest tennis strokes this audience had seen in years."

This type of planning is as applicable to the four-wall court game as it is to tennis. One word that was left out of the Ashe success formula was "patience." In setting up the game plan, the player must include the patience to stay with the blueprint, even though it might not lead to an immediate score margin.

We recall Stuffy Singer lob-serving Lou Russo into oblivion ... patiently we have witnessed Paul Haber pick apart the Gordy Pfeifer shooting game by getting him into a volleying duel ... and on the other side of the coin, we remember Gordy staying with a "serve right" plan against Haber that gained him the USHA national invitational singles crown several years ago.

Jim Jacobs, in his initial national USHA championship wins (1955-57) over Vic Hershkowitz, demonstrated how effectively the controlled ceiling shot to the left corner could counteract Vic's known ambidextrous shooting. Jim knew he had two basic weapons to neutralize Hershkowitz's talent and experience—the youth that enabled him to retrieve brilliantly, and the volley control to wear down his over 35-year-old opponent.

Don't play into your opponent's hands. Terry Muck would rather cope with the bombardments of a Steve August or Denny Hofflander, and put up his shooting percentages against theirs, than vie against the frustrating steadiness and controlled skills of Fred Lewis ... "and, invariably," as Terry puts it, "Fred will come up with the big serves or shots when most needed for those last few points leading to 21."

It isn't necessary to say that handball is the thinking man's game. We all know that. The trick is to get it all together and stay with it throughout the match. It takes maturity to keep from letting a referee's adverse decision upset your concentration, leading to two or three ensuing bad plays. Don't look for the "cop out" ... play your game and be satisfied at the end that you did exactly what you wanted to and did it to the best of your ability.

The tournament-wise performers learn with every frustrating loss. They can look back and analyze ... "Just what went wrong?"

In baseball we find managers turning grey and developing ulcers, lamenting about their pitchers. "Those walks will kill you." This, too, can be applied somewhat to handball, "The floor will kill you," meaning your errors will lose the match. Let your opponent make the errors. The combination of game plan and percentage handball go together.

What type of game is best suited to your abilities? You certainly don't want to copy a Haber, Lewis or Singer if you can't execute their shots properly. You take the best of your own game and plan accordingly.

Did it ever occur to you, when playing a right hander, that he is really experienced in defensively returning a serve to his right? Rather, he is attuned to shooting off the serve, eagerly going for the bottom board with his best weapon. But, in this quickness to take over the serve he doesn't realize he is shooting from a vulnerable position in deep court while the serving opponent commands the ideal short line area and can pounce on the return that isn't a kill.

Photo 4-6: **Fred Lewis serving to Dennis Hofflander in the 1976 National Singles Final at the Tropicana Hotel in Las Vegas. Lewis defeated Hofflander for his fourth National Singles Title.**

As National USHA Commissioner Ken Schneider points out, "As a righthander serving to a righthander, I personally find myself with a much better view of the play and can react more positively than when serving left and having to turn around to see what sort of a return is being made." Usually the serve right is made from the left side, short line, and fully three-quarters of the court is to the server's right.

We often watch good players routinely pound out a serve to their opponent's left, rarely varying with a lob, cross court, or serve right. Just think ... you have a full arsenal of serves at your command ... change of speeds, changes of locales where you will place the serve. Did you ever change the pattern by actually serving the ball right down the middle of the court, fat off the back wall? You know what will usually happen? The receiver in his bug-eyed eagerness to kill the so-called "fat serve," will either floor it or pound it in for a set-up for the server.

What we are trying to get at is: mix in the unexpected. We have been told about the 21st match point win over Gus Lewis by his fellow Buffalo opponent, Walter Plekan (who won the 1st USHA Nationals in 1951). Plekan, known for his big serve hooks, served the 21st point, a lob to the right, completely fooling Gus.

Let those big hitters try and put the ball through the wall ... It will never happen ... drive them crazy with slowed-up control. If you are the power player, learn to mix up the action. Don't fall into patterns that can be picked apart.

Never ... never ... never stop learning the lore of our "perfect game," because that's the fascination handball has ... it's a never-ending quest for perfection that will always remain out of our grasp. It is because of this that a plus-50 year old can give a comeuppance to the physical superiority of the 30 year old.

THE GAME PLAN
MORT LEVE

I'll never forget an intercollegiate match some years back involving Dr. Larry August, "kid brother" of Dr. Steve August. Larry was and still is a fine ball player in his own right, but never really took the dedicated hours necessary to hit the big tournament trail. But in this particular match Larry had decided upon a definite "game plan," revolving around the lob serve to the opponent's off-hand. He stuck with it tenaciously even though he fell far behind in the first game, as much as 1-14, if I remember correctly. Then, things started to fall in place. The slow pace took its toll; his opponent lost patience and started to blast away, trying to offense off the serve, leading to telling errors. Larry pulled up even, then went ahead to win. He took the second game easily over a frustrated and clearly rattled foe.

The game plan? Simply, prepare yourself mentally and physically before getting into the court. You can't function well mentally if the body isn't in prime physical condition, and most players will concede that it is difficult to concentrate when "sucking wind" badly.

Competitive exposure can acclimate a player to certain conditions and there's no doubt that time-after-time execution of various shots will ultimately become an automatic reflex action. The successful percentage ball players will generally fall into deep court defensive patterns that become most predictable to those of us who see them in action constantly. Paul Haber moving to deep right court invariably goes to ceiling left, and though his opponent may well anticipate such a shot, the pin-point control that brings the ball right down that left wall into the deep corner is mighty tough to return. Fred Lewis, with his strong overhand left, will go from deep left court to ceiling right. Other players do this also, but often are erratic and the ball will come off the right side wall without going deep and afford an offensive return for the opponent. In other words these top ball players can "telegraph" their shots, but with the all-important control practically challenge the foe to do something about it.

Haber, in particular, has been a master at the "Game Plan" both psychologically and physically. "Don't get into a volleying war with him," was always the sage advice given when Paul was ruling the roost. He would wear down the best of them and then would apply the percentage offensive shot. This, together with his off-hand abilities, made him a five-time national USHA singles champ, and brought him crowns in invitationals and three-wall tourneys. We're sure if he had worked at one-wall, he would have mastered that phase of the game too.

Haber has been one of the very few players I have ever seen who could alter his game to suit the occasion. Unlike the conservative percentage players, he would revert at times to a serve and shoot game with good success. This was his choice when he wanted to get in and out of the court fast and save himself for a grueling schedule. Over the years he changed from a scrambling, all-out, flashy but erratic, performer in his early 20's to the controlled percentage game player that started him on his national title binge when he was past 28 years of age.

Jim Jacobs, always a favorite subject amongst the all-time greats, would jump on opponents' weaknesses and exploit them to the fullest. In his prime, with tremendous stamina and all the assets of the complete handballer, Jim would usually be content to wear down his opponents patiently, much like a counter-puncher in boxing. He would let the foe throw his full arsenal at him, then completely deflate the confidence and at that juncture open up and destroy his man—this, of course, together with those wicked hooks that would cause the best of 'em to look like schoolboys.

To most of us the "Game Plan" usually consists of admonitions such as, "Keep the damned ball off the back wall" ... "Don't put a handle on the serve" (meaning you want to control the serve to the off-hand deep corner without the ball having enough acceleration to come around off the back wall to the opponent's strong hand) ... "Get the ball up to the ceiling effectively" ... "Move into the ball with hand, eye and foot coordination, getting low for the maximum power and volley ending trajectory" ... and, very important, in playing the percentages, remembering you only lose the serve, not the point, when you have the serve, so "If any chances are to be taken in going offense, do it when you have the serve, not when on the receiving end."

In working on the game plan make sure you are patient and don't panic if the opponent jumps off to a quick lead in the first game. The beautiful thing about handball is you can overcome such a handicap and, in coming back from the deficit, you get a big mental lift over your opponent. But you must have faith in your game plan; ultimately, if it isn't working, the worst that can happen is you will lose that first game; and then you start making adjustments if necessary.

Scouting the opposition: In my years of covering the Spalding Pro Handball tours I have noticed most pros will scrutinize matches carefully even when not playing themselves. Ask them about a pro opponent and they can give a complete rundown—they know their game from A to Z. You can always tell who the real pros are by the crying that takes place after they see the draw.

There are no doubts that the path to victory is made easy if you can greatly limit your opponent's number of serves and neutralize his battle plan with your own carefully thought out GAME PLAN.

Photo 4-7: **Stuffy Singer gets ready to shoot a mid-court set-up against Billy Yambrick in the quarterfinals of the 1966 Nationals in Salt Lake City.**

MAKE DECISIONS
FOR VICTORY:
PLANNED REACTIONS
STUFFY SINGER

"What did he hit? ... Where did he hit it? ... Where should I go? ... What shall I hit? ... Oh hell, I'll just end the volley!" You have just been witness to the thought pattern that goes on in every handball player's head during the course of almost every volley in handball he plays. That thought process is called decision-making, or the ability (or inability, in this case) to make up your mind and do something. Let me give you some case studies that will further demonstrate the futility of these exercises.

Case Study #1—Picture a situation where you have just committed the unpardonable sin of hitting the ball front wall, back wall on the fly, giving your opponent a spectacularly easy set-up, better known as a "lollipop." The typical ball player, having seen the upcoming result of his generosity, makes a futile decision, based on the following thoughts: "What will he do? Where will he hit it? Where should I go? How do I get there?" Suddenly, a light goes off in his head as he makes the one decision that will prove to be wrong 99 times out of 100. He goes to the center court at the short line.

Case Study #2—Your opposition is serving the ball, and he normally has a relatively good serve. You are standing back, getting ready to return serve and as is normal, your mind is a blank. Don't take that as an insult, but as a constructive evaluation of the circumstances involved. The following is a typical thought process of a player receiving service:
1. He served the ball.
2. It's going to the left.
3. I wonder which way it's going to hook?
4. Boy, that sure looks like a tough serve.
5. Should I play defense?
6. Should I punch the ball to the ceiling?
7. Should I hit it around three walls?
8. Should I just get it back any way I can?
9. It's not as tough as it looked.
10. Should I hit a killshot? To the right? To the left? Straight ahead?
After all this, he still has to execute whatever shot it was he finally decided to hit.

In both instances, despite the fact that the situations are completely dissimilar, our ball player makes exactly the same mistake— he refuses to make a commitment! His refusal to commit puts him in the dubious position of always being 50% wrong. The only thing that could right that situation is for his opponent to make a mistake.

Be prepared; don't ever count on your opponent to make a mistake. If you prepare yourself for your opponent's good shots, you'll also be able to handle his mistakes.

In Case #1, by placing yourself in the center court, you think you're doing the right thing. In actuality, your refusal to make a commitment means that the only way you can possibly hope to win the volley is for your opponent to make a mistake. The percentages dictate he won't make the mistake unless you force him to. When is the last time you ever tried to hit a set-up like this down the center of the court? Well, neither will your opponent, so why go to the one place on the court to which you know your opposition will never attempt to hit the ball?

Now I can't tell you where to go; I'm no mind reader, but go somewhere. Fake running to the left front and back up quickly to cover the pass shot, then move forward to pick up the kill. Do something that will force your opponent to think twice about which shot he's going to hit, and where he's going to hit it. Don't straddle the fence; make some commitments, force things to happen, dictate.

The important thing to remember is you're going to lose most of this type of volley anyway, but if you can force a few extra errors, or guess right a few extra times, you'll start winning a few more of those 21-20 games.

In Case #2, trying to figure out where the serve is going—then deciding whether to play offense or defense—then worrying over which offensive or defensive shot to hit and where to hit it—yet finally, still having enough time to execute effectively—well, that's asking too much of anybody.

My advice is to accept the fact that you are most vulnerable when returning the serve. By accepting your problem, and giving full commitment to making a good, effective defensive return of serve, and making these decisions before your opponent serves, you give yourself more time to concentrate on the pure execution of your defensive return.

Your thinking process prior to the serve might go something like this: "I'm in trouble, I've got to play defense. My first choice is to fist the ball to the ceiling. If I can't do that I must try to get the ball around three walls, and if all else fails, get the ball high and deep, and preferably soft."

The whole key to this theory is time. The more time you have and the fewer decisions you have to make in that time, the better the results will be.

"Fence straddling," or the refusal to make commitments and decisions, is basically the fear of being embarrassed. By establishing a neutral posture, you are never totally wrong and therefore never embarrassed, but you will lose the volley anyway.

Don't be afraid to commit; don't be afraid to be 100% wrong. I would rather be 100% wrong half the time and 100% right half the time and win, than be 50% wrong all of the time and lose.

Photo 4-8: **Jimmy Jacobs returning left wall, crotch serve with his back hand during his winning match against Kent Fusselman in the quarter-finals of the 1969 nationals at Austin, Texas.**

JACOBS ON
SERVE–SWING–VOLLEY
JIM JACOBS

Overswing

Make a determined effort not to "overswing." If handball players could grasp the enormous importance of this lesson it would certainly revolutionize tournament play. We practice all year long using certain "comfortable" strokes, and each of us learns to control our best shots using this stroke in our everyday workouts.

I have seen this pitfall literally "hundreds" of times. When that same practiced player gets into a tournament, he forgets about the comfortable stroke he has been using all year long and starts immediately to "overswing" (hit the ball harder by swinging much faster). That is when the ability of the individual falters and an "uncultivated type of zeal" takes over. I have witnessed this in countless matches of great importance, and I, too, have been a victim of my own enthusiasm in my early handball days. But I now realize there is nothing as important to "tournament play" as the ability to perform as well as you can in practice.

The biggest trap you have to avoid, and it takes a conscious mental effort, is changing your normal stroke once a year in a tournament because of the enthusiasm which always accompanies the contest. We all can hit the ball a bit harder than our accustomed strokes, but futility and inconsistency result from doing it once a year at tournament time.

Conceding a Point

Learn when to concede a point. This is an area which is seldom touched on, but since I put it into the practical application, allow me to pass an opinion on to you. We all admire the ball player who shows a lot of fire, a never-say-die spirit, who scrambles for everything which is "getable." I, too, love to win. And because there is just so much energy in each human body, I want to use every ounce of mine for one simple objective, "a winning effort." I have learned my lesson as most of us do, the hard way. There was a time in my handball life when, if an opponent passed me with a well-placed shot, I would streak after it, even if it took a supreme effort, merely to flip the ball back in a harmlessly soft arch to the front wall.

When my opponent took a look at the generous variety of places he had to hit the ball, after my "gift" return, he proceeded to send me on the same trip over again, and away I would streak like a greyhound after a rabbit. Naturally, whether I eventually won or lost, the rally was of little consequence. After a few dozen trips after the rabbit, I was melted down to a turtle chaser.

Now then, where is the line of demarcation? When should you "let it go" in the interest of "winning?" First let's rule out the natural objections to this novel suggestion. In any crucial rally towards the end of a game, you would, of course, do everything humanly possible to win the rally, which would include running all over the place if necessary.

The fact that you are passed on a shot most certainly does not mean you shouldn't go after the ball because you want to conserve your energy. To the contrary, I run hard when I'm passed—I always attempt to return the ball hitting one of the two side walls first, very high, which gives me an opportunity to get back into position while the ball is hitting all three walls.

If I go running after a well-placed pass shot, after catching it, I return the ball weakly because of the accuracy of my opponent's shot. Then if he chooses to send me on an extended trip over the same area, I only take that journey twice. If my second return of his pass shot is again poor, I will not take any more trips, unless the circumstances of the score demand that it's a "now or never" rally. But those rallies are few and far between, and there is nothing dishonorable in letting a point go when the rally gets out of hand, rather than proving you are a streak of lightning who can run for as long a period of time as your opponent can hit. This is a horrible thought. So think seriously of the logical possibility that giving up a rally, in preference to losing a substantial amount of energy, is at times an extremely wise choice.

PART II
LEARNING AND BEHAVIOR

PEAK PERFORMANCE AND FLOW: BEING ON

JOHN HOLTZWORTH

During a handball match held at a local YMCA tournament, Scot Lofthouse labored to win back the serve. The score stood 3-17. Walking heavily to the service zone, he reflected on the first game which he had lost 5-21. Lofthouse shook his head in apparent disbelief at his poor performance. Sweat dripped into his eyes. Anxiously, he waited for the referee to call the score. A glance at his opponent confirmed that he was taking his time getting ready to receive. Lofthouse risked another quick glance at the gallery. Suddenly, he loathed and feared the spectators. Their stalk-like eyes glared expectantly at him, watching intently, demanding to know what he planned to do next.

Photo 4-9: **Naty Alvarado raises his hands in triumph following his Open Singles victory over Lou Russo in 1979 National Three Wall Championships in Toledo.**

"Don't look at the spectators ... never mind the sweat dripping into your eyes ... don't think about it ... just play the game." Lofthouse's heart hammered erratically as he tried hard to shut his mind to distractions. He decided to call time out.

Lofthouse let the ball slip out of his hand, paused, took a long, deep breath, and exhaled slowly as if to clear his mind and body of conscious thought. He stood for a moment examining his present sensations. Gradually the tension lines in his face dissolved. He shrugged his shoulders, allowing his posture to become extremely relaxed while maintaining mental alertness. Lofthouse allowed his breathing to flow forth voluntarily from deep in his belly. With his finger, he pressed in an inch or two below his navel, feeling his belly expand and contract naturally like the rhythmic ebb and flow of the ocean tides.

Lofthouse felt an inner calm come over him. He allowed his hands to open and hang easily at his sides, and noticed a heightening of awareness in all of his extremities. Tension seemed to melt, releasing an energy-like flow through his arms to the tips of antennae-like fingers.

Lofthouse bent, picked up the handball and allowed his attention to become absorbed with it. At first, he became interested in its hard, dry surface. He touched it to his cheek and found it still warm from the preceding rally. The warmth felt comforting in contrast to the cool stares of the spectators. Out of curiosity, Lofthouse put the handball to his nose and smelled it. His nostrils flared slightly. The distinct rubber odor lingered for a few moments and seemed to draw his attention even deeper into the ball. He was surprised and delighted to discover these new sensations and allowed his awareness to continue its exploration. He thumbed the ball around his fingers. In previous volleys, its color appeared dull and gray with a hazy, indistinct shape. Now his attention became immersed in the clearly defined round shape of the handball. It appeared to advance with a vivid, black texture. Patches of the "Ace" red label were still visible and provided a focal point for his interest.

"Time in," barked the referee exactly 30 seconds later. "The score is 3 serving 17." Lofthouse's vision was following the seam around the handball when his sense of hearing made him aware of a distinct voice calling the score from somewhere above. His conscious attention was still immersed in the ball, thus allowing his subconscious to store away the score automatically. Lofthouse became faintly aware of a brief intervening thought that the time out seemed to have lasted a long time, but even this reflection faded as a clear mental picture of the serve developed in his mind's eye. The image materialized into a handball rolling gently off his fingertips, falling, bouncing back to the point of contact where his smooth, liquid serving stroke flowed through the ball—an artist immersed in his paint stroke.

The sound of the ball "cracking" around the walls was still echoing through the gallery as the spectators experienced a moving comeback performance. Lofthouse won the second game 21-18 and the third game 21-8. But it was not until some 15 minutes later in the searing heat of the steam room that the stale animal scent born of survival mixed with the nauseating sweat of competition to arouse Lofthouse's fatigued senses into a foggy awareness of the quality of his comeback performance. Even then, his awe was not so much for the win, but for the feeling which produced it.

Flow

This story comes to mind in view of recent research which is attempting to understand what makes up the quality of experience in which the player becomes completely immersed in an activity. In sports, the experience refers to a feeling of "being on" and generally results in the player realizing a peak performance. Artists, mechanics and athletes alike have reported a general feeling that mind, body, and spirit merge into a "flow" to produce a quality performance. The person who "drops into flow" experiences an intense centering of attention and heightened awareness. His sense of time is lost and external distractions fade. Concentration does not appear to improve by "trying harder" but seems to become absorbed in an event as naturally as a child's attention becomes immersed in playing a new game. A friend once told me that he "flowed" through each page of a new issue of *Handball* magazine.

Play and More Serious Matters

If we examine the qualities of handball, we discover that basically, like play, they are non-practical in nature and ask us to divorce ourselves from practical matters such as work in order to enjoy them. As children, we were absorbed and delighted by the elements of play. We were not concerned with the function or outcome of play when encountered, but enjoyed play as a quality of experience unique and marvelous in its own right. Our attitudes, skills, and potentials were not fixed but were constantly developing, flowing forth, and every moment of life was an adventure.

Michael Novak seems to have captured the spirit of play in his book, *The Joy of Sports*. He writes, "Sports are not merely entertainment, but are rooted in the necessities and the aspirations of the human spirit. They should be treated with all the intelligence, care, and love the human spirit can bring to bear." In an age of professional and technical emphasis, it is difficult to imagine handball or any sport as an end in itself rather than as a means to an end. But the true handball enthusiast, novice and professional, would do well to recapture some of the flowing adventure provoked by his earlier child-like immersion in play.

Peak Performance and Flow

What are some of the elements which make up the flow experience? Generally, there is a sense of being lost in the action. It is total absorption in the game which compels the player for eight points in a row before the feeling is disrupted.

A handball player describes the feeling. "Your energy is flowing smoothly and shot execution feels liquid. You frequently lose track of the score. The body feels relaxed yet the mind is alert. Sometimes the ball appears to be larger and moving slower than normal. Anticipation and execution of shots becomes as automatic as shifting gears while driving. You seem to float around the corner. There is no reflection on the other player or spectators when locked into flow. Thinking seems to block the feeling of flow."

The limitations of the printed or spoken word in fully describing the flow experience must be accepted as the natural inability of one medium to replace another. Most of us have felt the frustration which accompanies our attempt to describe a moving experience in handball to a friend. We are soon convinced that the only description lies in the experience itself.

The Art of Handball

An understanding of the flow experience may be further enhanced through an appreciation of art and handball. The spontaneous nature of flow is evident is LeRoy Neiman's painting of Jimmy Jacobs. The painting flows with color and energized motion for those who have had the pleasure of studying it. One can feel the elements of anticipation and execution flowing into place as Jacobs sets up to stroke the ball. Neiman's fluid strokes capture the flow experience by blending mood, tempo, and style to surface the true meaning of handball. Neiman's own comment: "By venturing into and penetrating the painting, the spectator discovers for himself new substances, and has a prolonged contact." In similar manner, players who lock into flow compel the spectator to become part of the experience. This is what Marshall McLuhan had in mind when he stated, "The medium is the message." Everything merges in the flow experience—the handball, players, and viewers.

Flow is Linked to Your Senses

Not all handball games will yield a deep, flow experience for the participants. Whether flow happens at all, and how deep the experience is, depends on the individual. Some seemingly gifted handball players possess what appears to be an inherent responsiveness to their senses which may increase the frequency and intensity of their flow experiences. These are players who continue to pay attention to the sensations in their bodies as they did during their childhood growth, and they continue to learn, change, and develop throughout their game. For most of us, however, increasing the spontaneous occurrence of flow has to be tied into some method of search and discovery which requires more than the casual use of our senses and capacity for introspection. This is true because our senses have lain dormant, undeveloped by passive acceptance of comfortable standards, inefficient habits and mellowed attitudes.

Beyond the Surface of Things

The newcomer to handball may ask if there is any genuinely reliable method to guide him or her in learning efficient and effective skills. A survey of various handball instruction books and observation of highly skilled players will confirm that techniques and emphases vary and change. Generally accepted teaching techniques never fail to be deceptively complex in their application to individual players. It appears that the more systematic, objective, and mechanical the instruction becomes, the more one overlooks the essential substance which facilitates learning. The novice, lacking in experience, has no other course than to let his senses provide the necessary feedback to develop his game.

Sensory awareness is a means to finer muscular control, as well as increased flow opportunities, because the player's senses, perceptions and action become totally immersed in the game. The following suggestions and exercises are not meant to be "How-to-do-it" instructions. They contain no rules, formulas or guarantees. The exercises are meant to be sensed and understood through experience for the purpose of expanding sensory awareness. None of the sensations, when experienced singly, is of any significance, but each sensation represents a part of what eventually occurs in the total flow experience.

SEE the ball. Easy to say but difficult to do as we have all learned. Habitually, we have learned to rely largely on our sense of sight to "watch the ball." This reminder generally focuses our attention on the obvious shape of the handball. The boundary or continuous edge of the handball, which stands out from the space and walls around it, give it the round shape we perceive. But even the round shape can appear soft and hazy, or sharp and distinct, depending on how near or distant the ball is. For the handball player to expand his sense of sight, he may find it helpful to look beyond the obvious round shape of the ball.

According to fundamental principles of art, contrasting and bright colors provide a focal point of interest and are associated with foreground or near positions. Concentration may be improved by allowing your eyes to focus, not only on a round, black ball, but on the contrasting red "Ace" label as you prepare to serve. See if you can focus your sight on the red label as the ball rotates through space during a volley. If your budget is like mine, you probably use the same ball for three months! In this case, either periodically paint your own label on the ball or forget this exercise. However, the argument for having a bright or multicolored ball with distinct seams would appear to be supported on the basis of facilitating the player's concentration as well as spectator considerations.

Another exercise which may help the player extend his sight of the ball is to visualize the line or path represented by the ball as it bounces around the court. It represents a path of action which links the player's strokes. The line moves and lives in the present, pulsating with emotions and conveying feelings, strategies, and intentions. In this sense, the ball's trajectory may appear as smooth and flowing, or as tense and erratic as the players themselves. The ball's abrupt and unexpected changes of direction create angular lines which our eyes find exciting and full of challenging interest. Watching the ball in this manner becomes visually entertaining and stimulating.

Photos 4-10: **Naty has his ''eye on the ball'' during match with Fred Lewis on the Pro Tour.**

As the player practices following the trajectory of the ball, his senses may give him the feeling that he is "riding with the ball" as it moves from one point of contact to another. Riding the ball becomes a self-renewing circuit which continually draws our attention deeper into the volley until it is ended. Concentration appears to be facilitated because the player's visual attention becomes totally absorbed in the ball's movement. It is the total absorption of our attention which increases the chances for spontaneous flow to occur.

Visual attention is but one sense which contributes to our total perception of the handball. Expanding sensory awareness requires the critical probing of the ball and ourselves with as many senses as possible.

FEEL the ball. Generally, smooth, light, and easy feelings accompany well performed strokes because these sensations yield greater sensitivity and finer muscular action. Excess tension and superfluous effort cause the body to draw itself together in defense, and prevent it from organizing itself properly for action. The tense player hinders himself to flow and improved performance as surely as an intentional hinder prevents him from executing a full, uninhibited stroke.

For example, some players are so hung up on winning every game to maintain their status in the local club pecking order, they will not allow themselves to relax and feel their strengths and weaknesses. They may lack self-confidence in their non-dominant side and adopt the "trying hard" style as an indicator of their will to win. Generally, these players will not relax because they feel to be relaxed is to be weak. Instead, they remain in a state of constant tension and execute stiff, robot-like strokes. Most of us have seen the type of driver who grips the steering wheel tightly and leans forward with his face set in a tight mask of concentration. Likewise, tense facial strains and muscular tightness give the handball player the feeling and appearance of "readiness" and "trying hard," but actually hinder the flow of sensory feedback necessary for improved performance.

With this idea in mind, allow your attention to focus on what it feels like to stroke the ball during warm-ups, practice, or even a game. You may have to give up a few points in order to notice the sensations generated when your hand meets the ball at point of contact, but awareness of this feeling is a means to increased accuracy. Can you distinguish the difference in feeling when the ball is contacted at the base of your fingers as opposed to your palm? Does the ball feel like it is rolling off your fingertips or does it feel like a collision at point of impact? Stroke the ball ten times with both sides and allow yourself to experience how it feels to stroke the ball. See if you can describe the quality of vibrations which are sent up your arms and through your body. Compare the subtle differences of these feelings with both right and left sides.

These feelings are experienced through the sense of touch but are interpreted in the mind. Awareness of these feelings is a means to finer muscular control, as well as increased flow opportunities. Because the mind and body are so completely absorbed with interpreting these feelings, it is less likely to be distracted by external events such as spectators, opponent's gestures, or thoughts about winning or losing. The total immersion of our mind and body yields a feeling of continued flow similar to the merging "steady state" a child's top achieves as it flows faster in the same direction. Our only concern should be with keeping the flow going. When thoughts of the next point or winning the game enter the mind, the flow is disrupted as surely as an outside force acting on the top causes it to lose its stability.

HEAR the ball. Discover the immediate effects of listening to the sound of the ball at its point of impact with your hand. Try to correlate this sound with the feelings you experienced in the previous exercise. While it is not probable that you can listen to the sound the ball makes upon contact with your hand and also be consciously aware of what it feels like on the same stroke, you can experience the different sensations singly through practice. Your mind and body will store these sensations in the subconscious. Later, as you expand sensory awareness, the composite of these sensations will surface for use in directing future strokes with little or no conscious effort at all.

Serve the ball and listen to the sound it makes at point of contact. Is the sound a soft click or a dull thud? Do your most effective serves sound the same as less effective ones? Was the served ball that seemed to "crack" off the front wall executed with a smooth, fluid serving stroke? Stroke the ball with the dominant side and listen to what the ball "has to say." Compare these sensations with the nondominant side. This kind of sensory awareness must be kept fresh by constant practice. Happily, the opportunities for this practice are present every day at your local club or YMCA. You have only to break the chains of past habits.

SMELL the ball? Well yes, I think it does make sense. Pun intended. The handball does have a distinct rubber odor. Go ahead, place the ball to your nose for curiosity's sake. Your sense of smell will distinguish the rubber odor immediately. You may even be surprised to discover that the smell lingers in your awareness and absorbs your attention for a few moments, or you may be asking yourself what all this has to do with stroking the handball. Here goes.

The fine art of allowing your attention to become completely absorbed with the ball is easily disrupted. Because we have aspirations, we can just as easily allow our attention to linger on thoughts of future goals such as winning the game. Likewise, we have a tendency to reflect on past experiences such as the last point we blew. Such thoughts usually enter our mind as we begin to serve, and we know full well that they contribute nothing to executing the present task at hand. Such thoughts only interfere with the flow of present sensory perceptions and actions necessary to stroke that elusive little ball. Thus when we have difficulty centering our attention on the ball, we might purposely place the handball to our nose. The distinct rubber odor should not fail to penetrate our minds and collect wandering thoughts for the few moments we need to focus our attention on the ball until it is served.

TASTE the ball! Foul play ... wait ... no fair ... hinder ... check the ball! No doubt the distinct taste of a handball would capture our attention not to mention the wonderful reverse hops a wet handball would impart. But we must kiss the sense of taste goodbye—a rule is a rule.

In summary, our senses are continually bringing in information on which we base our perceptions and actions in order to play handball. Our concern is with expanding sensory awareness so that our perceptions and actions related to handball will be more flowing and accurate. The spontaneous flow feeling we sometimes experience involves the harmonious merging of our sensations, perceptions, and actions made possible by our total concentration and absorption in the game. It appears that the player who probes and expands his sensory awareness through constant practice may be able to increase the occurrence and intensity of flow. That the player is able to realize improved performance near the outer limits of his skills almost seems secondary to capturing the true nature of the handball experience—flow.

Editors Note: *References for this article can be found in the original article in* **Handball** *magazine. See Chapter bibliography for reference.*

EMPIRICAL LEARNING PRINCIPLES APPLIED TO HANDBALL

RON BULLINGTON

Every handballer has an innate desire to improve his game as rapidly as possible, but a limited amount of time he can justify spending in this pursuit. This article was written to introduce to the reader certain learning principles derived from motor learning research which will enable him to utilize his practice time efficiently.

Motor learning is a branch of experimental psychology that deals exclusively with the learning of physical or motor skills. The learning principles that follow have been specifically related to the efficient learning and teaching of handball drills, but could be applied to almost any physical skill. For the reader to appreciate this article, there must be an understanding of the distinction made between the concepts of learning and performance.

A psychologist measures performance changes. The following graph will illustrate the above distinction: Let us assume we have a beginning handballer who diligently practices back wall kill shots every day for 25 days. Every fifth day he measures his performance by determining the percentage of 50 shots he is able to kill, and records this score as a point on the vertical axis of the graph. By connecting these performance measures (points) with a line, he has plotted a classical motor learning curve. The change between day 5 and day 25 is the inferred amount of learning that has occurred. In this example the handballer improved approximately 20% in kill shot accuracy over 20 days. *(Figure 4-1)*

Of the learning principles that should be utilized, the first and foremost principle is what a learning psychologist would refer to as a response trial, or in layman's language, practice. The more you practice a particular motor skill the higher the acquisition level. The classical research paper on extended practice was written by Crossman who tested industrial workers over a three year period with

Editors Note: *Ron Bullington has taught graduate level motor learning courses at the University of Iowa, Iowa City, Iowa. He is the current Colorado handball doubles champion, and is presently the club pro at the Vail Athletic Club, Vail, Colorado.*

millions of responses and found learning was still occurring. In essence there is no substitute for practice in the learning of a motor skill. Any top athlete will attest to the fact that it takes long, hard hours of practice to achieve championship performance. With the necessity for practice established, learning principles derived from other areas of motor learning will be introduced to enable him to efficiently utilize his practice time.

This brings us to a concept known as feedback, one of the strongest and most important variables controlling performance and learning. When a motor movement is made, you receive a wealth of sensory feedback from various sense organs regarding that movement. You may also receive feedback from a coach, instructor, or by watching a video tape replay. The practicing handballer should attempt to optimize all sources of feedback that are available to him. To utilize feedback effectively one needs to form a model (visual image in the mind) of the correct way to execute a given shot. Next, hit the

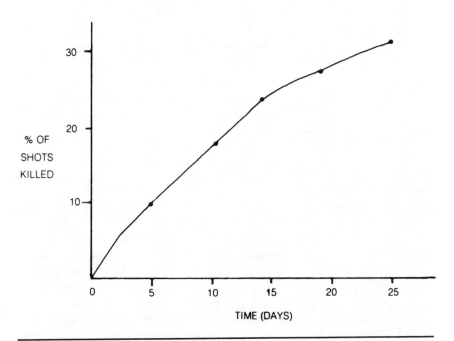

***Figure 4-1:* Classical learning curve.**

selected shot, receive feedback from the aforementioned sources, and use the feedback to compare the shot to the model (error measurement). Then make a cognitive decision as to how to reduce the error or variation from the model; hit the shot again and repeat this process until the error is essentially eliminated. Ask a club pro to provide the correct model for basic shots that can be practiced alone; it is more efficient to learn a skill correctly in the beginning, thus avoiding the need to break a well-learned bad habit at a later date. A video tape recorder with slow motion playback is an excellent source of feedback and can be used to compare your shot to the model. The recorder aids the club pro in spotting and pointing out fine details with fast movements and enables him to see, rather than having someone describe, how you look in action. Another excellent source of feedback that aspiring players should utilize are the top players in the club. Ask any of these players to observe your play and offer suggestions for improving your game. You will undoubtedly receive a multitude of suggestions and personal opinions which can only add to your overall knowledge of the game. *Figure 4-2* summarizes how to utilize feedback in learning a motor skill.

Feedback leads us to an area in motor learning known as social facilitation, which examines the effect of people upon people. Research strongly suggests that the presence of other persons during the early stages of learning has a detrimental effect upon skill acquisition. The literature also indicated that, once a skill is well-learned, the presence of other persons tends to elicit peak performance. A rather detailed theoretical explanation has been formulated to explain these results. Therefore, the literature suggests you practice alone or with just an instructor present. Once you have acquired a high skill level, play on an exhibition court where people are watching as this should get you up for a top performance. If you are trying to learn a new shot, go back to the secluded court to practice.

The next area of interest is concerned with the effect of "fatigue" on learning. To eliminate debate as to a suitable definition of fatigue, let us assume you have just played a vigorous hour-long match and are tired. Most players assume that if they are in a fatigued or tired state they cannot learn anything and practice would be futile. On the contrary, several researchers have indicated that fatigue is a performance variable rather than a learning variable. Your practice performance level while in a fatigued state will be depressed, but when you return to a rested state your performance level will increase to the same level it would have reached if you had practiced for an equivalent amount of time while in a rested state. During a vigorous match you receive a wealth of sensory feedback and should become aware of those aspects of your game which could use improvement. Practice before these invaluable feedback traces are forgotten. Prac-

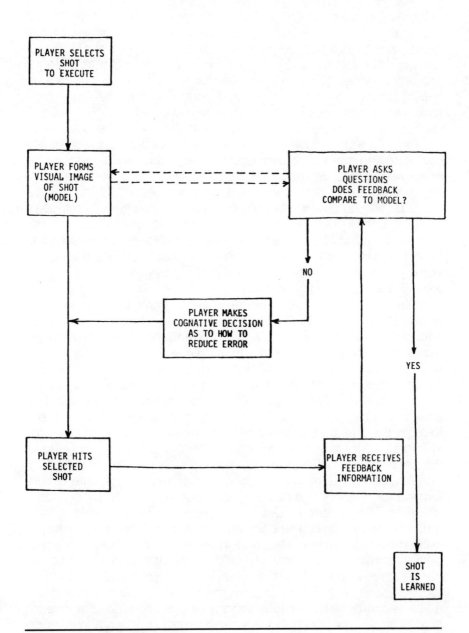

Figure 4-2: **Utilizing feedback.**

ticing while in a fatigued state may also increase your endurance for your next match. Remember that even though your practice performance is sub par, learning is still occurring and will manifest itself when you return to a rested state.

We will now concern ourselves with some of the mental aspects of learning a motor skill. Any champion athlete will attest to the fact that it takes tremendous mental concentration to elicit peak physical performance. Research reviews have shown that mental practice of a motor skill improves acquisition or learning of that motor skill. Mental practice is generally defined as cognitive rehearsal of a skill with no overt physical movement. To use mental practice effectively, you should find a quiet location, close your eyes and try to visualize yourself repeatedly hitting a specific shot, concentrating on all the factors you would if you were actually hitting the shot. The importance of mental concentration cannot be over-emphasized if this technique is to be effectively utilized. Several practice periods of 2 or 3 minutes each, with a short rest period, should aid skill acquisition. Mental practice could be utilized as a warm-up technique and has the advantage of enabling one to practice while injured or unable to obtain court time. The server in handball could use mental practice in the 10 seconds he has to initiate play. Many players fail to concentrate during the serve and seem to just put the ball in play. This nullifies the advantage they had in the serving position.

Next we shall concern ourselves with the area in motor learning known as retention. Maximizing retention of well-learned motor skills should also be of interest to the avid handballer. If you have spent the hours of practice necessary to learn a skill, you certainly wish to maintain this high level of proficiency. Research literature shows that motor skills are well retained over long periods of inactivity, but forgetting can and does occur over time. The research has shown that, after a long period of inactivity, it takes less practice to relearn a skill to a given level than it required to reach that level initially. You should spend an hour or two per week, in addition to playing, practicing all the basic shots to make these well-learned skills resistant to forgetting.

A second area of research dealing with retention is called short-term motor memory and has practical applications for learning handball skills. The research indicates we have short-term and long-term motor memory stores. The short-term store lasts from approximately five seconds to two minutes and measurable forgetting can occur during this short time interval. To utilize a skill or shot in a game situation effectively, the skill must be transferred from your short- to long-term memory store. Since forgetting has been shown to occur in just a few seconds, you should practice one specific shot at a time for at least fifty to one hundred trials, as opposed to hitting a few ceiling balls, a few shots righthanded, and a few shots lefthanded, etc. Using the latter method you may forget a shot before you have learned it. Use several balls while practicing to avoid spending time retrieving balls. Follow the advice of the top pros who recommend long periods of practice on specific shots. Once a skill is ingrained in your short-term memory store, it will gradually transfer into your long-term motor memory store.

Of course motivation is necessary for one to spend the hours of practice required for top level play. When a new skill is being learned, the rate of learning is comparatively fast. This rapid improvement is easy to recognize and acts as a motivation for the practicing player. As any handballer continues to improve he reaches a point of diminishing returns where a great amount of practice is required for a noticeable skill improvement. However, learning can still occur and only a slight skill differential separates many top club players from the pros. A player may utilize several techniques to maintain his motivation to practice. Set up a definite monthly practice schedule which lists the shots and amount of time you feel you should spend on various aspects of your game. Test yourself weekly by setting up an arbitrary scoring system and plot your results in the form of a learning curve.

For example, place a box in a back corner of the court and count the number of ceiling shots out of 50 that hit the box. Practice at various times during the day and vary the length of your practice sessions as repetition leads to boredom. Practice with various people on specific aspects of the game that require a partner, such as serving and the return of serve. One person may work on specific serves while his partner works on service returns. Finally, don't be discouraged if you are just beginning the game and other new players seem to posses superior skills. Researchers have shown that initial performance levels of individuals are insignificant after extended periods of practice. Stick with it. By utilizing efficient practice techniques you may surpass many players you had previously considered unbeatable.

This leads to an interesting phenomenon known as bilateral transfer which is applicable to handball due to the ambidextrous nature of the game. Researchers have shown that a skill learned with one hand transfers to the opposite limb. If you learn a shot with one hand a portion of this skill should transfer to your opposite hand. If one hand or limb is injured, practicing with the opposite hand should reduce any retention losses in the injured limb due to the forced inactivity.

A final area in motor learning known as warm-up has been given considerable attention by physiologists. They have pointed out that you should stretch and warm-up your muscles to improve flexibility, contraction velocity, and reduce the probability of muscle stiffness and injury. Viewing warm-up from a psychological perspective, researchers have observed that on motor tasks where injury is not a factor, a warm-up period will result in improved performance. Apparently one must acquire the right mental set before top performance can be elicited. The literature suggests a warm-up period of at least ten minutes during which you practice all the shots you might utilize in a pending match. This should follow your general physiological warm-up of stretching and jogging to improve flexibility and heat up the muscles for your match. Utilization of these experimentally derived motor learning principles should lead to efficient and rapid handball skill acquisition. Good luck and good handballing.

Photo 4-11: The picture of two great handball champions dates back to the 1950's. Johnny Sloan is on the left and Vic Hershkowitz on the right.

BEHAVIORAL ANALYSIS
OF HANDBALL INSTRUCTION:
AN OVERVIEW

DR. PHILLIP TOMPOROWSKI

Can Experimental Psychology Learning Principles Be Effectively Applied to Handball Instruction?

The role of psychology in sports has enjoyed increased popularity in the past few years. Both professional and amateur athletes in many sports stress the importance of using psychology during competition. During a match an athlete may "psych out" his opponent, develop a cerebral "flow" or "psych himself up." In many cases when the contest is close and the opponents are evenly matched, it is suggested that the use of psychology is the major factor which determines who wins and who loses.

Most investigators who have studied the psychology of sports have used the verbal report of highly skilled athletes as their main source of information. These verbal reports usually describe the sensations and feelings which existed during certain periods of the game or match. The reports are then analyzed in an attempt to understand what makes a winner. The method of examining these reported sensations in order to gain insight into psychological factors is known as the clinical method. Clinical researchers also use psychological tests, both written and oral, to gain additional information regarding an individual's personality. Going even further, several clinical psychologists have attempted to correlate personality "types" with success in specific sports.

The clinical approach has gathered valuable information regarding clusters of personality traits which correlate with success in competition; however, the clinical method fails to provide any information which will allow predictions to be made of the future performance of specific individuals. In many cases an athlete will excel in a sport even though his personality inventory or profile suggests otherwise. Also, findings obtained from psychological tests do not indicate which factors in an individual's environment are important for the development of particular skills. For example, how do various training procedures in handball affect later on-the-court performance? Does the self-taught handball player do as well as one who receives professional instruction? If professional instruction does produce more proficient handball players, when is the training most effective—at the novice level or after playing several years? If there do exist differences in long-term performance on the handball court which reflect varying methods of instruction, how can one best exploit the most effective teaching procedure?

These kinds of questions have resulted in the development of another method of studying the psychology of sports. This approach, known as applied experimental psychology, makes use of the observable behavior of an individual rather than verbal reports as the measure of psychological events. Instead of asking a handball player how he felt after making a dramatic backcourt kill shot, the experimental psychologist simply records the kill shot as an event which occurred during the progress of the match. The main interest of the experimental psychologist is the development of procedures which increase on-the-court behaviors such as kill shots, passing shots, well placed ceiling shots, or drop shots and reduce unwanted behaviors which result in errors on the court.

The reason for the interest in the development of such procedures in sports is based on evidence obtained from nonsport areas which have demonstrated repeatedly that skills are acquired faster, developed or altered with less trouble, and maintained for longer periods of time when certain training procedures are used. The main reason for the success of experimental psychology is its use of settings where the behavior under investigation is clearly defined and observable. Observable behavior has an advantage over verbal reports because changes in observable behavior can be measured and controlled. The study of the acquisition of highly refined motor skills such as flying an aircraft, driving an automobile, or performing industrial work, indicates the changes in reaction time, information processing (stimulus discrimination), and the force of a response can be altered through changes in the parameters of the training procedure.

In much the same way that an airplane pilot's reaction speed can be increased by training him to become knowledgeable of practicable changes in his environment, a handball player can also be trained to respond to the direction and speed of a handball coming off the front or side wall, thereby increasing the amount of time available to make a decision concerning the most effective return shot. Information processing, which is another way of asking what to do with the ball once you are in position to stroke it, can be improved by a training program which stresses the relationship between specific responses and their probability of success. Based on the findings obtained with other motor skills, it may be possible to train a handball player in a short amount of time to play the game using strategies which usually take months of court competition to acquire. One of the most beneficial effects of the applied behavioral method of instruction is the speed in which tasks are learned. It is not inconceivable that proper training techniques can reduce the amount of practice time required to become proficient in playing handball by fifty percent.

One example of instructing handball with an experimentally based methodology is a step-by-step program in which players are trained to become more proficient in playing handball. This method of teaching handball differs from the typical program in a variety of ways. First, the player learns specific tasks, such as the passing shot, kill shot, and various serves, as discrete items. Instead of beginning training by the student simply walking onto the court and starting to knock the ball around, the player is required to practice each task separately until he can demonstrate that his skill is at a level designated by the instructor. The individual's performance requirement for each task, which is known as the criterion level, is gradually altered throughout the training program.

Initially, response requirements for successful shots are quite low and can be performed easily; only as the individual's skills increase does the criterion level requirement become more difficult. Second, each player is required to demonstrate proficiency in each task before being allowed to play handball competitively. By doing this the individual learns all basic shots equally well and thereby avoids weak spots in his game prior to the beginning of actual competition. By having a well-balanced armament of responses prior to competitive play, the novice will not depend on one or two "favorite" shots. Finally, the teacher makes use of a players' bracket which can be entered only after a specific level of handball playing skill has been demonstrated. It has been shown that the entrance into the players' bracket will function as a reward (reinforcer) and will enhance learning speed.

While specific procedures which can be employed to train handball players have not been detailed in this article, it should be stressed that the methods involved are fundamentally different from those typically used to teach handball. Perhaps the most important point is that the progress of each player is continually monitored so skill requirements can be tailored to the individual. By altering requirements based upon the individual's change in handball proficiency, one can assure that the player will enjoy a history of success from the very first time he picks up a handball. It is a well-known fact that racquetball has enjoyed an increase in participation due to the ease with which the skills required to play the game are acquired. Individuals who begin playing racquetball usually have more initial success at the game than those players who start playing handball. Thus, many people choose racquetball over handball simply because it is easier to learn. The experimental method of teaching handball can increase the amount of success the novice handball player will derive and in doing so ensure that the student will continue to participate in the sport. It is the ability to engineer a history of success into the training program which makes the applied experimental method so effective as a teaching device.

The use of an applied behavioral analysis of sports in the United States is currently in its infant stage. Based upon the extent to which applied psychology has been demonstrated to be effective in developing skills in other areas, however, the benefits derived from a systematic teaching method, based upon experimentally verifiable findings, would be substantial. Once the technology is completely developed and put into use, it is certain the methods of instruction used in applied experimental psychology will be a powerful tool from which coaches of many sports, including handball, will be able to benefit.

Photo 4-12: **Paul Haber puts his body into shot during exhibition match in the two-side-wall-glass court at Lake Forest College, Illinois.**

THE PSYCHOLOGICAL PROFILE
OF THE SUCCESSFUL
HANDBALL PLAYER

DONALD SCHERRER AND
MITCHELL JACOBS

In any competitive endeavor a few individuals experience unusual success and rise to the top from within their group of peers. This success is attributed to several factors, not the least of which is hard work and dedication to the job or activity. For an individual in sports to excel to where he is recognized as an accomplished athlete takes more than mere dedication. Dedication will allow a person to develop to his own maximum potential in that sport, but will not automatically insure the success of a champion.

The question can be asked, "What are the attributes or the characteristics of those individuals who have excelled over other players and have experienced unusual success in handball?" Physically, they have developed themselves to a very high level of conditioning. Their cardiovascular systems, which includes the heart, lungs and circulatory system, have the efficiency to allow long periods of sustained intense activity.

Also, the muscles of the body have been developed to the point where there is sufficient strength to move in the court and execute all the shots. The muscles must have the endurance to perform in lengthy matches or even lengthy tournaments without appreciable fatigue or substantial muscle soreness that could interfere with effective playing.

The third attribute would be neuromuscular coordination. Strong muscles and an efficient cardiovascular system do not insure skill. Proper technique of all the essential shots must be perfected. A player's mind cannot be focused on such fundamentals as the proper way to hit the ball during the heat of a match, but rather must be concentrating on placement and strategy. The execution of the shot must be a coordinated reflex action, learned by many hours of practice and play in previous matches.

These three factors—cardiovascular endurance, strength, and neuromuscular coordination—are each vital for competitive success. However, these purely physical traits are not the only factors that are characteristic of success. If they were, handball success could be predicted on the basis of a physical fitness test.

Competition in sports also involves mental or psychological factors. It is difficult to assess a person's inner drive to win. And, certainly, there is varied drive from game-to-game or match-to-match. No athlete can remain at an emotional peak at all times during a game or match.

Each person, however, functions from within a certain personality framework unique to himself. An individual's personality profile has been developed from past experiences with family and environment and also from his own internally developed ideas. This psychological framework is not rigid, where a person becomes totally predictable, nor is it ever-changing, where a person's personality would be constantly changing. Investigations have been conducted studying the profiles of certain groups in order to determine if and how they differed from other groups or the population in general. For example, Olympic athletes have been found to demonstrate higher degrees of emotional maturity, calmness, and constancy in interests. These Olympic athletes are also more assertive, independent, headstrong, and admiration-demanding than the general population. Other personality characteristics which appear to distinguish these athletes from the "norm" are that they tend to be adventurous, impulsive, and have a carefree outlook on life. In another personality dimension, the Olympic champions appear to manifest a higher degree of self-confidence, cheerfulness and, as a rule, a lesser sense of inadequacy than the general population. College football players have also been compared to the average college population. In general, the results indicate that this type of athlete is more action-oriented, dominant, group-dependent, self-reliant, and "down-to-earth" than the typical college age adult.

The psychological inventory that is used in many investigations of personality characterists is one called Cattell's Sixteen Personality Factor (16PF). This inventory measures sixteen different identifiable traits based on the results of a written examination. Each of the traits is set up on a continuum where the extreme opposite characteristics are on each end of the scale and a normal range is in the center. As an example, in studying one of the traits, a low score would indicate shyness, restraint, and timidness, while a high score would be indicative of someone who is adventuresome, bold, and uninhibited.

Invitations to participate in this type of psychological inventory were extended to 32 of the nation's best handball players. There were 19 who completed the examination and the results are summarized in this report. Their responses to the examination were evaluated by the Student Counseling Services Testing Service of the University of Illinois at Chicago Circle.

On the basis of the test results, it is apparent that these handball players differed considerably from the general population on two of the 16 traits. Also, on two other traits the scores were consistent enough to indicate strong tendencies away from the population average. Of the remaining 12 traits, the inventory scores indicated the players scored within the normal range. One of the two traits in which there was a marked difference between the players and the general population is that describing the players as being very forthright, natural, and unpretentious, as opposed to shrewd, calculating and worldly. The scores of the players on this trait indicated that, as a group, they tended to be gregarious, had simple tastes, and were genuinely emotionally expressive. If one were to characterize how the typical handball player interacted socially with others from this psychological trait, he or she might use descriptive terms such as "completely direct" and "spontaneously outspoken." Thus, the typical handball player is more likely to be honest, open, and friendly. He also expects others to display a similar honest, open, and direct attitude when they interact with him. Compared to Olympic athletes, handball players are more unpretentious, open and friendly.

The second of the two traits where a significant difference occurred between handball players and the public at large was one indicating the players were abstract thinkers—a trait usually associated with more intelligent and bright persons—as opposed to concrete thinkers, associated with less intelligence. As a group, the handball players appear to be quite similar to Olympic athletes in this personality dimension. Both groups tend to be more perservering, fast-learning, and adaptable to changing events and times than the general adult population. This is probably the result of a higher level of education by the handball players and Olympic athletes. In fact, the scores indicated the group average was near the 90th percentile of the continuum, a very high rating.

Of the other two traits where moderately strong tendencies were revealed, the players tended to be more expedient about matters, disregarding rules and feeling few obligations, as opposed to being conscientious and moralistic. Interpretation of this psychological tendency is aided by the fact that Olympic athletes are quire similar to the handball players on this trait. Perhaps this indicates those in the population who are the "best" at what they do have to be expedient and disregard rules and norms. In other words, in order to become the "best," a person has to be different and not do "what is expected."

The second characteristic shows that the handball players tend to be self-sufficient, preferring their own decision making, and being resourceful to group dependency and being a "joiner." This finding seems logical since handball players are individual competitors and they must rely on their own talents and abilities as compared to members of a team.

The results of the scoring of one more trait also deserves mentioning, not for the group average that was attained, but rather for the variability of the individual scores. On this factor, extremely low scores indicate the subjects are humble, mild, and accommodating, while the opposite would indicate assertive, aggressive, and stubborn behavior patterns. It would appear that although the group average of handball players was close to that of the general population, handball players fall at both extremes of the personality dimension. Some players are very easygoing, considerate, and humble, while others are very assertive and aggressive.

In summary, there have been certain characteristics found that these highly skills handball players have in common. This is not to say, however, that each player of championship caliber is just like the other, but rather they tend to have similarities in their personalities. Because of their dedication to the game and the success they have had, one would expect their personalities to be different from the normal population, and as a group to have certain similarities.

The results of this study indicate that the highly skilled handball player tends to:

(1) be bright and intelligent,
(2) be quite open, natural, and unpretentious,
(3) be self-sufficient and prefer to live by his own decisions,
(4) feel few obligations, and
(5) deal with his problems as expediently as possible.

This investigation does not answer the question, "Does a person need this kind of profile in order to excel at the game of handball?" Or, "Does this type of profile evolve as a result of success in a sport?" Or, to put it another way, "Are champions born or are they made?" It is the authors' contention that an individual is not likely to achieve great success in handball unless he is a self-motivated individual possessing the traits identified in this investigation. These traits are a necessary ingredient and are just as important as the physical aspect of the game. It is still a debatable question, but at least we have gained some insight into the personality of the handball player at the point in time when he is a highly successful player.

HANDBALL–
CONCENTRATION/MEDITATION

MICHAEL D. BERNER

Meditation has become more popular as human-developed technologies create rapid changes over short periods, resulting in confusion and frustration for individuals.

Periods of meditation help to relieve the mind of the pressures of trying to keep pace and they promote a feeling of being able to cope with frustrations. Meditation takes a variety of forms. I prefer participation in strenuous mental and physical activity to stimulate my meditative activity—and I have found handball to be one of the most stimulating activities.

Photo 4-13: **Vern Roberts, Jr. shoots against Naty Alvarado in a recent exhibition match.**

Successful meditation requires undisturbed concentration. Handball, when properly played, requires complete concentration. The concentration of handball is a good exercise that prepares the mind for meditation.

Handball promotes meditation because it is a solitary game, not catering to the ego-centered desire to play before a crowd or to visions of gaining wealth. A good handball player is motivated primarily from a deeper sense of personal accomplishment.

Handball at its highest level is a psychological and physical battle between two determined athletes. It requires a high degree of mental and physical discipline—an almost pure state of being.

Properly played, handball requires a concentration into the thoughts of your opponent that allows you to anticipate his moves. A mutual respect is developed by handball players who are striving for and have reached high levels of the art of concentration.

Immersion of the whole being into the goal of winning a handball match can indeed be a form of meditation. After leaving the court, whether in victory or in defeat, life is perceived in a more clear and positive way. That is why handball is called by its enthusiasts ''The Perfect Game.''

CAN TM HELP YOUR HANDBALL GAME?

JOHN COFFEE

Complete Rest

Transcendental Meditation is a technique that allows the body and the mind to experience deep rest through resting the nervous system.

To be on top in business, in athletics, and in life, we all need our rest. With today's fast moving lifestyles, we all cannot attain a nightly average of eight hours of sleep. Even the people fortunate enough to get eight hours every night still tend to have a "run down" feeling, if they have compacted a day full of business worries, social entertainment and a vigorous hour and a half on the handball court. A full day can wear us down so we simply can't enjoy the day's events. Sometimes, we tend to go through the motions, like on those days we "just" show up on the court. Let's face it: when we are fully rested, we feel more energy, more energy to enjoy whatever we are doing to the fullest. The TM technique, when practiced only 20 minutes, is equivalent to 6-8 hours of restful sleep to the nervous system. This is a great little pick-me-up to help us enjoy a vigorous game of handball and the fun of going out dancing later that evening. The touring handball pro or the weekend local tournament player, who must go through some long, long down-to-the-wire matches two and three times daily, and for three days in a row, now has a beautiful and convenient way to rest up for the next round.

After 20 minutes of TM you feel refreshed, clear mentally and lighter physically, because of the release of stress from the nervous system. The game of handball is truly a running game and a game of expended energy and recovery time. Isn't it true that today's top pro circuit players all have the shots and it really comes down to a game of conditioning and who has more energy? We know where energy comes from: diet, conditioning and REST. TM is a convenient technique that can improve your handball game at its most critical point, your energy level and how long it lasts.

I started the Transcendental Meditation program because I felt like I wasn't doing anything for myself, for the growth of my system. I was wasting time. I wasn't reading. I wasn't really growing. So I started meditating because of the effects it has on your body and your mind, and it's done a great deal for me. It's made me feel like I am helping myself and through that I can get along with other people and maybe help them a little more with different situations or problems. The main thing though, I feel like it's helping me and that in itself it has done so much for my whole togetherness. I feel like I'm not wasting myself, that I am helping my mind and my body live life in the right way. And I've enjoyed it and I'm going to keep on enjoying it.

— Joe Namath, former quarterback, New York Jets

Athletes such as Joe Namath and twenty-five members of the Philadelphia Phillies are now experiencing the benefits TM grants to competitors in skillful sports. The benefits stem from faster reaction time in quick decision sports because of an increased alertness, improved coordination of mind and body, and greater awareness in overall participation. The increased motor performance from the TM technique simply means benefits such as hitting a target while performing in sports, something very much needed in a controlled game of handball, and also greater flexibility and resistance to disorientation, which is a must in a high velocity handball match of three games.

Psychologists believe that increased learning ability past late adolescence is difficult, but the "NEW TREND" in athletics, developed as a result of testing from the University of California at Berkeley, now has documented proof that we all can learn and progress faster, which is surely good news for us younger "green" players who want it all to happen today. Unfortunately, it takes many dedicated years to be a good handball player. TM is a helper that may make the day come sooner. My point is that many athletes in many sports, where a building process of skills is necessary, are searching and seeking for a "plus" that might help them be just a little better than the next guy. The TM technique is certainly not unheard of in the sports world, but I would like to help spread its gospel to the proponents of the greatest sport— HANDBALL.

Handball the Health Game

Handball is truly the health game, for it is physically and mentally demanding in nature. It is a tension reliever, a cardiac conditioner, a life expander and a mind and character builder. The game is truly a complete game. A complete game demands psychological stability involving stronger intellect, stability of attention, decreased anxiety and stabilization of an organized memory. These psychological factors would help anyone play a "control" game of handball.

Control, percentages and physical stamina—these are aspects of the complete game. Not only psychological but physiological stability is needed. TM can improve one's physiological condition by increasing respiratory efficiency, improve recovery from physical exertion, normalize weight and many other beneficial conditions. I would like to say to handballers both young and old everywhere, that the proof of TM's beneficial effects on athletic performance is here and should be valued as a positive addition to handball and other demanding sports. I would like this article to be counted among the first steps for a great beneficial plus to everyone's game, so handball players everywhere might reach their goals sooner.

TM advocates base their claim for reaction time improvement on studies such as the one done by Stuart Appelle and Lawrence Oswald, which was published in the *Journal of Perceptual and Motor Skills* (38: 1263-1268, 1974). They tested three groups of people for the time it took them to push a button after seeing a light signal. The test was carried out after one group meditated, a second group sorted columns of figures and a third group, the control group, simply rested. The meditators and figure sorters had significantly faster reaction times in the tests. The meditators were the fastest.

The important thing for handballers to note is the correlation between mental activity and reaction time. Mental alertness increases reaction time. Some people, for a variety of reasons, find meditation, or even the idea of meditation, inappropriate for them. These handballers, in preparing for matches, should find some alternative way of increasing their mental alertness, whether it be reading a book, balancing their checkbook, or simply holding a stimulating conversation. What must be avoided is going into matches "well-rested" so the mind is dulled and slowed. A slow mind makes a slow body.

PART III
CHAMPIONSHIP PROFILE

THE CHAMPIONS

TERRY MUCK

Thou great democratic God, thou who,
in all Thy mighty, earthly marchings,
ever cullest Thy selectest champions
from the kingly commons.

Champion. National champion. Paragon of handball, master of the kill shot, strategist nonpareil. The number one player in the world.

That's what champion means in the sport of handball. The best player in the country for one full year until the next national tournament rolls around. It's a title full of meaning, rich in tradition, a crown many a young handball player has dreamed of, spent hours practicing for, but achieved by only a few.

For the 60 years from 1919 when the AAU held the first officially recognized national tournament, to 1951 when the USHA took upon itself the task of determining the country's best player, until today after 29 USHA national events, only 28 men have been national handball champions.

A select group. Some won through consummate skill, some through backbreaking work, some through masterful thinking. Some champions overcame unbelievable barriers to win; some found good fortune smoothed the rocky course to the title. All of them, however, won their honors on the court against opponents who desired the national title every bit as much as they.

The champions were (are) men like the rest of us. From all walks of life, with all manner of personalities, of many different talents, they are distinguished by nothing more than this accident of fate, that they won a national crown. Does that mean we should honor them the less? Certainly not.

As handball players, they are our ideals. The champions deserve our respect for several reasons.

Take dedication for example. Joe Platak won the most national championships, nine. He won them because of dedication. He eschewed any kind of business career in favor of handball excellence.

His training regimen at Chicago's Lake Shore Club is legend. He strengthened his legs by moving up and down the Club's twenty flights of stairs—on one leg—with weights strapped around the ankles.

He hopped up the stairs on one leg and down on the other, and then reversed the procedure. He strengthened his heart and lungs by running miles and miles up and down the beach along Lake Michigan. He honed his handball skills alone in the court—Lord, the hours he spent in the courts, hitting righthanded shot after righthanded shot until you couldn't tell his natural southpaw swing from his grooved right side.

Joe dedicated himself to being the champion and he paid the price victory demands.

For another example, take courage. Winners conquer fear. Jim Jacobs won six national crowns, every one of them a triumph over fear: "When it came time to go to the courts for the national finals match, this match I had worked months and years to play in, I wanted to go the opposite direction from the courts. The intense apprehension I felt never left me until I forced myself in the court and the match began."

Championship courage conquered extreme leg circulation problems (Walter Plekan, 1951), knee surgery (Stuffy Singer, 1968), the loss of an infant daughter (Vic Hershkowitz, 1950), three straight years of final match defeats (Jack Clements, 1942); twisted ankles, broken fingers, bleeding heads mean nothing to the champion except one more minor hurdle to overcome.

The champions inspire us to greater action, to dedication and courage we alone could not muster ourselves, but because those who have gone before us have done it, we find some hidden reserve of strength to do it also.

The records of the champions will live on; they will be broken and superseded. But we'll remember them for the heights they reached and the examples they set.

Bill Ranft, 1890-1971
National Champion – 1919

In the first official national tournament, Bill "Murder Ball" Ranft defeated Joe Lacey for the title, 21-13, 21-11. The tournament was held at the Los Angeles Athletic Club with 13 players competing, most going both ways (singles and doubles). In fact, Ranft teamed with Lacey to win the doubles title.

Ranft learned his handball at Golden Gate Park in San Francisco, represented the Olympic Club for a time, and then moved to Los Angeles where he gained handball fame. He represented the Los Angeles Athletic Club in water polo, basketball, and track in addition to his excellent play on the handball courts.

He was a champion who gave back to the game. He tutored many young players, formed the Harold Lloyd Handball Club at Mr. Lloyd's spacious estate in Beverly Hills, and even after his playing days were over he kept current on the sport and its development.

The game was a little bit different in Bill's day. Two shorts were permitted, the third being a handout. Ceiling, back wall, and three wall serves were permitted. A hinder was allowed only if the ball did not reach the front wall, and body contact was generally overlooked.

Despite the roughness of the game, Ranft seemed to have been a popular player. Carroll Van Court, handball instructor at the LAAC describes "Murder Ball" as, "a very popular player because he never stalls, never loafs, always plays a fair, clean, hard, brilliant game, and gives the best he has."

Bill Ranft knew the game from soup to cigars and back again. He was as much at home in the handball court as a pickpocket in a crowd. He maintained a relationship with the game of handball all his life, which was 81 years long.

Max Gold
National Champion – 1920

Another Los Angeles Athletic Club member won the second national handball title held at the LAAC in 1920. Max Gold defeated George Klawitter in the finals, 21-7, 21-4. Gold had a hot tournament, with no one scoring more than 11 points on him in any single game.

He was also a fine doubles player, teaming with another stalwart of the era, Maynard Laswell, to win the doubles title two years later in Milwaukee. Gold played fine semi-pro basketball on the LAAC's national AAU team.

The game was still very rough at that time, with very few hinders called. Gold thought this should be changed, and perhaps influenced things in that direction by saying, "I think there should be a few changes in the rules. The hinder up I think should be changed to a hinder ball. Hinders should be decided by a referee if the opponent is hit by the ball when going towards the front wall."

Gold was an assistant director in the movies, and died at an early age when an airplane in which he was riding on location over Santa Monica crashed into the Pacific Ocean.

Carl Haedge, 1892-1947
National Champion – 1921

St. Paul Athletic Club star Carl Haedge defeated William Sachman, 14-21, 21-16, 21-12 for the national title in 1921 held at the Detroit Athletic Club.

Haedge, a St. Paul dentist, played a dig 'em up game with a wonderful combination of skill, stamina, and intelligence. He tried to run his opponents to death. Haedge himself was a very fast hand-ball player, perhaps the fastest in this particular tournament.

He put his physical skills to good use, starring in football and baseball at the College of St. Thomas, before turning to the four wall courts. He was a diligent trainer and conditioning fanatic.

Haedge played at a time when there was still a great diversity of court sizes, and a still greater diversity in the rules of the game. It was at this 1921 tournament that the players agreed upon the need for standardization and codification of the rules of the game, particularly the hinder rule.

Carl Haedge was killed in an automobile accident in St. Paul when he was 54 years of age.

Art Schinners
National Champion – 1922

On March 25, 1922 Art Schinners of the Milwaukee Athletic Club defeated Bill Sackman of the New York Athletic Club for the national handball title. Scores were 13-21, 21-18, 21-19.

The red-haired Schinners worked his way through sixty-four players, at the time the largest tournament field ever, for the championship. He played bare-handed which he claims was "really the exception at that particular time."

Another unusual feature of this tournament was the size of the courts: 20 ′ x 40 ′. At that time these were considered very small courts, and many contestants complained bitterly over the advantage the size gave to Schinners, since the tournament was at his home club. Max Gold wrote back to the Los Angeles Athletic Club: "In addition to being small the courts were wooden instead of cement, and had an overhang in the back court which caused some unusual shots to be played."

Schinners worked as a sports editor for the *Milwaukee News* at the time and actually covered the tournament he won. In his court skills he relied a great deal on his stamina and tenacity. Today he works as a warehouse sales agent, and still lives in Milwaukee.

Joe Murray
National Champion - 1923

One of handball's best-ever exhibitions of courage and staying power was that put on by Joe "Red" Murray, who fisted every ball he hit, against Maynard Laswell for the 1923 national singles title at the St. Paul Athletic Club. Murray, representing the San Francisco Olympic Club, won his first two matches easily, and then blasted defending national champion Art Schinners, 21-1, 21-8. He followed with a win over Al Hobelman, junior national champion, then eliminated another ex-national champ, Carl Haedge.

The finals pitted Murray against Maynard Laswell, destined to be a three time national champion. Murray recalls the match: "I will never forget the exciting and tense situations between two Californians for the national title. Laswell won the first game, 21-8, with a beautiful exhibition of kill shots and perfect placements. I just did not get going. The next game was a fight to the finish.

"The score was 20-20 for five consecutive hands. He would not give ground; neither would I. One mistake would finish me. Laswell, on the other hand, could still boot one and recover in the third game. I had two ace cards to play. When Laswell served, I laid a left hand kill from the back wall to put his hand out; then when I served, I laid another kill to win the game. I won the next game, 21-6, and the title. Maynard Laswell was strong, crafty and one of the best in the business. He was a great handball player, and, as the records show, he won the title three straight years."

Joe Murray remained active in handball at the Olympic Club and played for many years although he never won another title.

Maynard Laswell, 1896
National Champion – 1924, 1925, 1926

The first multiple winner of the national handball title was Maynard Laswell of the Los Angeles Athletic Club. He won the title three times, in Los Angeles in 1924, in Cleveland in 1925, and in St. Paul in 1926.

Laswell had just about everything in the way of handball "equipment" including one of the greatest underhand back wall drives in the sport's history. Laswell's back wall drive, one of the hardest of all time, was delivered almost effortlessly. That, combined with a fine overhand placing game and a side-arm fly kill plus great condition and competitive instinct, enabled him to win three years running.

Laswell had won the national doubles title the year before his first singles win, teaming with fellow club member Max Gold.

A fine all-round athlete, Laswell competed particularly well in basketball which he played on the national AAU level for many years.

After winning three straight national handball titles, Maynard Laswell retired to devote himself to business and founded a successful CO_2 fire extinguisher manufacturing company.

George Nelson
National Champion – 1927

The national title was finally brought East when George Nelson of Baltimore stunned the handball world with his famous hook serve.

Nelson had a very strong arm (he had been given a tryout as a pitcher with the New York Yankees), and had developed a hook serve that would jump five feet either way, an unheard-of practice at the time. St. Paul's Ed Pennig remembers the effect Nelson had on the rest of the players: "Most of us up to that time used a long, freestyle, underhand stroke, and when George threw the hook at us, we were dead ducks with most of us ending up with sore shoulders and arms trying to reach and return this new 'spook' ball. In that 1927 nationals he beat everyone in two straight, and ended up with an average of eight points per game per opponent."

Nelson had a well-rounded court game in addition to his super service, and was most effective on the small 20′ x 40′ courts that eventually became standard.

He remained active in handball, playing in some of the USHA Masters tournaments of the fifties. He wrote an instructional article for *Ace* magazine in 1953 on how to hook the ball, and performed in the first ever televised exhibition of handball in October of 1949. He was employed by the Baltimore and Ohio railroad.

Joe Griffin, 1905-1970
National Champion - 1928

Another great basketball player who became a national champion was Detroit's Joe Griffin, who won the title in Cleveland in 1928 by defeating defending champion George Nelson, 18-21, 21-16, 21-7.

Griffin, who won his title at the age of 23, featured very methodical tactics with accompanying steadiness, marked by effective placements and skill at playing to opponent's weaknesses. Joe was tall and had a wide stride. His side arm shot took advantage of that wide stride. He could drive a ball like a bullet, and his kill off the back wall was excellent. He had poise, and no one ever outfought him.

Griffin was a salesman for most of his life in Detroit, working for the Edison Company. He never lost his fervor for handball, and later when he moved to Ft. Lauderdale, Florida, he became the director of the Ft. Lauderdale YMCA Health Club, where he tirelessly promoted the sport amoung the youngsters there. Whenever a visiting handball player would look for a game, you could be sure he would be well taken care of by Joe.

By the way, when Joe won the title in 1928 a new handball cost $.35.

Al Banuet, 1909-1968
National Champion – 1929, 1930, 1931

Whenever handballers think about the greatest players of all time, the name of Al Banuet always pops up. He won the title three consecutive years, first in New York in 1929 at the age of 19, then in St. Louis in 1930, and finally in Minneapolis in 1931. In 1929 and 1930 Banuet also won the national doubles titles.

Because Banuet was such a great athlete, a boxing promoter talked him into a short-lived boxing career. This brief fling at professional sports caused him to be ever-after banned from AAU-sponsored handball competition, which at that time was the only game in town.

Banuet stories have become legendary. Angelo Trulio describes him this way: "Banuet was by all odds the most colorful player ever to come along. I've seen him literally run up a back wall like a monkey to return a shot. He could do things in retrieving a ball that are regarded as impossible."

W.O. McGeehan, sports editor of the *New York Herald,* said of Banuet after watching him win his 1929 championship: "He is the greatest champion in his chosen sport that I have ever seen. Greater than Babe Ruth is in baseball, greater than Bobby Jones in golf, greater than Jack Dempsey in boxing."

Banuet continued to play handball for a few years after his loss of amateur standing, then lost interest in favor of golf and tennis. It was not until he moved to Chicago for a spell in the early fifties that he began to play some handball again. In later life he was plagued with heart trouble.

Angelo Trulio, 1907
National Champion – 1932, 1946

Angelo Trulio won national titles fourteen years apart, in New York in 1932, and in San Francisco in 1946, the latter a tournament in which he defeated the legendary Joe Platak.

Trulio was absolute master of the big courts, a man who thrived on rally, rally, and more rally. He was a cover boy for strength magazines in his glory days, a dedicated weight-lifter and physical fitness model. He described his handball training regimen:

> In the age under thirty, I averaged fifteen to twenty games a day, from thirty to thirty-five it was twelve to fifteen games a day, and at thirty-five to forty I tapered off to ten games a day. The large courts (23' x 46', 24' x 48', 25' x 50') demanded a strictly different type of game than the small courts. In the height of my career my style of play for the large courts was considered ideal, combining unlimited stamina, anticipation, pin-point control, and a slower pace.

In 1932, Trulio also won the doubles title, teaming with Maynard Laswell. Angelo worked as a playground director for the City of New York.

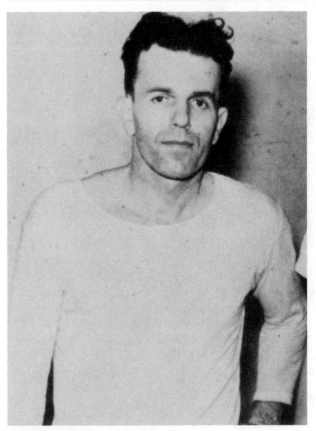

Sam Atcheson, 1902
National Champion – 1933, 1934

Sam Atcheson won the nationals in Chicago in 1933 and in New York in 1934. He added the doubles title in 1945 when he teamed with Walter Detweiler to win at age 43, eight years after his last tournament competition.

In the 1933 singles win, Sam played Al Hobelman. Sam was loose, limp, and relaxed as a rag doll. He came from behind to win both games. He made a run of 15 consecutive points in the first game, and 11 in a row to win the second. The next year he defeated Angelo Trulio on the big NYC courts, no mean feat considering it was the only loss for Trulio on those big courts in eight full years of play.

Actually, Sam's most impressive record was in YMCA play. The slender, wiry, and speedy perfectionist was a stellar national YMCA champion, winning 14 national titles over a period covering 1930-1945. In YMCA competition he was virtually unbeatable. He took the singles six times from 1931 through 1937, missing only in 1934 when George Nelson of Baltimore was the victor.

San lives in Memphis where they named the "Atcheson Courts" in honor of their hometown champ.

Joe Platak, 1909-1954
National Champion – 1935, 1936, 1937, 1938, 1939, 1940, 1941, 1943, 1945

The record book shows Platak, representing Chicago's Lake Shore Club, won seven national four wall singles championships in a row, added two more after Navy service in World War II, and took two national doubles championships in 1937 and 1944.

Joe's devotion to handball was complete. He spent literally hours in the courts alone building stamina, attaining dexterity, killing ball after ball, left, right, left, right, until it was almost impossible to detect that he was a natural southpaw. He spent hours running on the beach along Lake Michigan, hopping up and down the twenty flights of stairs at the Lake Shore Club, and skipping rope in the weight room.

In 1937, when Joe was at his peak, he made an exhibition tour. Meeting all comers, among them some of the finest players in the country, he played 136 separate games in 21 days in 17 clubs in 13 cities and 9 states, covering some 3,000 miles on the trip.

And he didn't lose a game in singles or doubles.

Platak developed his game in Armour Park just outside the left field wall of Comisky Park, and devoted his life to handball.

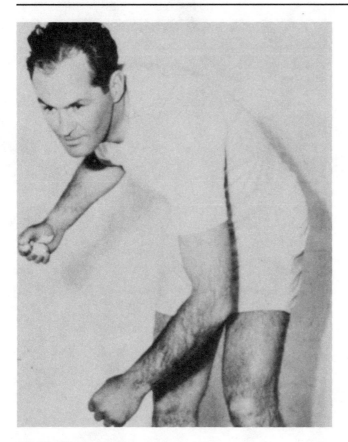

Jack Clements
National Champion – 1942

There's an old proverb that says: "All things come to he who waits," and Jack Clements learned of its truth in 1942 when Platak was in the Navy. Jack, the pride of San Francisco, and most certainly a great handball player, finally hit the jackpot. In the finals of the 1942 tournament, he defeated Dan Marble, a fellow townsman, 21-5, 21-10.

During the Platak era, many good players never got their shot at the spotlight because of Joe's domination, and Clements certainly seemed to be one of these. He reached the finals in 1938, 1939, and 1940 only to be defeated by the "Blonde Panther" from the Lake Shore Club.

In 1942, with Joe in the Navy, Clements finally got his chance, and he took advantage of it by playing terrific ball. Rarely has a national tournament been so thoroughly dominated by one player. Clements defeated his first round opponent by the scores of 7 and 3; his second round opponent managed 5 and 5; his quarter-final foe got 5 and 1; and his semi-final opponent got 6 and 1. That's an overall tournament average of 4.3, an all-time national tournament record.

Jack was a brewery worker in San Francisco.

Frank "Lefty" Coyle
National Champion – 1944

Frank "Lefty" Coyle had no peer when it came to the thinking man's handball. He was mainly known for his doubles play, but in 1944 he stunned the handball world with an upset victory over the seemingly invincible Joe Platak in Chicago, 21-15, 21-19.

Altogether he won seven national doubles titles, four with Eddie Linz in 1938, 1939, 1941, 1946, and three with Bill Baier in 1950, 1951, and 1952.

Lefty accomplished his great upset win over Platak by using a lob serve to Joe's right hand. As Lefty described it, "Although this type of serve was not too difficult for a player of Joe's caliber to return, it was tough for him to do anything with it other than return it. And, most of the time Joe gave me a setup, and I was waiting for the fly kill."

In doubles, Frank's style was to play a left front court with his two partners, Bill Baier and Eddie Linz. His partners worked the ball around until they could get a shot for Coyle's deadly left.

Frank was a championship water polo player in New York. Later he went to work for Bob Kendler in Chicago.

Gus Lewis, 1918
National Champion – 1947, 1948

Gus Lewis took advantage of his background as an acrobatic dancer to become a national singles champion in 1947 and 1948. His speed afoot gained him the nickname "Lightning Gus." He is considered one of the very best retrievers of all time and his all-around game was a delight to watch. Assorted physical setbacks kept Gus from more championships.

Gus wasn't a control player particularly, and certainly wasn't over-powering. He had an adequate off-hand. His real strength, in addition to his blazing speed, was a great fly kill which he used to great advantage along with his stamina and court coverage.

Originally out of Buffalo, New York, Gus later played in the Los Angeles area, and then moved permanently to Chicago, where he tutored many great national champions such as Johnny Sloan, Jimmy Jacobs, and Paul Haber.

After Gus's Open singles days were over, he compiled an outstanding Masters doubles record with another Bob Kendler employee, Ken Schneider. For many years Gus's speed and Ken's control made them an unbeatable combination in the Masters doubles ranks.

Vic Hershkowitz, 1920
National Champion - 1949, 1952, 1954

If a vote were taken to determine the greatest all-around handball player in one-wall, three-wall and four-wall, the probable winner would be Vic Hershkowitz. Vic won the four-wall title three times in 1949 at New York, in 1952 at Detroit, and in 1954 at Chicago.

He also won six one-wall singles titles, nine three-wall singles titles, three one-wall doubles titles, one three-wall doubles title, and one four-wall doubles title (in 1961 with Johnny Sloan at Denver).

No other player has ever so thoroughly dominated the entire sweep of handball competition.

In four-wall Vic displayed his tremendous single wall ability to the utmost, using a very powerful hop service. He combined maximum hitting power with either hand with unbelievable speed and accuracy. When Vic was right, his game was so strong that he seldom had to go to the back wall.

Vic worked in New York City as a fireman, and incidentally won several National Firefighters tournaments. All told, his national open titles number about 39, give or take a few.

Ken Schneider, 1921
National Champion – 1950

The door to national handball fame finally opened to Ken Schneider at the Town Club in 1950 when he defeated Walter Plekan in the finals 21-19, 21-13. Ken displayed amazing speed and court coverage, that indefinable sense of anticipation, a deadly back wall shot, and the art of digging up an opponent's apparent kill shot and rekilling it with a sidearm stroke.

If Ken had been endowed with the natural stamina of so many of his contemporaries, he could easily have gone down in handball history as one of the exceptional singles players of all time.

Ken's tournament career has spanned over thirty years. He was originally a product of the Castle Hill Club in the Bronx section of New York, and then was a member of an outstanding Al Stein team at the 92nd St. YMCA. He won three straight national doubles titles with Sam Haber in 1954, 1955, and 1956, and then he caught his second wind to win several Masters doubles titles with Gus Lewis.

Ken personifies good sportsmanship on the courts and has served as handball's national commissioner. He is Bob Kendler's corporate attorney at Community Builders in Chicago.

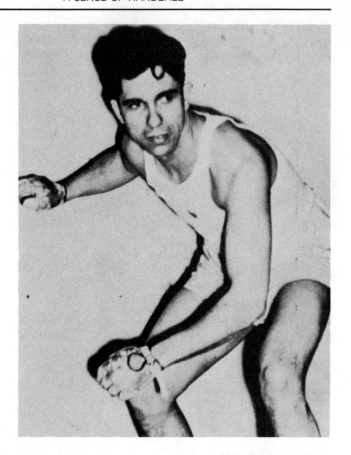

Walter Plekan
National Champion – 1951
In 1951 Walter Plekan was making what most experts considered his last serious bid for the Big One. Plekan, one of the cagiest players ever to grace a court, had been runner-up no less than three times. It was common knowledge that he was playing on damaged legs which literally quivered with every prolonged rally.

Hershkowitz trounced him soundly the first game, but someway, somehow, Plekan managed to retain his equilibrium and come back to take the next two from an unbelieving Hershkowitz. Final scores were 8-21, 21-16, 21-16.

The 1951 tournament was the first held by the United States Handball Association and marked the transition of handball administration from the AAU to the USHA. The AAU attempted to hold a competing tournament but could only manage to draw a third as many players as the fledging USHA. All the contending players of that time, with the exception of Bob Brady, entered the USHA tournament.

Plekan represented the Buffalo Athletic Club and has worked as a tool and die man in Buffalo for many years.

Bob Brady, 1922-1972
National Champion – 1953

Bob Brady learned his handball in Montana, and gained national attention playing out of San Francisco. "Bullet Bob" won his national singles title against Walter Plekan in 1953 at Houston, 21-10, 18-21, 21-16.

Brady's technique was not perfect so far as the stroke was concerned, but his headwork and control of the ball were marvelous. He used the old principle of "hit the ball where the other fellow ain't" with great success, making all his opponents run the wrong way many times. He never seemed to extend himself, but usually won without much trouble.

Brady was the bullish type, very determined. He used the Irish whip with his right hand, and stiff armed unorthodox punch shots with his left. He had a very deadly back wall kill shot.

Brady's finest hour probably came in the finals of the 1957 AAU on his home court at the Olympic Club in San Francisco, where he defeated the legendary Jim Jacobs after trailing 12-19 in the third game. Brady, a policeman, was selected to the handball Hall of Fame in 1965.

Jim Jacobs, 1929
National Champion – 1955, 1956, 1957, 1960, 1964, 1965

Jim Jacobs won the first of his six national titles in Los Angeles in 1955 when he beat Vic Hershkowitz 21-20, 21-7. In a 1979 poll taken by *Handball* magazine to select the all-time best players, Jacobs was the consensus "best" at the game of four-wall handball.

The term "complete player" has to apply to Jim. He had power, stamina, two-handed skills, speed, anticipation, and control. As a man who has accumulated the world's largest collection of fight films, he would understand our description comparing him to a champion counter-puncher in boxing. Jim was the one who developed the control rally game, using the percentage offensive shots, wearing down his opponents, and letting them make the mistakes.

Apart from his fabulous singles play, one of Jacob's more outstanding records was his doubles play with Marty Decatur. Together they won five national doubles titles and were never defeated, in tournament or in practice, as a doubles team.

Jim learned his game in Hollywood, prepped at Community Builders in Chicago, and starred in Los Angeles. He now lives in New York with his thriving fight film business.

354

John Sloan, 1936
National Champion – 1958, 1959, 1961

Total achievement in handball came to Johnny Sloan at an early age. He was 18 when he won the national YMCA doubles with Jack Gordin, and 22 when he pulled the game's "grand slam" by winning both the singles and doubles (with Phil Collins) in 1958, a feat he was to repeat twice more in 1959 and 1961. Overall he won three singles and five doubles titles.

John had lightning fast reflexes and court coverage in his early twenties. Jack Gordon taught him the importance of the fly shot in his apprenticeship at the Irving Park YMCA in Chicago. John copied Gus Lewis' pin-pointed right corner fly kill to a T. What Sloan had in addition was amazing control of his off-hand fist shots, keeping the foes away from the offensive in either singles or doubles. His partnership with Phil Collins demonstrated real teamwork, and they must be rated as one of the game's all-time great doubles teams.

The "Little Court General," as Bob Kendler so aptly tabbed Sloan, had a running battle with Jim Jacobs during his heyday, although the two never met in the finals of a national tournament.

John retired early and now lives in Honolulu.

Oscar Obert, 1929
National Champion – 1962, 1963

Oscar Obert developed into a champion four-waller comparatively late in his career, mainly because he had concentrated on one-wall, combining with his most talented brothers, Ruby and Carl, to stake a firm claim as the outstanding brother combine in the history of the game. Like Vic Hershkowitz, Oscar branched into four-wall after accumulating many national one-wall honors. It took several years of top tournament play to master the side and back walls and ceiling.

Obert's peak was the 1961-62 handball season when he started off with the one-wall victory, then beat John Sloan at Houston for his first four-wall title, and then capped it off with his first three-wall singles at Detroit, beating his brother, Carl, for that honor.

A second four-wall singles was annexed at Seattle in 1963 when Oscar again stopped Sloan.

Oscar Obert brought real crowd appeal to handball as a tremendous competitor, exciting all-out shooter, with championship killer instinct, demeanor on the court. He gave no quarter to any opponent, played clean, and performed superbly.

Paul Haber, 1937
National Champion - 1966, 1967, 1969, 1970, 1971

Paul Haber won five national championships, beginning with a win over Bill Yambrick in Salt Lake City in 1966. Only Jim Jacobs, Joe Platek and Fred Lewis have won more titles.

Twice more Haber defeated Yambrick in the finals, in San Francisco (1967) and Austin (1969), and then it was Lou Russo in Los Angeles (1970) and Steve August in Memphis (1971).

Paul left two things to handball: an uncanny use of the ceiling ball and a widespread media image that pictured him as a swinging playboy who still managed to win handball tournaments, even after a night of carousing.

It was the ceiling ball control that won Paul his five championships. He could drop the ball in the left rear corner from any place on the court with any stroke: overhand, underhand, or sidearm. Paul was the first to use the ceiling as an offensive weapon; his patience and determination with it were lengendary.

Paul was a professional golfer early in his career, and still works as a golf pro at clubs in the Chicago area.

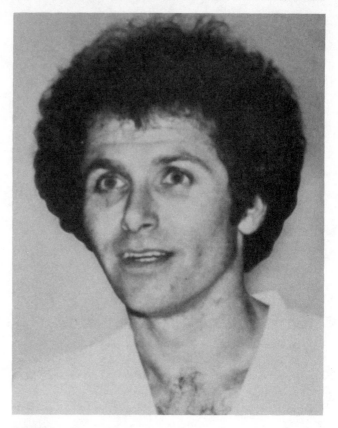

Stuffy Singer, 1941
National Champion - 1968

When Stuffy put his widely acknowledged skills together in 1968 to win the USHA Nationals in St. Louis, there were many who opined it would be the start of more to follow. But a series of physical setbacks kept him from reaching his full potential.

He has all the tools. His return of serve and rally game are as good as anyone's. Stuffy has extremely good front court quickness and excellent defensive shots. In fact, there isn't a shot in handball that Stuffy doesn't hit well.

His biggest problem was injuries. Several knee operations and severe Achilles tendon problems limited his play in his thirties. He was forced to compete more in doubles, and, playing with Marty Decatur, he won two national doubles titles in 1978 and 1979.

Stuffy has had a checkered career outside handball. He played table tennis well enough to be ranked among the top ten junior players in the nation. He was a child movie actor, playing Baby Dumpling on the "Blondie" television series.

Stuffy sells financial planning programs in his native Los Angeles where he lives with his wife Sunny and their two children.

Fred Lewis, 1947
National Champion - 1972, 1974, 1975, 1976, 1978, 1981

Fred Lewis upset the handball world's applecart in 1972 when he defeated Paul Haber in the semi-finals at Seattle and went on to defeat Terry Muck for the title.

Fred won five more titles and dominated the action on the early pro handball tour which started in 1974. He still tops the all-time prize money list with over $50,000 in earnings and has won 12 pro tournaments.

Fred personifies the "percentage handball" game, and couples this with the ability to defend superbly from deep court through controlled ceiling, round-the-wall, and driving shots. When presented with the rally-ending shot, "Steady Freddie" can shoot with the best of them.

Fred has also won four three-wall championships, a game he had adapted to very well, probably owing to his early training at the Castle Hill Beach Club in New York City which had outdoor four-wall and one-wall courts.

Fred is a very good handball instructor, and makes his living that way.

Terry Muck, 1947
National Champion – 1973

Terry Muck defeated Steve August in the finals of the national tournament in 1973 at Austin, Texas. Scores were 8-21, 21-17, 21-16.
He had previously defeated Paul Haber in the semi-finals 21-20, 21-18.

Haber calls Muck the "fastest handball player of all-time" and
certainly that was the asset that won a national title for Muck. He is
an all-out shooter and relies on his speed to make up for the high-
risk, offensive game he plays.

Terry's small stature limits his physical ability to have a stronger
serve; he has worked with hooks on the serve, but his lack of power
limits them. The other strong facets of his game, however, make up
for that shortcoming.

Muck is a player of whom it can truly be said he was developed
by the USHA's handball program. He played in the USHA's National
Junior, Intercollegiate, and Regional tournaments, and has benefited
from the generous travel allowances the USHA has provided to young
handball players.

He now works as editor of *Handball* magazine.

Naty Alvarado, 1955
National Champion – 1977, 1979, 1980

Alvarado has defeated Lewis three times for the national championship, once in St. Louis (21-15, 21-16), once in Miami (21-20, 21-8), and once in Tucson.

Naty's strengths are his speed and power. His playing style is to cut off everything he possibly can in the front court and kill in the front corners with both his right and left hands.

Naty came to the United States from Juarez, Mexico and is the first native of that country to win the USHA national title. He and his wife Lupe have two children and live in Pomona, California.

Naty won his first title when he was only 22, and is expected to rewrite the handball record books before he hangs up his gloves somewhere down the road.

He has talent, intelligence, and a desire to improve, so he should dominate the handball scene for quite a few years to come, if he continues to play.

BIBLIOGRAPHY

Berner, Michael D. "Handball - Concentration/Meditation." *Handball,* 1976, Vol. 26, No. 2.

Bullington, Ron. "Empirical Learning Principles Applied to Handball." *Handball,* 1978, Vol. 28, No. 6.

Coffee, John. "Can TM Help Your Handball Game?" *Handball,* 1977, Vol. 27, No. 2.

"The Game Plan." *Handball,* 1980, Vol. 30, No. 4.

Holtzworth, John. "Peak Performance and Flow: BEING ON." *Handball,* Vol. 30, No. 6.

Jacobs, Jim. Excerpts from "Jacobs' on Serve-Swing-Volley." *Handball,* 1973, Vol. 23, No. 6.

Leve, Mort. "The Game Plan." *Handball,* 1976, Vol. 26, No. 6.

Muck, Terry. "Apply Pressure to Win." *Handball,* 1977, Vol. 27, No. 6.

"The Champions." *Handball,* 1979, Vol. 29, No. 5.

"Percentages, Positioning and Conditioning." *Handball,* 1976, Vol. 26, No. 6.

Scherrer, Donald and Mitchell Jacobs. "The Psychological Profile of the Successful Handball Players." *Handball,* 1976, Vol. 27, No. 5.

Singer, Stuffy. "Make Decisions for Victory: Planned Reactions." *Handball,* 1977, Vol. 27, No. 3.

"Stuffy Singer's 3 C's of Handball." *Handball,* 1976, Vol. 26, No. 1.

Tomporowski, Dr. Phillip. "Behavioral Analysis of Handball Instruction: An Overview." *Handball,* 1977, Vol. 28, No. 2.

Tyson, Pete. "The Five Situations of Handball." *Handball,* 1976, Vol. 26, No. 5.

"Tyson's 3 H's - Hand, Head, Heart." *Handball,* 1976, Vol. 26, No. 3.

CHAPTER 5
HANDBALL RULES...
REFEREEING,
RULE INTERPRETATIONS
AND COMMENTS

IN THE END
THERE WERE RULES

JIM TURMAN

Although the rules are presented towards the end of this book, they are the beginning of understanding the perfect game. The essence of the game of handball is manifested in the rules that govern all phases of play. A complete and thorough understanding of the rules and a consensus interpretation of crucial rules, such as the avoidable hinder, will not only make the game more enjoyable to play, but will improve the conscientious player's game strategy, shot selection and performance. In addition, some rules appear to take on new meaning as a player's skill level and experience increase over the years. For example, the referee should consider interpreting the avoidable hinder rule that a ''C'' player may not watch the ball every moment due to experience and lack of body control. However, there are no excuses for the pros or national calibre players not understanding these rules and acting accordingly on the court.

Similarly, the new developments and changes in the techniques, strategies and, yes, the rules of the game, generally come from the top players and officials of the sport. Naturally, players tend to mimic the actions of the top flight handballers to improve their own games. Therefore, it is equally important to try to understand the interpretations of these rules by the people who are most responsible for affecting and making them. As a result, this chapter, in addition to the presentation of the rules of handball for your reference, includes selected rule interpretations by Neal Nordlund, USHA National Rules and Referees Commissioner, articles and comments directly related to the rules and refereeing.

Over time, the game of handball changes, sometimes drastically, sometimes imperceptibly; sometimes directly affecting rules, sometimes not. Usually any change will have an impact on your game. Two clear examples come to mind. Paul Haber demonstrated that the punching shot to the ceiling could be controlled and used as an offensive, as well as a defensive, weapon. His expertise with this shot not only helped him win five national championships but also drastically changed handball by affecting in some way how everyone now plays the game. However, this particular innovation of Haber's did not perceptibly affect any rules. On the other hand, Haber's mastery of the lob serve, effectively "wall papering" the side wall, clearly stirred controversy and various interpretations surrounding the responsibilities of the server and receiver in this situation. Questions arose concerning the five foot restraining receiving lines, encroachment on the short line, service screens, follow through on fly returns of the lob serve, etc.

Times do change, as do our perception and understanding of ourselves, our surroundings and the rules by which we play handball. Whether you agree or disagree with them is not the issue in this chapter. So, read the rules and their interpretations for clarity and understanding and reread them periodically since they do affect your game in many ways. Remember, in the end the rules are the beginning of the fundamental principles for the game of handball and should be learned to perfection.

Photo 5-1: **Vern Roberts shooting the left corner kill against Fred Lewis in 1981 Pro Stop at Austin, Texas. Sometimes shooting ball in front of yourself can hinder the view of the ball by your opponent and result in a screen ball hinder.**

OFFICIAL U.S.H.A.
FOUR-WALL HANDBALL RULES

Part I. The Game

A. Types. Four-wall handball may be played by two, three, or four players. When played by two it is called "singles," when played by three, "cut throat," and when played by four, "doubles."

B. Description. Handball, as the name implies, is a competitive game in which either hand or either fist may be used to serve and return the ball.

C. Objective. The objective is to win each rally by serving or returning the ball so the opponent is unable to keep the ball in play. A serve or rally is won when a side is unable to return the ball to the front before it touches the floor twice.

D. Points and outs. Points are scored by the serving side when it serves an ace or wins a rally. When the serving side loses a rally it loses the serve. Losing the serve is called an "out."

E. Game. A game is won by the side first scoring 21 points or, in the case of a tie breaker, 11 points.

F. Match. A match consists of two 21 point games, with an 11 point tie breaker if the first two games are split. For the 11 point tie breaker, the player with the most points scored in the first two games is awarded the first serve. If the points are tied in the first two games, a flip of the coin determines the server.

Part II. Court and Equipment

A. Court. The specifications for the standard four-wall court are:

1. Dimensions. The dimensions are: 20 feet wide, 20 feet high, and 40 feet long with back wall recommended minimum height of 12 feet.

2. Lines and zones. Handball courts shall be divided and marked on the floors with 2 inch wide lines. Recommended color is white. The lines shall be marked as follows:

a. Short line. The short line is parallel to the front and back walls. Its outside measurement is 20 feet from the front wall.

b. Service line. The service line is parallel with the short line and its outside measurement is 5 feet in front of the outside of the short line.

c. Service zone. The service zone is the area between the outer edges of the short and service lines.

d. Service boxes. A service box is located at each end of the service zone by lines whose outside measure is 18 inches from and parallel with each side wall.

e. Receiver's restraining lines. Five feet back of the short line (outside measure), lines should be marked on the floor extending 6 inches from the side wall. These lines are parallel to the short line. See rule IV. B. 1.

B. Ball.

1. Specifications. The specifications for the standard handball are:

a. Material. The material should be rubber or synthetic material.

b. Color. Color is optional.

c. Size. 1⅞ inch diameter, with ⅟₃₂ inch variation.

d. Weight. 2.3 ounces, with a variation of .2 ounces.

e. Rebound. Rebound from freefall 70 inch drop to a hardwood floor is 46 to 50 inches at a temperature of 68 degrees F.

Photo 5-2: In match against Fred Lewis, Vern Roberts, Jr., moves into defensive position close to Lewis but far enough away to allow Freddy a direct shot to the front wall.

C. Gloves.

1. General. Handball may not be played barehanded. Gloves must be worn.

2. Style. Gloves must be light in color and made of a soft material or leather, and form fitting. The fingers of the gloves may not be webbed, connected, or removed.

3. Foreign substances. No foreign substance, tape, or rubber bands shall be used on the fingers or on the palms of the gloves. Metal or hard substances should not be worn on the hand under the glove. For sensitive, bruised, or sore hands, surgical gauze or tape may be wrapped around palm of hand with or without thin foam rubber for protective purposes.

4. Wet gloves. The gloves must be changed when they become sufficiently wet to moisten the ball. This is the referee's decision. It is the player's responsibility to have an ample supply of dry gloves for each match.

D. Uniform.

1. General. All parts of the uniform, consisting of a shirt, shorts, socks, and shoes should be clean. Only customary handball attire, in the referee's judgment, can be worn. Players may not play without shirts. Shirts must be full length (not a shirt cut off in the torso).

2. Color. Color is optional, provided, in the judgment of the referee, it does not affect the opposing player's view of the ball. (Some very dark colors or unusual pattern may do this).

3. Wet shirts. Referee may request wet shirt be changed. Players should have ample supply of dry shirts.

4. Lettering and insignia. Names of the players may appear on the back of the uniform shirts. Lettering or insignia in poor taste are not allowed.

Part III. Officials and Officiating

A. Tournament chairman. All tournaments shall be managed by a tournament chairman, who shall designate the officials. (The officials shall include a referee and a scorer if available. Linesmen should be used whenever possible).

1. Responsibilities. The chairman is responsible for overseeing the entire tournament. He, or his delegated representative, shall be present at all times.

2. Rules briefing. Before all tournaments, all officials and players shall be briefed on rules and on local court hinders or other regulations. Referee clinics should be held prior to all USHA-sanctioned tournaments.

B. Referee's chairman. The referee's chairman is in charge of assigning referees to all tournament matches.

C. Referee.

1. Pre-match duties. Before each match commences it shall be the duty of the referee to:

a. Playability. Check on adequacy of preparation of the handball court with respect to playability.

b. Equipment. Check on availability and suitability of all materials necessary for the match such as handballs, towels, scorecards, and pencils (or marking pens).

c. Assisting officials. Check readiness and provide instructions to assisting officials.

d. Court hinders. Explain court hinders, if any, to players. (see rule IV. E. 1a)

e. Inspect gloves and uniforms. Remind players to have an adequate supply of extra gloves and shirts. Inspect compliance of gloves and hands with rules.

f. Start game. Introduce players, toss coin to determine order of serve, and signal start of game.

g. Time. The assigned referee should be present 15 minutes before match time.

h. Two-minute warning. He should give a two minute warning before the match and before each game.

2. Decisions. During games the referee shall decide all questions that may arise in accordance with these rules. On all questions involving judgment and on all questions and situations not covered by these rules, the decision of the referee is final. This might include changing a call.

3. Appeal calls. When linesmen are used the server may appeal a serve called short (or a foot fault) by the referee, if he thought it was a good serve. If both linesmen disagree with the referee's call the server is awarded the serve over. If he had one short, the call would cancel the previous short call, and he could be awarded two serves, because he was judged to have made a legal serve.

If, in the opinion of the referee, the ball could not have been re-turned, a point should be awarded the server. If the appeal was not upheld, the call would be two shorts, a side out.

On rally ending calls, either player may appeal on a double bounce call, kill shots called good, or kill shots called no good. The outcome may result in a point being awarded, a side out, or a replay, depending on the linesman's opinion. If both linesmen disagree with the referee's call on a double bounce ball, the call is reversed or replayed. Other rally ending appeals permitted are court hinders. No other hinder or technical calls are appealable.

The receiver, during the serve, may appeal calls on short balls, foot faults, and skip serves not called by the referee: in order to make these appeals, he must stop play before he returns the ball to the front wall. In so doing he assumes the risk of losing a point should his appeal not be upheld. If he wins the appeal, he is awarded the appropriate call. Once the ball has been legally returned to the front wall, no appeals may be made.

During the rally if a player feels his opponent did not return the ball legally (double bounce, wrist ball, or carry), he must stop play and appeal. He then accepts the consequences of the appeal.

4. Protests. Any decision not involving the judgment of the referee may be protested and then decided by the head referee (if a rules question) or tournament chairman (if a question regarding tournament administration).

5. Forfeitures. A match may be forfeited by the referee when:

a. Unsportsmanlike conduct. Any player refuses to abide by the referee's decision or engages in unsportsmanlike conduct.

b. Leaving the court. Any player leaves the court at a time not allowed by these rules without permission of the referee.

c. Failure to report.

i. No show. Any player for a singles match, or any team for a doubles match, fails to report to play.

ii. Late start penalty. The opponent shall be awarded one point for each minute of delay of game up to ten minutes. The match shall then be forfeited. This applies to the start of the match, be-tween game time outs, time outs during a game, and glove change time outs. Players should stay within earshot of the referee's call to help prevent the delay of game penalty. It is the obligation of the players to be ready to resume play on time even if the referee failed to give time warnings.

If the matches are on, or ahead of schedule, the players should be in the court warming up at least ten minutes before the assigned match time to assure a prompt start. If running behind, the players should be dressed and ready to enter the court for a maximum ten-minute, in-court warm up. If a player shows up five minutes late, "he" has restricted "himself" to a five minute warm up, etc. The tournament chairman may permit a longer delay if circumstances warrant such a decision.

6. Technical. If an argument develops, or if too frequent complaints are made against the referee's judgment calls, the "Referee's technical" will be invoked. If the referee says *"Play ball,"* and the player does not return to his respective serving or receiving position within ten second a technical will be called. A point will be deducted from the offending player's score. If, in the opinion of the referee, the appeal privileges afforded the players are being abused, the technical can be utilized. A technical warning is to precede the penalty of a technical.

D. Linesmen. If possible, two linesmen will be used in all matches, positioned at the most advantageous viewpoints.

1. Appeal responsibility. Players make appeals to the referee. The referee requests the opinion of the linesmen.

The linesmen's opinion is based on his agreement or disagreement with the referee's call. If a linesman is uncertain, he should abstain from making an opinion.

2. Procedure. The Linesman's judgment is conveyed by a visual signal of "thumbs up," if in agreement with the referee's call, "thumbs down," if in disagreement. If abstaining, a horizontal extension of the open hand, palms down, is given.

If one or both linesmen agree with the referee's call, the call stands. If both linesmen abstain from an opinion, the referee's call stands. In case of a tie, one linesman disagrees and one abstains, the referee has the final decision. He may either make his call stand, call for a replay or reverse the call. If both linesmen disagree with the referee, the call is reversed or replayed, depending on the situation.

E. Scorers. The scorer, when utilized, shall keep a record of the progress of the game in the manner prescribed by the committee or chairman. As a minimum, the progress record shall include the order of serves, outs, and points. The referee or scorer shall announce the score before each serve.

F. Floor manager. The floor manager readies players for their court assignments, times and their readiness to play.

Part IV. Play Regulations

A. Serve.

1. General.

a. Order. The player or side winning the toss becomes the first server and starts the first game.

b. Start. Games are started by the referee calling, *"play ball."*

c. Place. The server may serve from any place in the service zone. No part of either foot may extend beyond either line of the service zone. Stepping on the line (but not beyond it) is permitted. Server must remain in the server zone until the served ball passes short line. Violations are called "foot faults." See Rule IV.A.3.b.i.

d. Manner. A serve is commenced by bouncing the ball to the floor in the service zone. After the serve is commenced, on the first bounce the ball must be struck by the server's hand or fist so that it hits the front wall and on the rebound hits the floor back of the short line, either with or without touching one of the side walls.

e. Readiness. Serves shall not be made until the receiving side is ready. "Ready" means receiver has at least one full second in the receiving position. Server must also stand in the "ready" position for one full second before serving.

2. Doubles.

a. Server. At the beginning of each game in doubles, each side informs the referee of the order of service, which must be followed throughout the game. Only the first server may serve the first time up and continues to serve first throughout the game. When the first server is out, the side is out. Thereafter, both players on each side shall serve until an out for each occurs. It is not necessary for the server to alternate serves to his team's opponents.

b. Partner's position. On each serve, the server's partner shall stand erect with his back to the side wall and with both feet on the floor within the service box until the served ball passes the short line. Violations are called "foot faults."

3. Defective serves. Defective serves are of three types, resulting in penalties as follows:

a. Dead ball serves. A dead ball serve results in no penalty and the server is given another serve without cancelling a prior illegal serve. Dead ball serves do not cancel any previous illegal serve. They occur when an otherwise legal serve:

> *i. Hits partner.* Hits the server's partner on the fly on the rebound from the front wall while the server's partner is in the service box. Any serve that touches the floor before hitting the partner in the box is a short. See Rule IV.A.3.c.ii.

ii. Screen balls. The ball passes so close to the server or the server's partner that the view of returning side is obstructed. Any serve passing behind the server's partner and the side wall is an automatic screen. See Rule IV.E.1.d.

iii. Straddle balls. A legally served ball between the legs is an automatic hinder.

iv. Court hinders. Hits any part of the court that under local rules is a dead ball. See Rule IV.E.1.a.

b. **Fault serve.** Two fault serves results in an out. The following serves are faults and any two in succession result in an out:

i. Foot faults.

(a) Leaving the service zone. When the server leaves the service zone before the served ball passes the short line.

(b) Partner leaves the service zone. When the server's partner leaves the service box before the served ball passes the short line.

ii. Short serve. A short serve is any served ball that firsts hits the front wall and on the rebound hits the floor in front of the back edge of the short line either with or without touching one side wall.

iii. Three-wall serve. A three-wall serve is any served ball that first hits the front wall and on the rebound hits two side walls on the fly.

iv. Ceiling serve. A ceiling serve is any served ball that touches the ceiling after hitting the front wall either with or without touching one side wall.

v. Long serve. A long serve is any served ball that first hits the front wall and rebounds to the back wall before touching the floor.

vi. Out-of-court serve. Any ball that goes out of the court on the serve. See Rule IV.D.6.

c. **Out serves.** An out serve results in one-out.

i. Missed ball. Any attempt to strike the ball on the first bounce that results either in a total miss or in touching any part of the server's body other than his serving hand or fist.

ii. Non-front wall serve. Any served ball that strikes the server's partner or the ceiling, floor, or side wall, before striking the front wall.

iii. Touched serve. Any served ball that on the rebound from the front wall touches the server, or touches the server's partner while his feet are out of the service box. This includes the ball that is intentionally caught. See Rule IV.A.3.a.i.

iv. Out-of-order serve. In doubles, when either partner serves out of order or one player serves both serves. The violation must be detected before the next team serves.

v. Crotch serve. Any served ball that hits the crotch in the front wall shall be considered the same as a ball that hits the floor and is an out. A crotch serve into the back wall is an ace, as is a three-wall crotch serve.

vi. Delay. A server fails to serve the ball within ten seconds after he and the receiver have assumed the ready position.

B. Return of serve.

1. Receiving position. The receiver or receivers must stand at least 5 feet back of the short line, as indicated by the 6 inch restraining line, until the ball is struck by the server. Any infraction of this rule results in a point for the server.

2. Fly return. In making a fly return, the receiver must play the ball after it passes over the short line and no part of his foot may extend on or over the short line. A violation results in a point for the server. After contact the receiver may step on or over the short line without penalty.

3. Legal return. After the ball is legally served, one of the players on the receiving side must strike the ball either on the fly or after the first bounce and before the ball touches the floor the second time, to return the ball to the front wall either directly or after it has touched one or both side walls, the back wall, or the ceiling, or any combination of those surfaces. A returned ball may not touch the floor before touching the front wall. A ball may be played off the back wall as well as the front wall provided the ball does not touch the floor a second time.

4. Failure to return. The failure to return a serve results in a point for the server.

5. Touching receiver. See Rule IV.D.5.

C. Changes of serve. A server is entitled to continue serving until he makes an out. When the server or the side loses the serve, the server or serving side becomes the receiver, and the receiving side, the server; and so alternately in all subsequent services of the game. Outs are made by:

1. Out serve. He makes an out serve under Rule IV.A.3.c.

2. Fault serves. The server makes two fault serves in succession under Rule IV.A.3.b.

3. Hits partner. The server hits his partner with an attempted return before the ball touches the floor the second time.

4. Return failure. The server or his partner fails to keep the ball in play by returning it as required by Rule IV.B.3.

5. Avoidable hinder. The server or his partner commits an avoidable hinder. See Rule IV.E.2.

6. Second-out. In doubles, the side is retired when both partners have been put out, except on the first serve as provided in Rule IV.A.2.a.

D. Rally. Each legal return after the serve is called a rally. Play during rallies must accord with the following rules (each violation results in an out or point):

1. One hand. Only the front or back of one hand may be used at any time to return the ball. Using two hands to hit a ball is an out. The use of the foot or any portion of the body, other than the hand or fist, is an out.

2. Wrist ball. The use of any other part of the body to return the ball, including the wrist or arm above the player's hand, is prohibited.

3. One touch. In attempting returns, the ball may be touched only once by one player. In doubles, both players may swing at, but only one may hit, the ball.

4. Return attempts.

a. **Singles.** In singles, if a player swings at but misses the ball in play, the player may repeat his attempts to return the ball until it touches the floor the second time.

b. **Doubles.** In doubles, if one player swings at but misses the ball, both he and his partner may make further attempts to return the ball until it touches the floor the second time. Both partners on a side are entitled to attempt to return the ball.

c. **Hinders.** In singles or doubles, if a player swings at but misses the ball in play, and in his, or his partner's, continued attempt to play the ball there is an unintentional interference by an opponent, a hinder is called. See Rule IV.E.

5. Touching the ball. Except as provided in Rule IV.E.1.b., any touching of a ball before it touches the floor the second time by a player other than the one making a return is a point or out against the offending player.

6. Out-of-court ball.
a. After return. Any ball returned to the front wall that on the rebound or on the first bounce goes into the gallery or through any opening in a side wall is declared dead and the serve replayed.

b. No return. Any ball not returned to the front wall but which caroms off a player's hand or fist into the gallery or into any opening in a side wall either with or without touching the ceiling, side, or back wall, shall be an out or point against the player failing to make the return.

7. Dry ball and gloves. During the game, and particularly on service, every effort must be made to keep the ball dry. Deliberately wetting the ball results in an out or point. The ball may be inspected at any time by the referee during the game. If a player's gloves are wet to the extent that they leave wet marks on the ball, the player must change to dry gloves on a referee's time out. This is strictly a referee's judgment. If a player wishes to change to dry gloves, he must hold the palms of his hands up to the referee and obtain the referee's permission to change. He may not leave the court without the referee's permission. Two minutes are allowed for glove changes. The referee should give a one minute warning, but the player is still responsible for returning to the court within two minutes. Deliberately wetting the gloves results in an out or point.

8. Broken ball. If there is any suspicion that a ball has been broken on the serve or during a rally, play continues until the end of the rally. The referee or any player may request the ball be examined. If the referee decides the ball is broken, a new ball must be put into play and the point replayed. Once the succeeding serve is begun (or attempted) the previous rally stands.

9. Play stoppage. If a player loses a shoe or other equipment, or foreign objects enter the court, or any outside interference occurs, the referee must stop the play immediately.

E. Hinders. Hinders are of two types: "dead ball" and "avoidable."

1. Dead ball hinders. Dead ball hinders as described in this rule result in the point being replayed. When called by the referee, the following are dead ball hinders:

a. Court hinders. If in the referee's opinion an erratic bounce, caused by a court obstruction, affected play, it should be called a "court hinder." The player should not stop play at any time in anticipation of a call, nor influence the call.

Included in court hinders is the unplayable, wet, skidding ball that hits a wet spot on the floor. This is the referee's, not the player's, call.

b. Hitting opponent. When a returned ball touches an opponent on the fly before it returns to the front wall, and the shot obviously would not have reached the front wall on the fly, the player who is hit by the shot will be awarded the rally. If there is any doubt in the official's mind as to whether or not the ball would have reached the front wall, a dead ball hinder will be called.

c. Body contact. When any body contact with an opponent interferes with seeing or returning the ball.

A player should not stop play, except on physical contact on the backswing by the offensive (shooting) player. He should immediately call "contact" if he wants the contact hinder. If he elects to shoot, no contact call will be permitted. At no other time should the players stop on physical contact. Physical contact is not an automatic hinder. It is the judgment of the referee if the physical contact impeded the play.

d. Screen ball. When any ball rebounds from the front wall close to the body of a player on the side that has just returned the ball in such a way as to interfere with or prevent the returning side from seeing the ball. See Rule IV.A.3.a.ii.

e. Straddle ball. When a ball passing between the legs of a player on the side that just returned the ball, if there is no fair chance for the opposing player to see or return the ball. This is not automatic.

f. Avoidance. While making an attempt to return the ball, a player is entitled to a fair chance to see and return the ball. It is the duty of the side that has just served or returned the ball to move so that the receiving side may go straight to the ball and not be required to go around an opponent. On the other hand, the receiver must make a reasonable effort to move towards the ball. The referee should be liberal in calling hinders to discourage any practice of playing the ball in such a way that an opponent cannot see it until it is too late. It is no excuse on an attempted kill, unless in the opinion of the referee the player cannot return the ball. Hinders must be called without a claim by a player, especially in close plays and on game points. It is not a hinder when a player hinders his partner.

g. Doubles. In doubles, both players on a side are entitled to a fair and unobstructed chance at the ball.

Either one is entitled to a hinder even though it naturally would be his partner's ball and even though his partner may have attempted to play the ball and have already missed it.

h. Effect. A call by the referee of a "hinder" stops the play and voids any situation following, such as the ball hitting a player. No player is authorized to call a hinder, except the shooting player on the backswing and such call must be made immediately.

2. Avoidable Hinders. An avoidable hinder results in an out or a point depending upon whether the offender was serving or receiving. Player intent need not have bearing on an avoidable call. Avoidable hinders are called when:

a. Failure to move. A player does not move sufficiently to allow his opponent his shot.

b. Blocking. A player moves into a position that effects a block or crowds his opponent about to return the ball; or in doubles, one partner moves in front of an opponent as his partner is returning the ball.
c. Moving into ball. A player moves in the way and is struck by the ball just played by his opponent.
d. Pushing. A player forcibly pushes or shoves an opponent during a rally.
e. View obstruction. Deliberately moving across a player's line of vision just before he strikes the ball.
f. Distraction. Any avoidable intimidation or distraction that would interfere with the player playing the ball such as stomping feet, shouting, whistling or loud noise.

F. Rest periods.

1. Delays. Delays exceeding 10 seconds by server or receiver shall result in an out or point against the offender. Server and receiver must be in ready position within 10 seconds of the end of the preceding rally.

2. Time outs. During a game each player in singles, or each side in doubles, either while serving or receiving may request a time out. Each time out must not exceed one minute. No more than three time outs in a game may be granted each singles player or to each team in doubles. Two one-minute time outs are allowed during the tie breaker.

A player may not call a time out after, in the judgment of the referee, the players have taken their ready positions as server and receiver.

A player may leave the court during a time out. Time outs may be called consecutively.

3. Equipment time out. At the discretion of the referee, equipment time outs may be granted for lost shoes, broken shoelaces, torn equipment, wet shirts, wet floor, etc. Player is not charged for this time out.

4. Injury. No time out shall be charged to a player who is injured during the play. An injured player shall not be allowed more than a total of 15 minutes of rest. If the injured player is not able to resume play after a period totalling 15 minutes per match, the match shall be awarded to the opponent or opponents.

For any injury, the tournament director, if present, or committee, after considering any available medical opinion, must determine whether the injured player may be allowed to continue.

5. Between games. Five minute time outs are allowed between the first and second game, and before the tie breaker. Players may leave the court.

Part V. Tournaments

A. Draws. If possible, the singles draw shall be made at least two days before the tournament commences. The seeding method of drawing shall be approved by the committee or chairman.

B. Scheduling.

1. Preliminary matches. If one or more contestants are entered in both singles and doubles, they may be required to play both singles and doubles on the same day or night with little rest between matches. This is a risk assumed on entering both singles and doubles. If possible the schedule should provide at least a one hour rest period between all matches.

2. Final matches. Where one or more players have reached the finals in both singles and doubles, it is recommended that the doubles match be played on the day preceding the singles. This would allow more rest between the final matches. If both final matches must be played on the same day or night, the singles match should be played first, and a rest period of not less than one hour be allowed between the finals in singles and doubles.

C. Notice of matches. After the first round of matches, it is the responsibility of each player to check the posted schedule to determine the time and place of each subsequent match. If any change is made in the schedule after posting, it shall be the duty of the committee or chairman to notify the players of the change.

D. Tournament management. In all USHA sanctioned tournaments the tournament chairman and/or the national USHA official in attendance may decide on a change of courts before, during or after any tournament game, if such a change will accommodate better spectator or player conditions.

E. Tournament conduct. In all USHA-sanctioned tournaments the referee is empowered to default a match if an individual player or team conducts itself to the detriment of the tournament and the game.

F. USHA Tournament.

1. Regional tournaments. Regional tournaments are held each season. A map defining the boundary lines of each region will be drawn and made available to USHA Regional Commissioners.

a. Residence. Only players residing in the area defined can participate in that regional tournament.

b. One event. When several events are held at one time in a regional tournament, players can participate in only one event.

2. Intercollegiates. The purpose of the USHA-sponsored intercollegiate competition is to give the more advanced college players a chance to showcase their talents under ideal conditions, and to assist in the promotion of college handball.

3. Juniors. The purpose of the USHA Junior program is to promote a worthwhile competition, both on the local and national levels, to stimulate an ideal introduction to the game.

G. Pick-a-Partner. The essence of the "Player's Fraternity" has been to allow players to select a partner regardless of what organization or city he might represent.

Photo 5-3: Naty Alvarado "plays it close" on this shot by Dennis Hofflander. Moving into your opponent's shot and hindering his swing/follow through is an avoidable hinder.

DISSECTION OF
AVOIDABLE HINDER RULE
NEAL NORDLUND

The most confusing and sensitive rule in handball for beginners and veterans alike is the avoidable hinder. It is a rule that has plagued players and referees since its inception, and it will probably continue to do so for many years.

Once this rule was called the "intentional hinder." It was changed in nonmenclature to eliminate a certain element of stigma, so to speak, and to clarify as much as possible the point that the referee does not have to prove intent to impose the penalty. To control the game better we have added the "technical" penalty rule that can be invoked by a referee for flagrant unsportsmanlike conduct by a player.

Obviously, there are various plateaus of skills in handball competition and the referee must guide his avoidable hinder call accordingly. For example, many C players do not watch the ball at all times and the referee must take this into consideration.

There are two common misunderstandings concerning the Avoidable Hinder Rule that should preface the interpretation of the specifics of this rule. First, many handball players incorrectly assume that once a player has established "court position," it is his to hold. No player at any time during a match "owns" a position on the court.

Secondly, it is the obligation of any player to move sufficiently to allow his opponent a clear and unimpeded shot at the ball. The purpose of this article is to help all handballers understand the avoidable hinder better, the reasons for its presence in the rule book, and interpretation of it for competitive purposes.

The avoidable hinder has six specified areas within the rules.

Editor's note: *The references to the rules in the original article have necessarily been changed to coincide with the numbering of the specific rules in the previous article printed herein.*

Rule IV.,E.,2. Avoidable hinders. An avoidable hinder results in an "out" or a "point" depending upon whether the offender was serving or receiving. Player intent need not have bearing on an avoidable call. Avoidable hinders are called when:

a. Failure to move. A player does not move sufficiently to allow his opponent his shot.

b. Blocking. A player moves into a position that effects a block or crowds his opponent about to return the ball; or in doubles, one partner moves in front of an opponent as his partner is returning the ball.

c. Moving into ball. A player moves in the way and is struck by the ball just played by his opponent.

d. Pushing. A player forcibly pushes or shoves an opponent during a rally.

e. View obstruction. Deliberately moving across a player's line of vision just before he strikes the ball.

f. Distraction. Any avoidable intimidation or distraction that would interfere with the player playing the ball such as stomping feet, shouting, whistling or loud noise.

The first such specified offense is *Failure To Move.* The interpretation of this section is clear. You must get out of the way of your opponent. It makes no difference if doing so will almost assuredly result in your losing the rally. You have undoubtedly put yourself in this position due to a poor shot and now you must pay the consequences.

All players at one time or another have hit a shot that seems to come back at them. You have to move out of the way. Many players claim they have no idea where their opponent is, that they are afraid to move for fear of a violent collision. Again, this is no excuse, for just as it is your obligation to move out of the way, it is also your obligation to know where your opponent is, if that is what is necessary to make you move.

For example, the biggest single threat to safety on the court among beginning handball players is that player who never takes his eyes off the front wall. This player will strike the ball and crouch down, facing the front wall, waiting to his opponent's return to come into view. Not only is this practice poor fundamentals, it is also extremely dangerous.

If that ball he just hit should carry to the back wall on the fly, it could very easily rebound back to center court. And, if the opponent is playing correctly, his total concentration will be on striking the ball and that's where his eyes will be focused. It is the obligation of the first party to look over his shoulder and, if necessary, get out of the way to allow his opponent this shot. If there is a collision, or if this player is struck by the ball, or in any way hinders his opponent's shot, such a hinder is avoidable and the rule applies.

Many players do not look over their shoulders because they are afraid the return will strike them in the face. Fundamentally, the player should keep his eye on the ball at all times. Note: it is highly recommended that all players wear protective eye guards!

This brings us to the second specified offense, *Blocking.* The first part, devoted primarily to singles, is the opposite offense of *Failure to Move.* This is moving too much. The player who is guilty of moving into another player and effecting a block is unquestionably the dirtiest of players. I would rather contend with the player who occasionally forgets that double bounce pick-ups are illegal than with the blocker.

This is the guy who, when you have him out of position, doesn't care—he'll get to the position he wants, even if it means putting shoe rubber on your chest. The blocker realizes at all times what is happening. He is watching the ball sizing up every situation. When his poor shot results in a virtual set-up for his opponent, there he is with his block, claiming "hinder, hinder," when no movement on his part would have enabled his opponent a clear shot.

If you have hit a poor shot from deep court, giving your opponent a mid-court set-up, do not rush directly at him in a frantic attempt to get back into play. It is your own fault. You must allow your opponent his shot. Many top players, when forced into this situation, just choose to cover one side of the court. They make this decision based on the assumption that if their opponent kills the ball, there is no way to retrieve it anyhow; secondly, if they were to attempt to climb their opponent's back for center court position, this move would block their own vision.

I remember one player whose favorite ploy was to run directly to the point behind his opponent who had a set-up. Every time his opponent would kill the ball, he'd throw up his hands yelling, "hinder, hinder, I never saw the ball." Of course, this is not a hinder when created by that player. In other words, you cannot create a hinder for yourself. He had poor position because he hit a poor shot and that's all.

The line in this portion of the avoidable hinder rule commenting on doubles play is one of the most difficult avoidable hinders to detect. Veteran doubles teams have thoroughly frustrated their opponents and confounded rookie referees by this tactic.

As an example, when your partner strikes the ball, say from the right side of the court, you at that moment move directly in front of your opponent on your side. Your partner's shot, if it is a pass cross court, will never be seen by the player you have just blocked. Not only is it dirty play, it is an avoidable hinder. A block of this type is asking for trouble and the leading reason for bad feelings between some doubles teams. Doubles play is close enough with four players inside that 20 X 40 box. More blocking is unnecessary.

In one of the first tournaments I ever attended, I watched the most unusual and disgusting displays of handball imaginable. I witnessed a player who dressed himself in thick gray sweat pants, a long sleeved thick gray sweat shirt and even wore a hat. Every time his opponent had a shot off the back wall, this player would move directly into the path of the ball, be struck by it, and claim hinder. Unfortunately, the referee was inexperienced and allowed the player to continue this practice. I believe the player won his match, but ran into a more competent referee the next round and was continually given avoidable hinders.

The above extreme example shows clearly what is meant in the third section of this rule, *Moving Into Ball.* This avoidable hinder can be created at almost any spot on the court, but it is usually done off the back wall, when the player has time to move into this blocking position.

Moving into the ball is perhaps the most easily detectable of all avoidable hinders. It is a blatant attempt on the part of one player to prohibit his opponent's shot from following its natural course. I imagine that our friend in the sweat suit had calculated the risks involved, wore his outer coating of protection, and just decided to take his rips. It was embarrassing to watch.

The next avoidable hinder, *Pushing,* is called when one player is deliberately pushing or shoving an opponent during a volley. This avoidable hinder is not as easy to detect as one might imagine. Some top players have reputations for being able to push an opponent subtly without detection by the referee.

However, the most common pushing done is by the rookie player, who really does not know any better. He is the one who rushes in to cover your shot and when you anticipate this move and hit a ceiling or pass return, he puts his hand on your back and pushes off as he changes direction. The reason for making pushing off an avoidable hinder is the effect it has on both players. First, it gives the player doing the pushing an unfair start on his retrieving efforts. Secondly, it often results in putting the player who is pushed off-balance and thus in an awkward position to retrieve the subsequent shot. The third reason, of course, is the possibility of injury.

Remember, at no time are you allowed to push your opponent. It is always an avoidable hinder. What then should you do if your opponent is in the way? Well, whatever you do, don't push. If you get boxed in and he's in your way, just take a hinder and forget it. Pushing will lead to hard feelings on the court and probable rough play and more injuries. If your opponent is not moving out of your way, his actions are an avoidable hinder, and if the match is refereed, it should be called as such.

The fifth section, *View Obstruction,* not to be confused with a "screen" ball hinder, can be a difficult call to make. Generally, this type of hinder occurs after you have hit the ball and find yourself out of position or pinned against the side wall by the ball rebounding either off the front wall or the back wall to your opponent. Realizing too late that you are out of position, a desperate attempt is made to move into a better court position across the eventual path of the flight of the ball just prior to reaching your opponent, thereby obstructing your opponent's view of the ball. This is an avoidable hinder.

The last section, *Distraction,* is very clear and needs no further explanation.

Although the aforementioned circumstances fall directly under the avoidable hinder rule, there are a number of others that might so be interpreted also. It must be pointed out that at no time is the avoidable hinder meant to infer intentional hinder. Although any intentional hinder would, in fact, be an avoidable. There are cases in which the player does not deliberately hinder his opponent, yet it can still be called avoidable.

One of the most sensitive calls occurs when one player dives for a ball and is successful in returning it to the front wall. Many players with intense competitive desires often dive for balls, especially late in a close match. That is not the problem. The problem is when that player attempts to get up from the floor. In the event that the return after the dive rebounds at or near the fallen player, he still has every right, of course, to regain his feet. He does, that is, unless in doing so he creates an avoidable hinder.

In other words, if in regaining his feet, the player effects a block on his opponent, or moves into the path of the ball, or fails to move as the ball rebounds toward him, he must lose that point, or a handout must be called. We all have compassion and admiration for the player who can make this desperate lunge for the ball and get it. However, he does not have unlimited freedom in regaining his feet. He must let his opponent have his shot. Even though this seems a pretty tough interpretation, remember, that player probably would not have had to dive had he not hit an earlier shot poorly. The opponent cannot be discriminated against for showing superior control in making the rally reach the point where he has finally maneuvered his opponent into the ultimate poor position—prone on the floor. To allow the fallen player complete freedom in regaining his feet might take away a well earned point from his opponent.

Another example of an avoidable hinder not clearly spelled out in the rules, but encompassed by interpretation, is that player who yells or stamps his feet as his opponent is about to strike a shot, particularly a set-up. This is not only an avoidable hinder, it is also unsportsmanlike conduct and can be punishable under Rule IV.E.2.f.

Usually, one or at most two avoidable hinder calls will stop a player from continuing his illegal on-the-court antics. There are some players who attempt to see how far they can go in intimidating a referee along these lines. Thus, in the final analysis, it is the referee's duty to see that avoidable hinders are called. Many refs are too timid to take what they consider to be such drastic action, the awarding of a point or serve to one player. Yet it must be done. For the game to continue to evolve as a clean, sportsmanlike and enjoyable sport, the avoidable hinders must be called and just as important, they must be understood by the players and referees.

OTHER SELECTED RULES
INTERPRETATIONS
AND COMMENTS
NEAL NORDLUND

Editor's Note: *This article is a selection of rules interpretations, comments, and questions and answers regarding handball rules that have appeared in various issued of "Handball" magazine since 1975.*

The Lob Serve – The lob serve has become very popular around the country the last few years. Many questions have been asked regarding the responsibilities of the receiver and the server.

The receiver must remain behind the five foot receiver restraining line until contact of the ball by the server. An infraction results in a point for the server. He may then advance up to, but not on or over, the short line with either foot. No part of his body may encroach over the outside edge of the short line in the attempt to return the serve. It is as though an imaginary piece of glass extended from the outer edge of the short line. If any part of the receiver's hands or feet extend beyond this point it is illegal, and the penalty is a point for the server.

When contact of the ball is made behind the short line, any follow through by the feet or hands that carry the receiver over the short line is permitted. The calls on this situation can vary from no call, which means in the referee's judgment there was enough room for the server to return the serve fairly, to a screen hinder, or the possibility of an avoidable hinder being created by the server for serving too close to the side wall, and "not moving sufficiently" to permit a fly return. (Rule IV.E.2.a.)

Another situation is that of the server who bounces the ball as if preparing for a lob serve, so that the defensive player moves over to one side to get ready to come in for the fly return. The server then catches the ball, bounces it again quickly, and serves to the opposite side. This is an illegal ploy to draw the receiver from his normal receiving position. Rule IV.A.1.e. reads: "Serves shall not be made until the receiver is ready." In this case the first bounce was not the serve. The second bounce was the actual serve and the receiver was not in his "ready" position, a position to which he is entitled. Should this situation occur, the referee must stop play and call for a replay, because the receiver was not ready to receive. It is the responsibility of the server to determine if the receiver is ready to receive.

The server may not back over the short line until the ball has crossed the short line. This is a foot fault and the penalty is one short. Once the server has contacted the ball, it is the duty of the serving player to give the receiver a fair chance to see and return the ball. Some players are of the opinion that once they have contacted the ball they may remain in their stationary position as long as they are in the service zone. Not so. No server is entitled to a defensive position as long as it may interfere with the return of service by the receiver. If the receiver chooses to fly return the lob serve, it is his right to have an unobstructed view and return. Some feel because it is on the serve and not the volley, they are not obligated to move to allow the shot as is necessary in the volley. Again, not so.

Screen Ball Hinders – Certainly one of the more difficult of the many difficult calls a ref is confronted with is the screen ball hinder. The rules state the ball may not be "so close to the body" that the view of the ball "is obstructed." What is "so close?" As some kind of guideline the ball should be at least 12 inches from the player as it passes his body. The speed of the ball, the angle from which the player is returning the ball, the closeness of the players, the speed of the returning player, are all factors to consider in assessing a screen hinder. This could increase the distance of the ball from the body. Compounding the call of the screen hinder is that one player may feel he is entitled to a screen call, while another may feel he is not hindered in the same situation. Just one more of the many 50/50 calls (half right and half wrong) where the burden of judgment is placed on the referee.

Note that the player returning the ball should be making every effort to follow the direction of the ball to get into position to return it. Also, it is the obligation of the player who has made the shot or serve to move to allow the receiving player an unimpeded view of the ball.

Uniforms – One question which used to be asked frequently was can a player wear a half cut-off shirt? The answer was that in the interest of safety, it was not permitted. It could cause more perspiration to fall on the floor, creating a slippery and dangerous condition. This interpretation applies to all USHA tournaments.

Outside Interference – As a rally was continuing in court three, a referee in court four called a hinder, loud enough to make the player who was about to hit the ball in court three stop play. He thought his referee had called a hinder. The referee in court three called for a replay. This was the proper call due to outside interference.

Server Slipped – A player slipped and fell after he served. He yelled "Wait." The ball was legally served over the short line, and he remained within the service zone. The referee properly did not stop play, because the ball had been legally put into play.

Serving – While starting the serve, a player's back foot is a couple of inches outside the short line. This foot drags across the line so that when he actually contacts the ball, he is inside the service zone. This is still a foot fault with the penalty of one short. The server must be completely within the service zone and in a set position (one second) before he commences the serve.

Hinder – A ref started to call a hinder on a crowded play. He only said "Hin..." and the ball hit the player who had just returned the ball. The ref then changed his call to a point, since the player's opponent was serving. The interpretation is as soon as a ref begins to call a hinder it stops any ensuing situation. The hinder should have stood as the call.

Quick Serve – Many young players start to serve before the referee gives the score. The server should always wait for the ref to announce the score. And refs should realize they should announce both scores before every serve. The players often do not look back to see if their opponent was ready to receive. The receiver is entitled to a set position before the serve (also one full second). If the server starts to serve before the receiver is ready the ref can stop play.

Avoidables – The more familiar avoidables are failure to move, blocking, moving into the ball, and pushing. It should be explained that there are other violations of the avoidable hinder rule. Three of them occurred during a particular tournament.

As a player bounced the ball to start a lob serve, the opponent loudly stamped his feet. He was "avoidably" attempting to distract his opponent. This can definitely be called an avoidable hinder.

A player when he missed his shot and set up his opponent would "avoidably" reprimand himself vocally. This, also, can cause distraction to his opponent, and can be called an avoidable hinder. There should be no conversation during play except in doubles where "yours" and "mine" are permitted.

A player was against the left wall after hitting the ball directly back to his opponent, who was about five feet from the left wall, at the short line. As the ball was on the rebound from the front wall, he "avoidably" ran between the ball and the receiving player to gain center court position. If definitely caused an obstructed view and was clearly avoidable.

In effect, if a player voluntarily creates a distraction, an intimidation, an interference, or a hindered situation that in the referee's judgment affects his opponent's play, the violator has committed an avoidable hinder. These and other situations not specifically covered in the rules may come up during a match. It is the referee's prerogative and duty to administer fair play through common sense.

Dear Mr. Nordlund,
At a recent tournament, in the finals of the "A doubles," I got in a dispute with one of my opponents, a personal friend of mine, who argued that the referee should have called an avoidable hinder on me in the preceding rally. The situation was this: My opponent was returning the ball by taking it off the back wall in the left corner. To get out of his way I flattened up against the left wall just behind the server's box or about fifteen feet from him but the ball still hit me. My opponent insisted that this was an avoidable hinder because I had not given him the shortest shot to the front wall. In other words, the shortest distance between him and the front wall would be a straight line which ran parallel to the side wall from the point at which he made contact with the ball to the front wall. My opponent, who graduated from the Univ. of Texas, explained that this was the position that Pete Tyson took on the matter. I contended, and the referee backed me, that all I had to give him was a straight line but that line didn't have to be the shortest one possible. Do you think you might give a ruling which would settle our debate?

Neal's Reply:
You have posed a difficult question. The timing element is so important to the calling of an avoidable hinder that in identical situations one call could be a hinder, and the other could be an avoidable. Let us review the rules on avoidable hinders that would most likely apply to this situation: failure to move (IV.E.2.a.) or blocking (IV.E.2.b.).

Most players when shooting a back wall setup along the walls prefer to shoot straight ahead close to the wall or side wall-front wall. By assuming a stationary, or blocking position in the direct line you referred to, a player is preventing this shot selection. Similarly, if a player was about to shoot a back wall setup in center court and his opponent was standing just back of the short line in center court, a blocking situation is created. It is difficult to evaluate a situation when not actually observing the play. However, in my judgement I would consider the ruling an avoidable hinder.

Dear. Mr. Nordlund:

Please answer a question for me. We are playing one-wall handball, doubles. Players A and B versus C and D. Player A sends a shot to the wall which bounces off the wall to player C. Player C hits the ball off the side of his hand causing the ball to go backwards from the wall. The ball strikes Player B who is standing three feet behind Player C. Player B says that the ball has not been hindered because he is behind Player C and the ball has no possibility of reaching the front wall. What is your ruling?

Neal's Reply:

First, when you say "player A sends a shot to the wall" I am assuming you mean the front wall. You have brought up a rule that has long been a controversial one among many players. It is a rule that may have to be changed. the rule is IV.E.1., dead ball hinders. Section b of this rule, hitting opponent, reads, "when a returned ball touches an opponent on the fly before it hits the front wall." This means it is an automatic replay. The rules applies if the opponent is in front of, or to the side of, or even behind, his opponent. It also applies whether or not "the ball has no possibility of reaching the front wall" as you mentioned. Your letter is very timely because we are in the process of reviewing the rules and this is certainly one that will be thoroughly discussed.

I personally believe that the rule should be changed so that it would be the judgment of the referee whether the ball would have made it to the front wall. On the fairly close calls a liberal approach would have to be taken, so that if there was any chance the ball would reach the front wall, a replay should be called.

Legal Gloves – There were a couple players who played with holes in their gloves. This is illegal and the ref should request a change of gloves.

Dry Glove Change – A player only a couple minutes into the match requested a glove change. The referee asked to see his gloves, which when shown were dry. The ref denied his request. He said he might change his gloves, but would be charged a time out. The player claim-ed he had the right to change his gloves under an equipment time out because they didn't fit right. The ref was correct in his decision. It is the player's responsibility to be properly prepared to play when the match starts.

Play Stoppage – A player's shoe came off in deep court. He was forced to finish the rally with one shoe. The ref should have immediate-ly stopped play when the player's shoe came off.

Side Out or Automatic Hinder – A very spirited game of doubles was being played without a referee. The second man was serving with one short. His second serve went behind his partner and barely landed short. The happy receiving side came in to assume the serve. The serving side refused to leave the serving zone claiming they had another serve coming. They reasoned it was an automatic hinder since it went behind the server's partner before the ball landed short, nullify-ing the short. Then the sparks began to fly. The discussion went on for several minutes with neither team relinquishing the serving area. Finally the receiving team reluctantly gave in and went back to receive, protesting they had been cheated.

The interpretation here is the serve must be a legal serve (over the short line) before the automatic hinder rule would apply. The appli-cation is similar to a ref calling a screen hinder on the server and the ball falling short. He would, or should, change his call to a short ball. Yes, the receiving team was cheated.

Illegal Serve – After the server and the receiver were ready, a player bounced the ball on the short line and served, which is legal. He was cautioned by the ref he can only bounce the ball inside the service zone. A few minutes later he bounced the ball outside the short line. The referee called a side out to the dissatisfaction of the player. He was reminded that he was given a caution (which is not required) and that it is the responsibility of the players to know the rules.

REFEREEING IN HANDBALL: HOW TO IMPROVE THE PLAY

PAUL HABER

After the many years that I have played handball, watched handball, refereed handball and talked handball to thousands of players, I have come to the conclusion that there is one thing about handball that needs to be improved at every level of play. That is refereeing. Over the years, it's a fact that the level of efficiency has not increased a sufficient amount to term it improved. The reasons for this are many. Most importantly, there has never been any type of educational program conducted for refereeing on any large scale basis. Plainly, funds for this type of program have not been available. The USHA has had to spend untold thousands of dollars on many important projects to better the growth of handball, and somehow, a program for refereeing has not yet surfaced as one of those projects. This is certainly not to place a blame on USHA or anyone else, but it remains a fact in our world of handball.

After attending the recent USHA Nationals in Coral Gables, Florida and watching many, many matches throughout the week, I became very distressed with the general calibre of the refereeing, especially during many of the doubles matches. Throughout this article, I will try to get you on the right track for refereeing in the future. Most importantly, be sure to have an updated USHA rule book handy during your reading to use it as a check list. That is your handball "bible." I truly hope this article will help each and every one of you.

Preliminary matters

At the start of any given tournament, a referee's chairman should be elected by the local handball committee. That person should then select the number of referees he feels will be needed for the tournament. A meeting should be scheduled by the group, to which each person brings a copy of the current USHA rule book. All rules should be reviewed thoroughly and the chairman should try to impress upon all committeemen the importance of following these rules to the letter.

Each player entered in the tournament should be given a pamphlet that includes all the up-to-date USHA rules. If they're smart, they'll read it carefully.

Once a match begins, there should be no excuses made by the players or, especially, the now well-versed referees. If all of these

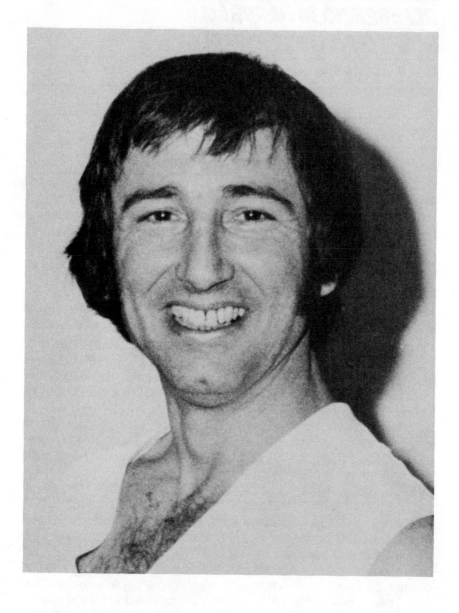

Photo 5-4: **Paul Haber, five-time National Open Singles Champion and one of the greatest handball players of all time, gives his thoughts on refereeing.**

preparations have been made for your next tournament, you are well on your way to having a good one.

All tournament players, of course, should have an ample supply of dry gloves available for each match. Frequently, a player may be told by the referee to change gloves although the player may think they are dry enough to use as is. But many times a player will strike a ball on the outer edge of the glove (where it gets wet first) and the result is a wet ball in play. We all know how a wet ball acts when it hits a side wall. Having at least three pairs of gloves available for change will eliminate problems for you. As defined in the rules, a referee may forfeit a match for a player who cannot change into dry gloves.

Ready to play ball

The referee should flip a coin to determine who will be first server. The flip should occur during the time that the players are warming up. Immediately after the coin flip, the referee *may* warn the players about a few of the lesser known and followed rules. He is not required to do this, but if he wishes, he may do so. Bear in mind—*any infraction* at any point during the game is subject to penalty.

As play begins, a sharp lookout for "foot faults" should be made by the ref. If a player is even a "smidgeon" beyond the back or front line, the calls should be made. A decision by a referee to "overlook" this minor infraction will penalize the player receiving service—he is, in effect, allowing the server at least three serves. Wouldn't you love it if, after you served one short ball, the referee yelled: "One short, two serves coming!" So you see, it is important to watch this seemingly unimportant phase of refereeing.

Once the ball is legally in play (no fault or screen ball being called), total concentration on the part of the referee is still needed. Any of a variety of rule infractions may occur and he must be able to make a call instantly. Unfortunately, many refs fail to make a call until after 2 or 3 continuing shots, and then confusion and often an argument ensues. *Remember, all calls should be made loudly and quickly.* During the course of the rally, the ref is responsible for all calls. I have often heard a ref say to the players: "Help me with your doubles bounces and wrist balls, fellas." Well, that's just plain bunk! If you, as the ref, think that a player has returned a ball after two or more bounces, you should call it as such. *That is why you are there.* If, on the other hand, a player *does* volunteer to call an infraction upon himself, of course you accept his call. Perhaps in a future article, however, I will explain why I think a player should *not* make any call against himself.

From past experience, I have noticed and concluded that about 75% of all improper calls made are those concerning "hinder" calls, "avoidable" hinder calls and various "body contact" calls. These situations occur most often in doubles, but also a surprisingly large number of times in singles play. These particular areas of refereeing seem to be the problem ones for refs when, in all frankness, they are really no problem at all. Again, a handy copy of the USHA rule book will greatly aid you in determining how and when to make the proper call.

Photo 5-5: **Paul Haber zeroes in on back court set-up on route to winning his first National Open Singles Championships in 1966 at Salt Lake City against Billy Yambrick. Haber was the surprise winner as he was sixteenth seed and had to beat Phil Elbert, Dave Graybill, and Marty Decatur to reach the finals against Yambrick. In addition, Haber and Paul Morlos took second in Open Doubles.**

Hinder Ball A – In general terms one variety of hinder ball occurs when one player cannot move far enough out of the way of the ball or the opposing player to allow the opponent a clear view of the ball and/or be able to move his total body into a normal swinging position. Usually this occurs on a ball hit rather hard, but misdirected to its intended path. This type of hinder will find the ball bouncing on the floor at some point between the shooter and the front wall, and the ball coming toward the player in a direct manner. It most often occurs in lower skill level games, usually because the player has opted for a poor choice of shots.

Hinder Ball B – Another hinder ball occurs when one player, trying to retrieve an opponent's rally shot, runs into the opponent in such a manner that balance is lost, momentum of the swing is impeded, or vision of the ball is lost. Of great importance here, in order to determine if it truly is a hinder, is whether the retrieving player was actually headed in the proper direction when the collision occured. If, in your estimation as the ref, you think the player was headed the "wrong way," you can feel secure in calling the play in favor of the player who struck the ball.

Hinder Ball C – This last hinder is almost never called, yet I am sure occurs every day in many courts throughout the country. During the course of play, if a ball hits any protruding area outside the confines of the court, (an overhand light fixture, a faulty rim of a glass panel, a faulty edge of any rim of a sill or the like) and then travels in an unusual manner, a court hinder must then be called. On the contrary, many clubs I have visited even have signs posted indicating there are no court hinders. That is just not correct. The USHA rule book will back you up when you make this decision.

Avoidable Hinders – These hinders can occur in so many ways I will not list them as A,B,C, etc. I will, though, explain what constitutes an avoidable hinder in simple terms. Of course it's not quite as easy to describe the action in words as it would be on the court, so you'll have to visualize the various circumstances as you read on.

To understand better the various situations on the court, I would ask that you apply one sentence that is printed in the USHA rule book—the defensive player *may not* assume a position on the court. As I watch refs during a match, I can plainly see that this particular group of words is not understood. Translated into very simple terms, they mean that a player may not "guess" or "judge" or "hope" an opponent is going to strike a ball to one particular spot on the court, and then occupy the space between the opponent and wall before opponent strikes the ball. Sound confusing? Well, it's not. This usually occurs as one player hits a set-up ball to his opponent and then decides to cut off his lane for the kill or pass shot. Many times this occurs as a back wall setup is about to be struck. Part of this problem stems from the player on the defensive not following the ball visually as it goes to the rear court. *Usually that player just bends over while gazing directly at the front wall.* All of a sudden he is struck in the back or head or leg, then mutters something like: "Sorry, but at least I stopped the kill." Well, guys, he has just committed an avoidable hinder—the offensive player was penalized and, here's the crux of the matter—the ref very calmly says "hinder, play it over." Wrong, bucko!

Another situation occurs when a defensive player moves from one position, a position clear of the ball and opponent, to another, in effect causing the ball to strike him on the way to the front wall. That is *always* an avoidable hinder and should be called. In another instance player A, in the front court hits a rather low, soft shot just about in front of his body. Most players describe this action as playing "cute"—but when the ball bounds off the front wall, and player B comes in for the return, B finds himself stymied by player A because A has not moved sufficiently and quickly to allow player B an unobstructed view and swing at the ball. Fellas, that is an avoidable hinder. You *must* allow your opponent room at all times. In the simplest language possible, an avoidable hinder is a hinder which could have been avoided by one course of action or another. The next time you're just watching a pick-up game and two players concur on a hinder call, ask yourself if there was any way at all for the defensive player to have prevented that hinder from occurring. If it suddenly dawns on you that he could have moved more quickly or to just another area, then you will have discovered the avoidable hinder.

Errors in judgement by defensive players do not prevent an avoidable hinder. If he runs into an opponent who is in the act of swinging, he is guilty of an avoidable hinder. Bear in mind, most avoidable hinders are not such because a player means to disrupt the play intentionally. Nonetheless, they are always to be called avoidable hinders.

You've occasionally seen a player stamp his feet on the floor as his opponent is about to swing at a set-up shot. That, too, is an avoidable hinder.

Well, handballers, this should be some help to you for your coming handball season. Do the best you can and good luck at it.

HOW TO WATCH
A HANDBALL MATCH
MORT LEVE

In the conventional standard courts the viewing area is from a balcony behind the back wall. With the use of glass you can view directly behind the back wall or side walls. There are now several facilities that have glass front walls.

I have found the best view of the action on the non-glass court to be in the middle of the balcony first row. This is where the referee is usually stationed so a seat on either side is next best. With glass to the floor on the back wall, viewing is excellent in most of the seating area, but when you are at floor level you are "hindered" by looking directly at the backs of the players. While seated six or seven rows up, you can get the clear view. On the side glass walls I have found the viewing best at the deep court areas rather than toward the middle or front of the court. In the middle of the court you must turn your head from side to side to watch the play. With glass in the front wall, your best view would be up six or more rows, looking down on the action right into the front of the players, enjoying the full "agony and ecstasy" of our game.

By watching the better players, you can give yourself a valuable lesson. Don't just watch the typical serve and volley routine. Note where the receiver stations himself, how he returns the serve, watch his foot placement, his anticipation. If you watch through a point with the receiver, you'll have an excellent idea of what you should be doing when you're out there on the court.

You can do the same thing with the server. Don't take your eyes off the server after he finishes his serve. Follow him as he turns to watch his opponent, and then as he moves to position himself for his shot. Study his tactics.

A handball match allows for much flexibility, but most spectators never bother to probe a match to study the "chess-like intricacies" that may ultimately help them.

In watching doubles, spend some time on the partner who is not involved in returning a ball. See what he does, how he maneuvers, his shifting in certain instances, what balls he "leaves" because his partner can position better and probably use his strong hand. Watch the teamwork and the strategy. All this will not only make the role of spectator more enjoyable, but will also help improve your game as a player, particularly if you're the type of player who lacks the opportunity for consistent practice sessions.

We don't ask you to copy the style of any one top ball player. You can, instead, pick up some facet of his game that can be adapted to your own particular physical abilities. You'll find it works.

BIBLIOGRAPHY

Haber, Paul. "Refereeing in Handball, How to Improve the Play." *Handball,* 1979, Vol. 29, No. 4.

Leve, Mort. "How to Watch a Handball Match." *Handball,* 1977, Vol. 27, No. 1.

Nordlund, Neal. "Dissection of Avoidable Hinder Rule." *Handball,* 1977, Vol. 27, No. 6.

"Other Selected Rules Interpretations and Comments." *Handball,* 1975-81 (selected from various issues).

APPENDIX

THE COMPLETE HANDBALL BIBLIOGRAPHY

Books and Magazines

Aberdare, (Lord). *Rackets, Squash-Rackets, Fives and Badminton.* Philadelphia: J.B. Lippincott Company, 1933.

Brokaw, James T. *How to Play American Handball.* New York: American Sports Publishing Company, 1916.

Deshong, Maurice W. *Handball and How to Play It.* New York: American Sports Publishing Company, 1893.

Doherty, Ray. *Handball.* Wicklow, Republic of Ireland: Lithographic Universal Ltd., Bray Co., 1970.

Egan, Michael. *Handball and How to Play It.* New York: American Sports Publishing Company, 1913.

Haber, Paul. *Inside Handball.* Chicago, Illinois: Reilly and Lee, 1970.

Lowy, Lance. *The Handball Handbook: Strategies and Techniques.* Boston, Massachusetts: American Press, 1979.

Mann, Charles L. *Handball Fundamentals.* Columbus, Ohio: Charles B. Merrill Publishing Company, 1976.

Melarland, Wayne and Philip Smith. *Sports Illustrated Handball.* Philadelphia and New York: J.B. Lippincott Company, 1976.

Nelson, Richard C., and Harlan S. Berger. *Handball.* Englewood Cliffs, New Jersey: Prentice-Hall, Inc., 1971.

O'Connell, Charlie. *Handball Illustrated.* New York: The Ronald Press Company, 1964.

O'Connell, Charles J. *How to Play Handball.* New York: American Sports Publishing Company, 1935.

Pfeifer, Gordy (editor). *A Lifetime Handball and Racquetball Reference Guidebook.* Tacoma, Washington: G. Pfeifer, 1975.

Phillips, Bernath. *Fundamental Handball.* New York: A.S. Barnes and Company, 1937.

Phillips, Bernath. *Handball: Its Play and Management.* New York: The Ronald Press Company, 1957.

Plotnicki, Ben A., and Andrew J. Kozar. *Handball.* Dubuque, Iowa: Kendall/Hunt Publishing Company, 1970.

Reznik, John W. *Championship Handball by the Experts.* West Point, N.Y.: Leisure Press, 1976.

Roberson, Richard and Herbert Olson. *Beginning Handball.* Belmont, California: Wadsworth Publishing Company, Inc., 1962.

Shaw, John H. *Handball.* Boston: Allyn and Bacon, Inc., 1971.

Tyson, Pete. *Handball.* Pacific Palisades, California: The Goodyear Publishing Company, 1971.

Tyson, Pete and Mort Leve. *Handball.* Chicago: The Athletic Institute, 1972.

United States Handball Association. *Handball* (Magazine). The United States Handball Association, 4101 Dempster Street, Skokie, Illinois 60076.

United States Handball Association. *Official Four-Wall Handball Rules.* The United States Handball Association, 4101 Dempster Street, Skokie, Illinois 60076.

Van Court, Carroll. *Scientific Handball Course.* Los Angeles, California: Carroll Van Court, 1935.

Yessis, Michael. *Handball.* Dubuque, Iowa: Wm. C. Brown Company Publishers, 1966.

Zafferano, George J. Handball Basics. New York: Sterling Publishing Company, Inc., 1977.

Theses and Dissertations

Atkinson, James Riley. "Predicting Performance in Tennis, Badminton and Handball from Certain Physical Traits." Ed.D., University of Arkansas, 1976.

Bethe, Donald Ray. "Success of Beginning Handball as a Function of the Theory of Achievement Motivation." Ph.D., The Ohio State University, 1968.

Bryant, F.O. "Effect of Handball on the Physical Fitness of the Adult Male." Unpublished Master's thesis, The University of Illinois, 1950.

Carter, Charles N. "A Preliminary Investigation of a Handball Skill Test." Unpublished Master's thesis, The University of Tennessee, 1963.

Charouhas, Desmond. "The Opinions of Selected Experts with Regard to the Design and Construction of Handball Courts." Unpublished Master's thesis, University of Washington, 1964.

Davies, Donald Bertrand. "A Comparative Study of the Whole and Part Methods of Teaching Handball to Beginning Students." Ph.D., University of Oregon, 1971.

Griffith, Malcomb Anstett. "An Objective Method for Evaluating Ability in Handball Singles." Unpublished Master's thesis, Ohio State University, 1960.

Haynes, Frederick J. and Thomas J. Romanello. "The Development of Materials for a Filmstrip and Manual on the Techniques and Strategy of Handball Play." Unpublished Master's thesis, Springfield College, 1950.

Holt, Lawrence E. "A Comparative Study of Handball Techniques." Unpublished Master's thesis, Springfield College, 1963.

Leinbach, C.H. "The Development of Achievement Standards in Handball and Touch Football for Use in the Department of Physical Training for Men at the University of Texas." Unpublishes Master's thesis, The University of Texasa, 1952.

McCachren, James R. "A Study of the University of Florida Handball Skill Test." Unpublished Master's thesis, The University of North Carolina, 1949.

Railey, Jimmy Howard. "The Effects of Imitative Resistance Exercise and Direct Practice on Handball Serving Skill." P.E.D., Indiana University, 1969.

Sattler, Thomas Peter. "The Development of an Instrument to Measure Handball Ability of Beginning Level Players in a Physical Education Class." Ed.D., Oklahoma State University, 1973.

Savage, David Earl. "The Comparative Effects of a Beginning Boxing Class and a Beginning Handball Class on Physical Fitness." Unpublished Master's thesis, Brigham Young University, 1963.

Schiff, F.S. "A Test of Skills Performed in the Game Situation of Handball." Unpublished Master's thesis, Ohio State University, 1938.

Simos, Thomas. "A Handball Classification Test." Unpublished Master's thesis, Springfield College, 1950.

Taylor, Richard A. "A Study of Whole and Part Methods in Teaching Handball Skills." Unpublished Master's thesis, The University of Tennessee, 1965.

Turnbull, Lawrence Myron. "A Comparison of the Cardiorespiratory Changes as Determined by Treadmill Performance Occurring in Selected University of Washington Males Enrolled in Two Selected Physical Education Activities." Unpublished Master's thesis, University of Washington, 1964.

Tyson, Kenneth W. "A Handball Skill Test for College Men." Unpublished Master's thesis, The University of Texas at Austin, 1970.

Articles

Banister, E.W., P.M. Ribisl, G.H. Porter and A.R. Cillo. "The Caloric Cost of Playing Handball," Research Quarterly, 35:236-240 Part I, October, 1964.

Bischoff, D.C. "Skill Grading System Using a Modified Ladder Tournament." *Journal of Health, Physical Education and Recreation,* 34:10-11, April, 1963.

Clevett, Melvin A. "The Fundamental Technique of Handball." *Journal of Physical Education,* 30:3ff., September, 1932.

Cornish, Clayton. "A Study of Measurement of Ability in Handball." *Research Quarterly,* 20:215-222, May, 1949.

Friermood, H.T. "A Handball Classification Plan." *Journal of Health and Physical Education,* 8:106-107, 127, February 1937.

Holt, Lawrence E. "Comparative Study of Selected Handball Techniques." *Research Quarterly,* 40:700-703, December, 1969.

Kutzer, B. "Advanced Handball Drills." *Journal of Physical Education,* 71:16-17, September, 1973.

McKinney, Wayne C. "Handball: A Philosophic Interpretation." *The Physical Educator,* 20:63-64 No. 2, May, 1963.

Montoye, Henry J. and John Brotzman. "An Investigation of the Validity of Using the Results of a Doubles Tournament as a Measure of Handball Ability." *Research Quarterly,* 22:214-218, May, 1951.

Ostrow, Andrew. "Goal-Setting Behavior and Need Achievement in Relation to Competitive Motor Activity." *Research Quarterly,* 47:174-183, May, 1976.

Pennington, G. Gary, John N. Drowatzdy, James A.P. Day, and John P. Hansen. "A Measure of Handball Ability." *Research Quarterly,* 38:247-253, May, 1967.

Railey, Jimmy H. "Effects of Imitative Resistance Exercise and Direct Practice on Handball Serving Skill." *Research Quarterly,* 41:523-527, December, 1970.

Schreiber, M. "Group Variation in Handball." *Journal of Health, Physical Education and Recreation,* 15:220-222, April, 1944.

Shaw, John. "How to Rate Your Handball Players." *Journal of Physical Education,* 72:116-117, March, 1975.

Sheets, Normal L. "Facilities for Handball." *Journal of Health, Physical Education and Recreation,* 39:76-77, May, 1968.

Van Slooten, Philip and Marian Kneer. "Performance by College Students in Handball Being Taught by Three Different Teaching Methods." *Research Quarterly,* 47:484-489, October, 1976.

Waglow, T.F. "Effect of School Term Lengths on Skill Achievement in Tennis, Golf and Handball." *Research Quarterly,* 37:157-159, March, 1966.

BIOGRAPHICAL STATEMENT
PETE TYSON

Pete Tyson received his B.S. degree (1960) in Physical Education from the Southern Methodist University (SMU) at Dallas, Texas and his M.E.D. degree (1970) in Education from the University of Texas (UT) at Austin. Pete is a former #5 ranked singles player in the United States and former National Open and Masters Doubles Champion.

During his senior year in high school, Pete started playing handball at the Dallas Athletic Club. His first teacher and mentor was George Lee, who was the Athletic Director at that time. After learning to play under Mr. Lee, Pete went on to become a National Intercollegiate Doubles Champion at SMU.

Pete has been the handball instructor and coach in the Department of Physical Education at UT for the past 22 years. During that time his teams have won the USHA National Intercollegiate Team Championships eleven times. In addition to his duties at UT, Pete travels around the country giving handball clinics, has authored two other handball books and written many of the articles in this text.

BIOGRAPHICAL
STATEMENT
JIM TURMAN

Jim Turman received his B.S. degree (1970) in Printing Technology and Management from the California State Polytechnic University (Cal Poly) at San Luis Obispo and his M.A. degree (1973) in Physical Education from the University of California (Cal) at Berkeley. As a graduate student he wrote papers on the kinetics/biomechanics of the handball stroke, the principles of motor learning and the teaching of handball. Jim has taught elementary, intermediate and advanced handball while on the faculty of the Department of Physical Education at Cal in the early 1970's.

After retiring from high school, collegiate and A.A.U. wrestling, Jim began playing handball on the "cement" courts at Cal Poly in 1967. During those first handball years, Jim contributes his early development, particularly of his left hand, to the encouragement and patience of Robert Swett, a local San Luis Obispo architect, who currently lives in the state of Washington. Since that time Jim has played many local, regional and national open singles and doubles tournaments. Jim is the current #6 ranked singles player in the United States in the Open Senior Singles Division.

In addition to his current duties as the Budget and Administrative Officer for the Department of Recreational Sports at Cal, Jim is the United States Handball Association's National Intercollegiate Commissioner. Jim lives in Albany, California with his wife, Barbara, his son, Adam, and his daughter, Karen.

Pete Tyson, left, and Jim Turman, right.